ROBERT BURNS: SELECTED POETRY

Robert Burns was born in 1759, the son of a struggling tenant farmer in Ayrshire, who nevertheless joined with neighbours to employ a university-trained tutor for their children. When very young, Burns read the Bible, the English Augustans and Gray; later he learned some French and a little Latin. The surrounding countryside was rich in folklore, but Scots literature came his way only by chance and it was later in his life that he realized the possibilities of contemporary literature in Scots. Meanwhile the privation and overwork of subsistence farming began the rheumatic heart-disease that was to cause his premature death. His father died bankrupt in 1784 and Burns, as head of the family, leased a farm at Mossgiel. He began to circulate verse satires on Calvinist extremists, and in July 1786 the Church avenged itself by exacting public penance from him and Jean Armour who was pregnant by him and whom he acknowledged as his wife in 1788. *Poems, chiefly in the Scottish Dialect* was published in 1786 and enthusiastically received and Burns spent the winters of 1786–7 and 1787–8 in Edinburgh, acting out with increasing unease the role of child of nature and untutored poet of the plough in which the Edinburgh gentry had cast him, seeking relief in the city's hard-drinking low life. An admirer leased him a farm at Ellisland and in 1789 he was appointed to the Excise Division in nearby Dumfries. The farm failed, through lack of capital, and Burns devoted his main energies to the collection and rewriting of Scots songs. He moved to Dumfries in 1791, where, after official investigation into his sympathies for the American and French Revolutions, he was promoted in the Excise and helped to organize local Volunteer units. His health gave way and he died in 1796.

ROBERT BURNS

Selected Poetry

EDITED BY
ANGUS CALDER
AND
WILLIAM DONNELLY

PENGUIN BOOKS

PENGUIN BOOKS

Published by the Penguin Group
Penguin Books Ltd, 27 Wrights Lane, London w8 5tz, England
Viking Penguin, a division of Penguin Books USA Inc.
375 Hudson Street, New York, New York 10014, USA
Penguin Books Australia Ltd, Ringwood, Victoria, Australia
Penguin Books Canada Ltd, 2801 John Street, Markham, Ontario, Canada l3r 1b4
Penguin Books (NZ) Ltd, 182–190 Wairau Road, Auckland 10, New Zealand

Penguin Books Ltd, Registered Offices: Harmondsworth, Middlesex, England

First published 1991
1 3 5 7 9 10 8 6 4 2

Printed in England by Clays Ltd, St Ives plc

'Your Immortal Memory, Burns!' on pp. xi–xii is reprinted from
Complete Poems 1920–1976 by Hugh MacDiarmid, by kind permission of
Martin Brian and O'Keefe Ltd and Michael Grieve. 'Mrs Abernethy:
Burns the Hero' on pp. xii–xiii is reprinted from *True Confessions and
New Clichés* by Liz Lochhead, by kind permission of Polygon and
Liz Lochhead.

CONTENTS

❦

PART ONE: SONGS

Part Two: Poems, Epistles, Epigrams

INTRODUCTION

Robert Burns, during his own lifetime, became a mythical hero – the ploughman poet, the peasant of sensibility, not quite a shepherd but very nearly the real embodiment of the pastoral dream that had haunted the literary imagination of Europe. After his early death, mythologizing had freer rein. 'The rank,' he had written, was 'but the guinea's stamp.' The man was 'the gowd for a' that'. Long after the guinea had passed out of use, the effigy of the man, Burns, would adorn Scottish five-pound notes. 'Burns Night', the celebration of the poet's birthday on 25 January, would be a far more important fixture in the calendar of Scots, at home or in exile, than the Hallowe'en of which he had recorded the rites in verse. All over the world – not least in the Soviet Union, where Burns had been translated into numerous languages – that humble mythical beast the Haggis would be addressed in Burns's words; 'Tam o' Shanter' would be recited from memory.

C. M. Grieve, 'Hugh MacDiarmid', tried to blow the whistle in the 1920s:

> Thought may demit
> Its functions fit
> While still to thee, O Burns
> The punctual stomach of thy people turns.
>
> Most folks agree
> That poetry
> Is of no earthly use
> Save thine – which yields this Annual Excuse! . . .
>
> Be of good cheer
> Since once a year
> Poetry is not too pure
> A savoury for shopkeepers to endure!
>
> And, dined and wined,
> Solicitors find

Their platitudes assume
The guise of intuitions that illume

The hidden heart
Of Human Art [1]

To no avail ... A casual check in Edinburgh two centuries after the Kilmarnock edition of *Poems, chiefly in the Scottish Dialect* first appeared revealed that bookings of hotel function-rooms for Burns Suppers were unabated. A building in the West End of the city was under scaffolding. Someone, presumably the contractor, had put up a blackboard to cheer passers-by: 'Scots word of the day – Cutty Sark = a witch'. A glance at the splendid new *Concise Scots Dictionary*, however, would have revealed that 'cutty' means 'short' and 'sark' is 'a woman's shift or chemise'. But a witch in 'Tam o' Shanter' wears a cutty sark ...

Branches of all political parties hold Burns Suppers. The Scottish National Party can legitimately hail the author of 'Robert Bruce's March to Bannockburn' ('Scots, wha hae'). Labour can with equal legitimacy claim the author of 'For a' that and a' that' as a spiritual ancestor of the working-class movement, and Tories have no problem – never had – with the poet who celebrated Jacobite loyalty to kings by divine right. But the archetypal Burns cultist is Mrs Abernethy, the minister's wife in Liz Lochhead's monologue, who is organizing the Women's Guild Burns Supper:

Don't you think it would of been absolutely Super to have been Immortalised by Robert Burns? What a man, eh? [...] Such Passion. And such eyes! I mean, have you seen the portrait, you know the Kilmarnock Edition one, the one you see on all the ashtrays, the one on all the dishtowels [...] He ... Felt Things, don't you feel that? [...]

Of course some of Our Guild Members are dare I say it just that wee bit narrow minded [...] I just says to Mrs Sneddon that she needed a new battery for her hearing aid and that a daimen-icker in a thrave didny mean whit she thought it did! And anyway Burns had always been Very Frankly Spoken about that kind of thing. Before his time really. Of course somebody, Who Shall Be Nameless, would bring up the subject of Burns-And-You-Know-What, and how many of his children were born on The Wrong Side Of The Blanket, What Right Had We to look down on Brown Owl for her shotgun wedding when we were all supposed to look up to Rabbie Burns as Our Big Hero? I tried to tell her, don't be daft, everybody knows Artists Are Different.

Anyway, every time I hear 'Ae Fond Kiss' I Melt Inside, I really do . . .[2]

2

The success of Burns-as-myth has in fact obscured the vast merits of Burns the poet. When the Kilmarnock and Edinburgh editions appeared in 1786 and 1787 it was not couthy Scots sentiment that impressed such good judges as the English poet Cowper – it was the abundance of technical skill, the clear evidence that in Scots or English this farmer still in his twenties could deliver the goods. He opened with brilliant octosyllabic couplets ('The Twa Dogs'). He showed he could handle not only such familiar forms, but also the fiendishly difficult stanzas peculiar to Scottish tradition – the 'Standart Habbie' and the 'Chrystis Kirk on the Grene' stanzas and the all but impossible 'Cherrie and the Slae' fourteen-liner. He not only had more interesting things to say than that predecessor, Allan Ramsay, whom he revered, his technical fluency was amazing. So easily conversational is the Burns voice that one must, as it were, stand back and pinch oneself before such a routine achievement as 'Tam Samson's Elegy' and admit that one has been bewitched into hearing as casual and occasional an extraordinary feat of practised skill. It is only when the voice falters – as for many readers, now, it does in 'The Cotter's Saturday Night' – that one is aware of Burns's technique at all. Yet this very poem, with its crafty modulations between Scots and English lexicon, its blend of 'universal' Christian sentiment with precise 'manners-painting' of a vanishing rural Scotland, was justly central to Burns's nineteenth-century reputation.

That reputation, it should be stressed, was by no means confined to Scotland. In the north of England, where in 'Resolution and Independence' Wordsworth had celebrated

> Him who walked in glory and in joy
> Following his plough, along the mountain-side,

cheap editions of Burns outsold Wordsworth by far. His dialect had no terrors for working people in England. It is twentieth-century ideology that has marginalized Burns as a 'regional' exception in 'English' literature and has made him seem, to nationalistic Scots like MacDiarmid, charming but brainless, like a nice old dog. In the 1920s New Criticism arose at the same time as 'English Literature' was canonized as a tool of the Westminster-dominated 'UKanian' state, for which 'standard English' was a self-evident good. For the New Critics, the freely discursive nature of Burns's epistles was as much a problem as the stripped directness of his best songs. Neither appeared to offer the richness and complexity which it was the priestly task of criticism to unpack. Burns has received astonishingly little attention from the great minds appointed to minister to the young at Oxford and Cambridge and their Scottish satellites. Had it not been for activity on his behalf by one Scottish New Critic, David Daiches, and the brilliant scholarly labours of Thomas Crawford and James Kinsley, he might have altogether dropped out of 'Literature', as received in schools and universities, and have been left to Mrs Abernethy. These are sad days for Burns's reputation when an American scholar, Carol McGuirk, in her book *Robert Burns and the Sentimental Era*, feels compelled to defend Burns on the grounds that he is more 'universal', less merely 'Scottish', than he looks.

> O, why the deuce should I repine
> And be an ill foreboder?

Burns is safe in the bosom of his people. You walk into a Scottish pub which advertises folk-singing. A youth with a guitar is murdering 'Such a parcel of rogues'. The yowes are ca'ed to the knowes and love is compared to a red, red rose so spontaneously that many people do not realize that the words were written – or, at least, delivered – by Burns, him on the ashtrays and dishtowels. It is perhaps Scottish culture's most important quirk that 'Such a parcel of rogues' along with Hogg's 'Maclean's Welcome', Scott's 'Bonnie Dundee', Byron's 'Dark Lochnagar' and Henderson's 'Fare Ye Weel, Ye Banks o' Sicily' has passed into the currency of casual song, rendered by people who never think of its having an author.

3

R. L. Stevenson was one of the most eminent of those who have complained that after Burns's brilliant débuts in Kilmarnock and Edinburgh, he frittered his talents away. It was, Stevenson wrote, 'typical of his loss of moral courage that he should have given up all larger ventures ... that a man who first attacked literature with a hand that seemed capable of moving mountains, should have spent his later years in whittling cherry stones'.[3] Here a debatable aesthetic judgement – songs are less important than odes – gets mixed up with moralizing. Before confronting Burns the song-writer, we had better consider Burns the Moral Problem and his relative stature compared with Brown Owl of the shotgun wedding.

Compared with his aristocratic contemporary James Boswell, Burns, both as drinker and womanizer, seems remarkably wholesome. He worked very hard indeed all his life. He enjoyed himself in taverns in his scanty spare time, at a period when tea was only just ceasing to be a luxury and no prudent person trusted water. Unlike Boswell, he did not pay for sex. A man with his verbal and musical gifts, and good looks, would always find female admirers, and the flattery of their eyes would be hard to resist. He took a job in the Excise, against his principles, to secure the necessities of life for his young family. He died not of drink, but of a rheumatic heart condition probably caused by overwork on the farm in his youth. That early posthumous editor, Thomas Stewart, who first printed 'Love and Liberty' and 'Holy Willie's Prayer', judged the poet fairly:

> An approach to licentiousness in some pieces exposed Burns, when alive, to the scoffs of the illiberal, which still insult his ashes. But let the self-sufficient who asperse the memory of a son of genius for some slight deviations from decorum, remember to appreciate his merits also, and to be more attentive to a declaration sanctioned by greater than human authority, that *To the pure all things are pure.*[4]

But by the time this was published, in 1801, the damage had been done. James Currie, whose life of Burns, attached to his pioneering edition of the works, would be incessantly reprinted, had delivered the judgement underlying Stevenson's belief that the bard had lacked 'moral courage'. Burns, Currie averred,

> had in his constitution the peculiarities and the delicacies that belong to the temperament of genius ... In his moments of thought, he reflected with the deepest regret on his fatal progress, clearly foreseeing the goal towards which he was hastening, without the strength of mind necessary to stop, or even to slacken his course. His temper now became more irritable and gloomy: he fled from himself into society, often of the lowest kind. And in such company, that part of the convivial scene, in which wine increases sensibility and excites benevolence, was hurried over, to reach the succeeding part, over which uncontrolled passion generally presided. He who suffers the pollution of inebriation, how shall he escape other pollution? [5]

At very best this means, as Mrs Abernethy would have it, that 'Artists Are Different'. At worst – and the evangelical nineteenth century was very willing to believe the worst of people – it suggests that Burns betrayed his own great gifts in favour of drunkenness and lechery. 'Whittling cherry stones' would be as much as such a degenerate could manage.

Yet Burns's meeting with the Edinburgh engraver James Johnson in 1787 was arguably as fruitful for Western culture as Eliot's with Pound or Stravinsky's with Diaghilev. For the rest of his life Burns worked, unpaid, as virtual editor of *The Scots Musical Museum*. 'Many beautiful airs,' he noted, 'wanted words; in the hurry of other avocations, if I could string a parcel of rhymes together anything near tolerable, I was fain to let them pass.' [6] He was scrupulous in distinguishing between what he had from tradition – as he heard it in tavern and town and field, or found it in such collections as David Herd's *Ancient and Modern Scottish Songs* – and what he added himself. If we accept his own word, he did not 'write' the best-loved lyrics associated with his Immortal Memory, 'Auld lang syne' and 'A red red Rose'. Yet to say this is to magnify, rather than diminish, his achievement. He was the Very Humble Servant of the musical traditions of his people. His prime concern was that good tunes should live, with 'tolerable' words to assist them. And without his intervention, the two songs mentioned as well as many others would not be part of Scotland's contribution to European, and world, culture.

He had a wonderful ear, and was assisted by his wife's fine singing. His touch was not infallible – his words for 'Hey, Johnny Cope' are less pithy and stirring than those attributed to Adam Skirving. He was not fighting a lone battle: as Thomas Crawford has abundantly shown, the 'song culture' of eighteenth-century Scotland was the common property of rich and poor. But whether building a wonderful song upon a fragment, as in 'McPherson's Farewell', devising something wholly new, as in 'Oh wert thou in the cauld blast', or transmitting what he had heard, deftly tinged with his own voice, Burns produced an astonishing number of outstanding songs.

Even as zealous, disinterested song collector, Burns has been criticized. Dave Harker, in his aggressively named book *Fakesong*, sees Burns as serving up the songs of the poor in forms agreeable to his rich patrons. His editing, Harker says, was 'directed consciously at getting tunes taken up by the culture to which he partly aspired, by the strategy of patching up original texts to fit the aesthetic ideals of their culture of destination'.[7] William Donaldson is, by implication, equally severe about Burns's handling of Jacobite material. He notes, correctly, the 'labyrinthine tortuousness' of Burns's politics. He notes, further, that Burns's 'editing' of Jacobite song in fact spawned a new genre – the 'Bonny Prince Charlie' ditty fit to be sung in middle-class households. Burns emerges in an unexpected light. Creating Jacobite songs, he served the aims of Scottish Toryism. The valiant feats of Highland Gaels fighting for Britain against France were a conspicuous anomaly. 'The typical way round the problem was to generalise dynastic loyalty to the Stuarts into an expression of abstract monarchist legitimism and then transfer it lock, stock and barrel to the House of Hanover.'[8] When Walter Scott was drilling with the Edinburgh Volunteers a few years after Burns's death, these lads loved nothing better, after exercise, than to bawl out Jacobite ditties.

4

Which leads us to the vexed question of Burns's politics. His attraction to Jacobitism may have partly stemmed from his family's roots in the

Episcopalian north-east, but represented a revolt against his father's Presbyterian, 'Whiggish' values. His responses, though, seem to have been governed by the strength of Jacobite tradition in the singing he heard as he went about Scotland:

> It is singular enough that the Scotish muses were all Jacobites
> ... For myself I would always take it as a compliment to have
> it said that my heart ran before my head. And surely the
> gallant though unfortunate house of Stewart, the kings of our
> fathers for so many heroic ages, is a theme much more interest-
> ing than an obscure beef-witted insolent race of foreigners
> whom a conjuncture of circumstances kickt up into power and
> consequence.

But, having very reasonably said this, he further noted:

> To tell the matter of fact, except when my passions were
> heated by some accidental cause, my Jacobitism was merely by
> way of, *Vive la bagatelle*.[9]

Having denounced the auld-farrant 'Whiggery' of the likes of 'Holy Willie', the heirs of the ultra-Presbyterian Covenanters, Burns himself became a Whig and a supporter of the biggest of Scots Whigs, the Edinburgh lawyer Henry Erskine, who was fellow mason, friend and patron. His political waverings during his last years are easily explained by that fact and by his total financial dependence, as provider for his family, on a job with government. In 1792 his well-known support for the French Revolution nearly cost him that job. His association with Erskine implied that he jumped with the big Whigs, who were themselves frightened and discomfited by the strength of anti-French feeling. Familiar passages in Cockburn's *Memorials of His Time* are borne out by other documents: it was less safe to be a Whig in Scotland in the 1790s than to be a Communist in the 1930s. Furthermore, what happened in France was not satisfactory. There is no real discrepancy involved when Burns, in the same brief period, writes 'For a' that and a' that', his great democratic anthem, and 'The Dumfries Volunteers', a patriotic song expressing the will to resist the French power, which was now reverting to French traditions of despotism.

5

Finally, a word about Burns's religious background. There is a tendency for poetry to come into contact with religion, be the relationship complementary, antagonistic or tangential. In the case of Burns, this tendency is indeed self-evident, the urge to 'puzzle Calvinism' being prominent in many of the major poems. Beyond this, however, there are less direct ways in which the entire tone of Burns's work is influenced by the specific nature of his country's religious inheritance.

The unique feature of the religious climate in post-Reformation Scotland is without doubt the extent of the Calvinist presence. In its own terms, Calvinism may be seen as an aspect of Renaissance thought, in that it represented the application of logical rigour to Christian practice, subject, of course, to the fundamental truths of Scripture. This saw the rejection of all that was thought to fail the test, which meant in effect the denial or downgrading of the medieval church's role as mediator through its ritual, symbolism and sacraments. Yet since such mediation existed in response to the needs of human fallibility, its abolition bestows a heavy psychological burden on the espousal of Calvinist logic. In its absence, fallen man remains fallen and all are therefore damned – except for those who have been predestined, or elected, to salvation from the beginning of time. In a later century Burns would have great fun with all this, but Calvinist conviction of election in an otherwise reprobate world was first to fuel the religious fanaticism that devastated the seventeenth century.

So how do we get from there to Burns? More broadly, how does a nation so theologically obsessed translate itself in the course of the eighteenth century into one of the major centres of the Enlightenment? It may be readily understood how, as a direct reaction, gradual exhaustion and ultimate revulsion against the fruits of religious excess might turn a people to the solid moderation offered by rationalism and empirical facts. Thus blossomed the Scotland of Hume, Smith, Ferguson and the rest. Indirectly, though, it is also worth considering how far this reaction was facilitated by the logical emphasis of Calvinism itself, which now, in the Age of Reason, made the fundamental adjustments that science and logic demanded. So, where once intolerance was nothing short of a duty and damnation an imminent probability, the professors of theology preached toleration under a distant but benevolent Creator.

As said, in Burns's poetry all these influences are directly or indirectly reflected. As with many a post-Calvinist Scottish writer, we find in his work something of the fatalism which was that theology's psychological heritage – 'Winter, A Dirge' and 'Man was Made to Mourn, A Dirge' being two examples. His more typical response, however, is an often hilarious defiance. The ultimate inversion of the notion of universal reprobation comes near the end of his 'Address to the Deil', where the Devil is advised that, were he to clean up his act, even he might just escape the consequences. Burns was a supporter of the 'Enlightened' New Licht theology. But in deepest Ayrshire there remained many Auld Licht or traditional Calvinists, who no doubt lived to rue the day they made an enemy of 'Rab the Ranter'. The notion of predestination was, understandably, a great promoter of hypocrisy. In the face of the bleak alternative it is pretty tempting to consider oneself elected, with all the trimmings. It is a condition, though, that would never fully recover from Burns's onslaught in poems such as his 'Address to the Unco Guid' and, the ultimate deflation, 'Holy Willie's Prayer', to which, of course, Willie himself remains oblivious.

So much for his anti-Calvinism. The other side of this, Burns's positive vision, celebrates the good sense, the toleration and the democratic impulse that were at the core of the eighteenth-century Enlightenment. Looking forward, Burns's liberation of the language and subject-matter of poetry would prove a crucial bequest to the Romantic movement. But for reasons already suggested, the values of the Enlightenment had particularly deep roots in Scotland, and Scottish writing continued to reflect the fact. Certainly, this is so of Burns's work, and that of Byron and even Scott might lend weight to the point. The implications of this bring us back to where we started. A feature of such a poetic vision is accessibility, and this in turn produces a level of popularity on the one hand and critical neglect on the other – the parallel examples of Byron and Scott continue to hold good. As a highly refined vehicle for articulating meaning, poetry is often concerned with the difficult, and indeed the intangible, which may account for the relationship with religion discussed above. It is therefore to be expected that criticism too will address such matters.

But to an exceptional degree post-Calvinist Scotland represents a set of values that are themselves a reaction against the excesses of transcendental preoccupations. In articulating these values, Burns gives expression to the other side of what is perhaps the ultimate debate about life. He does so, superbly, in many poetic modes as well as in the songs, an achievement that surely merits the recognition of serious criticism. We hope that the present volume will assist the process.

REFERENCES

1. Hugh MacDiarmid, 'Your Immortal Memory, Burns!', *Complete Poems 1920–1976*, vol. 1, London, Martin Brian and O'Keeffe, 1978, 77–9.
2. Liz Lochhead, 'Mrs Abernethy: Burns the Hero', *True Confessions and New Clichés*, Edinburgh, Polygon, 1985, 6–7.
3. Quoted in Thomas Crawford, *Society and the Lyric: A Study of the Song Culture of Eighteenth-Century Scotland*, Edinburgh, Scottish Academic Press, 1979, 1.
4. 'Advertisement', in Thomas Stewart, ed., *Poems Ascribed to Robert Burns*, Glasgow, 1801.
5. James Currie, *The Works of Robert Burns; with an account of his life*, vol. 1, London, 1802, 218–19.
6. Davidson Cook, ed., *Notes on Scottish Songs by Robert Burns*, 24, printed with James C. Dick, ed., *The Songs of Robert Burns*, Harboro, Pa., Folklore Association, 1962.
7. Dave Harker, *Fakesong: The Manufacture of British Folksong 1700 to the Present Day*, Milton Keynes, Open University Press, 1985, 36.
8. William Donaldson, *The Jacobite Song: Political Myth and National Identity*, Aberdeen University Press, 1988, 73, 91.
9. Cook, *Notes on Scottish Songs*, 4–5, 27.

BURNS'S LIFE:
A CHRONOLOGY

(Quotations are from Burns's letters and journals)

ᴄᴏꙨᴏꙨᴏ

1759   Robert Burns born on 25 January at Alloway, near Ayr, where his father, William Burnes, is gardener on a small estate.

1765   Together with his brother Gilbert, Burns attends the school run by John Murdoch at Alloway. At the same time he is absorbing 'from an old woman who resides in the family . . . the largest collection in the country of tales and songs'.

1766   The family moves to Mount Oliphant, a small farm near Alloway: 'a ruinous bargain'.

1768   Murdoch leaves the area. Burns's education continues under his father's guidance.

1774   Burns is working on the farm. He first commits 'the sin of Rhyme'.

1777   The family moves to Lochlie, a larger farm on the banks of the river Ayr.

1783   The landlord serves a writ of sequestration on Burns's father. Robert and Gilbert rent Mossgiel, a farm near Mauchline, 'as an asylum for the family in case of the worst'.

1784   William Burnes dies. Robert moves to Mossgiel, where many of his major poems will be written in the course of the next two years.

1785   A daughter, Elizabeth, born to Elizabeth Paton, his mother's servant girl. Burns meets Jean Armour. He begins to 'puzzle Calvinism' with 'much heat and indiscretion'. This is most evident in the many epistles and 'kirk satires' written at this time.

1786   *Poems, chiefly in the Scottish Dialect* printed at Kilmarnock on 14 April. Twins born to Jean Armour on 3 September. Burns abandons what ideas he had of emigrating to Jamaica.

In December he travels to Edinburgh to 'try for a second

edition'. He is taken up by Henry Mackenzie and capital
society in general.

1787   Second edition of *Poems* published in Edinburgh. From his
base in the capital, Burns spends much of the time from May
till late October touring the Borders and the Highlands. In
autumn the first London edition of the *Poems* is published,
and he begins to contribute songs to James Johnson's *Scots
Musical Museum*. In December he meets Mrs McLehose,
'Clarinda'.

1788   Despite Clarinda, Burns returns to Ayrshire, where Jean
Armour once more produces twins. After a brief return to
Edinburgh he leases a farm at Ellisland, near Dumfries, and
resolves to give Jean 'a *legal* title to the best blood of my
body; and so farewell Rakery'. In September Burns takes up a
post as exciseman, while his literary energies centre increas-
ingly on his work for the *Musical Museum*.

1790   Burns's health begins to suffer as he struggles to maintain a
farm and the extensive travel entailed in his work for the
Excise. Work on the songs continues, however, while Nov-
ember sees the completion of 'Tam o' Shanter'.

1791   Further offspring born to Jean, as well as a daughter, Elizabeth,
to Ann Park of Dumfries. Burns gives up Ellisland and settles
as an exciseman in Dumfries. He contributes towards a fourth
volume of the *Musical Museum*.

1792   Fourth volume of *The Scots Musical Museum* published. Burns
also begins contributing to George Thomson's *Select Collection
of Original Scotish Airs* (1793–1818). Accused of political
disaffection, he resolves to 'set, henceforth, a seal on my lips,
as to these unlucky politics'.

1793   In February a second Edinburgh edition of the *Poems* is
published. In May the first part of Thomson's *Collection* is
published.

1794   Burns ill in winter, but continues to send songs to both
Johnson and Thomson. In December he is appointed acting
supervisor of the Excise, raising false hopes of financial
security.

1795   Ill in winter with rheumatic fever.

1796   Illness continues, though he strives to maintain the flow of songs. On 12 July he appeals to Thomson for a loan of five pounds to cover a debt. Thomson does not respond.

On 21 July Burns dies at Dumfries. His youngest son is born on the day of his funeral, 25 July.

NOTE ON THE TEXTS

❧❧❧

We have generally followed James Kinsley's edition of *The Poems and Songs of Robert Burns* (Oxford, 1968). Kinsley's texts are found in, or collated from, 'Burns's holographs and transcripts revised in his own hand; the authoritative Kilmarnock (1786) and F 'inburgh (1787–94) editions of his *Poems, chiefly in the Scottish Dialect* ... Johnson's *Scots Musical Museum* (1787–1803) and Thomson's *Select Collection of Original Scotish Airs* (1793–1818); transcripts of manuscripts which are not at present accessible; and early printings in newspapers, periodicals and tracts'.

Most of our departures from readings preferred by Kinsley are trivial, and we do not advertise them. Not without thought, however, we have restored passages in 'The Author's Earnest Cry' and 'Tam o' Shanter' to their state in the earliest printed editions, and have inserted the 'Merry Andrew' passage into the main text of 'Love and Liberty'.

Eighteenth-century writers used asterisks in place of full names (e.g. W*****m P**t) for deliberate effect, as well as on grounds of prudence. When Burns writes about men famous in his day, we have retained this feature of his style. But his Ayrshire epistles and satires cannot be read aloud, or even scanned, without the full names of local personalities, which we have supplied.

All footnotes printed with the text are Burns's own.

PART ONE

❧❧❧

SONGS

BEFORE 1788

❦

O Tibbie I hae seen the day

❦

Tune, Invercald's reel – Strathspey

CHORUS

O Tibbie I hae seen the day
Ye wadna been sae shy
For laik o' gear ye lightly me
   But trowth I care na by –

Yestreen I met you on the Moor
Ye spak'na but gaed by like stoor
Ye geck at me because I'm poor
   But fien' a hair care I. –

When comin' hame on Sunday last
Upon the road as I cam' past
Ye snufft an' gae your head a cast
   But trouth I caretna by. –

I doubt na lass, but ye may think
Because ye hae the name o' clink
That ye can please me at a wink
   Whene'er ye like to try –

But sorrow tak' him that 's sae mean
Altho' his pouch o' coin were clean
Wha follows ony saucy Quean
   That looks sae proud and high –

Altho' a lad were e'er sae smart
If that he want the yellow dirt

Ye'll cast your head anither airt
    An' answer him fu' dry –

But if he hae the name o' gear
Ye'll fasten to him like a breer
Tho' hardly he for sense or lear
    Be better than the ky –

But Tibbie lass tak' my advice
Your daddie's gear mak's you sae nice
The de'il a ane wad speir your price
    Were ye as poor as I –

There lives a lass beside yon park
I'd rather hae her in her sark
Than you wi' a' your thousand mark
    That gars you look sae high –

An' Tibbie I hae seen the day
    Ye wadna been sae shy
An' for laik o' gear ye lightly me
    But fien' a hair care I.

Corn rigs are bonie

I

It was upon a Lammas night,
   When corn rigs are bonie,
Beneath the moon's unclouded light,
   I held awa to Annie:
The time flew by, wi' tentless heed,
   Till 'tween the late and early;
Wi' sma' persuasion she agreed,
   To see me thro' the barley.

II

The sky was blue, the wind was still,
   The moon was shining clearly;
I set her down, wi' right good will,
   Amang the rigs o' barley:
I ken't her heart was a' my ain;
   I lov'd her most sincerely;
I kiss'd her owre and owre again,
   Amang the rigs o' barley.

III

I lock'd her in my fond embrace;
   Her heart was beating rarely:
My blessings on that happy place,
   Amang the rigs o' barley!
But by the moon and stars so bright,
   That shone that hour so clearly!
She ay shall bless that happy night,
   Amang the rigs o' barley.

IV

I hae been blythe wi' Comrades dear;
   I hae been merry drinking;

I hae been joyfu' gath'rin gear;
    I hae been happy thinking:
But a' the pleasures e'er I saw,
    Tho' three times doubl'd fairly,
That happy night was worth them a',
    Amang the rigs o' barley.

CHORUS

Corn rigs, an' barley rigs,
    An' corn rigs are bonie:
I'll ne'er forget that happy hour,
    Amang the rigs wi' Annie.

John Barleycorn*. A Ballad

I

There was three kings into the east,
   Three kings both great and high,
And they hae sworn a solemn oath
   John Barleycorn should die.

II

They took a plough and plough'd him down,
   Put clods upon his head,
And they hae sworn a solemn oath
   John Barleycorn was dead.

III

But the chearful Spring came kindly on,
   And show'rs began to fall;
John Barleycorn got up again,
   And sore surpris'd them all.

IV

The sultry suns of Summer came,
   And he grew thick and strong,
His head weel arm'd wi' pointed spears,
   That no one should him wrong.

V

The sober Autumn enter'd mild,
   When he grew wan and pale;
His bending joints and drooping head
   Show'd he began to fail.

* This is partly composed on the plan of an old song by the same name.

VI

His colour sicken'd more and more,
    He faded into age;
And then his enemies began
    To show their deadly rage.

VII

They've taen a weapon, long and sharp,
    And cut him by the knee;
Then ty'd him fast upon a cart,
    Like a rogue for forgerie.

VIII

They laid him down upon his back,
    And cudgell'd him full sore;
They hung him up before the storm,
    And turn'd him o'er and o'er.

IX

They filled up a darksome pit
    With water to the brim,
They heaved in John Barleycorn,
    There let him sink or swim.

X

They laid him out upon the floor,
    To work him farther woe,
And still, as signs of life appear'd,
    They toss'd him to and fro.

XI

They wasted, o'er a scorching flame,
    The marrow of his bones;
But a Miller us'd him worst of all,
    For he crush'd him between two stones.

XII

And they hae taen his very heart's blood,
    And drank it round and round;

And still the more and more they drank,
   Their joy did more abound.

XIII

John Barleycorn was a hero bold,
   Of noble enterprise,
For if you do but taste his blood,
   'Twill make your courage rise.

XIV

'Twill make a man forget his woe;
   'Twill heighten all his joy:
'Twill make the widow's heart to sing,
   Tho' the tear were in her eye.

XV

Then let us toast John Barleycorn,
   Each man a glass in hand;
And may his great posterity
   Ne'er fail in old Scotland!

Mary Morison

Tune, Duncan Davison

O Mary, at thy window be,
  It is the wish'd, the trysted hour;
Those smiles and glances let me see,
  That make the miser's treasure poor:
How blythely wad I bide the stoure,
  A weary slave frae sun to sun;
Could I the rich reward secure,
  The lovely Mary Morison!

Yestreen when to the trembling string
  The dance gaed through the lighted ha',
To thee my fancy took its wing,
  I sat, but neither heard, nor saw:
Though this was fair, and that was braw,
  And yon the toast of a' the town,
I sigh'd, and said amang them a',
  'Ye are na Mary Morison.'

O Mary, canst thou wreck his peace,
  Wha for thy sake wad gladly die!
Or canst thou break that heart of his,
  Whase only faute is loving thee!
If love for love thou wilt na gie,
  At least be pity to me shown;
A thought ungentle canna be
  The thought o' Mary Morison.

In Mauchline there dwells

∿✕∿✕∿

Tune, Bonie Dundee

In Mauchline there dwells six proper young Belles,
    The pride of the place and its neighbourhood a',
Their carriage and dress a stranger would guess,
    In Lon'on or Paris they 'd gotten it a':
Miss Miller is fine, Miss Murkland 's divine,
    Miss Smith she has wit and Miss Betty is braw;
There 's beauty and fortune to get wi' Miss Morton,
    But Armour 's the jewel for me o' them a'. –

O leave novels

O leave novels, ye Mauchline belles,
  Ye're safer at your spinning wheel;
Such witching books, are baited hooks
  For rakish rooks like Rob Mossgiel.
Your fine Tom Jones and Grandisons
  They make your youthful fancies reel;
They heat your brains, and fire your veins,
  And then you're prey for Rob Mossgiel.

Beware a tongue that 's smoothly hung;
  A heart that warmly seems to feel;
That feelin heart but acks a part,
  'Tis rakish art in Rob Mossgiel.
The frank address, the soft caress,
  Are worse than poisoned darts of steel,
The frank address, and politesse,
  Are all finesse in Rob Mossgiel.

Green grow the rashes

CHORUS

Green grow the rashes, O;
Green grow the rashes, O;
The sweetest hours that e'er I spend,
  Are spent amang the lasses, O.

I

There's nought but care on ev'ry han',
  In ev'ry hour that passes, O:
What signifies the life o' man,
  An' 'twere na for the lasses, O.
                              Green grow, &c.

II

The warly race may riches chase,
  An' riches still may fly them, O;
An' tho' at last they catch them fast,
  Their hearts can ne'er enjoy them, O.
                              Green grow, &c.

III

But gie me a canny hour at e'en,
  My arms about my Dearie, O;
An' warly cares, an' warly men,
  May a' gae tapsalteerie, O!
                              Green grow, &c.

IV

For you sae douse, ye sneer at this,
  Ye're nought but senseless asses, O:
The wisest Man the warl' saw,
  He dearly lov'd the lasses, O.
                              Green grow, &c.

V

Auld Nature swears, the lovely Dears
Her noblest work she classes, O:
Her prentice han' she try'd on man,
An' then she made the lasses, O.

Green grow, &c.

The rantin dog the daddie o't

O Wha my babie-clouts will buy,
O Wha will tent me when I cry;
Wha will kiss me where I lie,
The rantin dog the daddie o't.

O Wha will own he did the faut,
O Wha will buy the groanin maut,
O Wha will tell me how to ca 't,
The rantin dog the daddie o't.

When I mount the Creepie-chair,
Wha will sit beside me there,
Gie me Rob, I'll seek nae mair,
The rantin dog the Daddie o't.

Wha will crack to me my lane;
Wha will mak me fidgin fain;
What will kiss me o'er again,
The rantin dog the Daddie o't.

There was a lad

❧❧❧

Tune, Daintie Davie

There was a lad was born in Kyle,
But what na day o' what na style,
I doubt it 's hardly worth the while
   To be sae nice wi' Robin.
        Robin was a rovin' Boy,
           Rantin' rovin', rantin' rovin';
        Robin was a rovin' Boy,
           Rantin' rovin' Robin.

Our monarch's hindmost year but ane
Was five-and-twenty days begun,
'Twas then a blast o' Janwar' Win'*
   Blew hansel in on Robin.

The Gossip keekit in his loof,
Quo' scho wha lives will see the proof,
This waly boy will be nae coof,
   I think we'll ca' him Robin.

He'll hae misfortunes great and sma',
But ay a heart aboon them a';
He'll be a credit till us a',
   We'll a' be proud o' Robin.

But sure as three times three mak nine,
I see by ilka score and line,
This chap will dearly like our kin',
   So leeze me on thee, Robin.

Guid faith quo' scho I doubt you Stir,
Ye'll gar the lasses lie aspar;
But twenty fauts ye may hae waur –
   So blessins on thee, Robin.

* Jan. 25th 1759, the date of my Bardship's vital existence.

Ca' the ewes (A)

Ca' the ewes to the knowes,
Ca' them whare the heather grows,
Ca' them whare the burnie rowes,
    My bonie Dearie. –

As I gaed down the water-side
There I met my Shepherd-lad,
He row'd me sweetly in his plaid,
    And he ca'd me his Dearie. –
        Ca' the &c.

Will ye gang down the water-side
And see the waves sae sweetly glide
Beneath the hazels spreading wide,
    The moon it shines fu' clearly. –
        Ca' the &c.

I was bred up at nae sic school,
My Shepherd-lad, to play the fool;
And a' the day to sit in dool,
    And naebody to see me. –
        Ca' the &c.

Ye sall get gowns and ribbons meet,
Cauf-leather shoon upon your feet,
And in my arms ye 'se lie and sleep,
    And ye sall be my Dearie. –
        Ca' the &c.

If ye'll but stand to what ye've said,
I'se gang wi' you, my Shepherd-lad,
And ye may rowe me in your plaid,
    And I sall be your Dearie. –
        Ca' the &c.

While waters wimple to the sea;
While Day blinks in the lift sae hie;
Till clay-cauld Death sall blin' my e'e,
   Ye sall be my Dearie. –
           Ca' the &c.

AFTER 1788

I'm o'er young to Marry Yet

I am my mammy's ae bairn,
   Wi' unco folk I weary, Sir,
And lying in a man's bed,
   I'm fley'd it make me irie, Sir.
     I'm o'er young, I'm o'er young,
      I'm o'er young to marry yet;
     I'm o'er young, 'twad be a sin
      To tak me frae my mammy yet.

Hallowmass is come and gane,
   The nights are lang in winter, Sir;
And you an' I in ae bed,
   In trowth, I dare na venture, Sir.
     I'm o'er young &c.

Fu' loud and shill the frosty wind
   Blaws thro' the leafless timmer, Sir;
But if ye come this gate again,
   I'll aulder be gin simmer, Sir.
     I'm o'er young &c.

McPherson's Farewell

Farewell, ye dungeons dark and strong,
   The wretch's destinie!
McPherson's time will not be long,
   On yonder gallows-tree.

CHORUS

Sae rantingly, sae wantonly,
   Sae dauntingly gae'd he:
He play'd a spring, and danc'd it round
   Below the gallows-tree.

O what is death but parting breath?
   On many a bloody plain
I've dar'd his face, and in this place
   I scorn him yet again!
     Sae rantingly, &c.

Untie these bands from off my hands,
   And bring to me my sword;
And there's no a man in all Scotland,
   But I'll brave him at a word.
     Sae rantingly, &c.

I've liv'd a life of sturt and strife;
   I die by treacherie:
It burns my heart I must depart
   And not avenged be.
     Sae rantingly, &c.

Now farewell, light, thou sunshine bright,
   And all beneath the sky!
May coward shame distain his name,
   The wretch that dares not die!
     Sae rantingly, &c.

What will I do gin my Hoggie die

꧁꧂

What will I do gin my Hoggie die,
  My joy, my pride, my Hoggie;
My only beast, I had nae mae,
  And vow but I was vogie. —

The lee-lang night we watch'd the fauld,
  Me and my faithfu' doggie;
We heard nought but the roaring linn
  Amang the braes sae scroggie. —

But the houlet cry'd frae the Castle-wa',
  The blitter frae the boggie,
The tod reply'd upon the hill,
  I trembled for my Hoggie. —

When day did daw and cocks did craw,
  The morning it was foggie;
An unco tyke lap o'er the dyke
  And maist has kill'd my Hoggie. —

Up in the Morning Early

Cauld blaws the wind frae east to west,
  The drift is driving sairly;
Sae loud and shill 's I hear the blast,
  I'm sure it 's winter fairly.
Up in the morning 's no for me,
  Up in the morning early;
When a' the hills are cover'd wi' snaw,
  I'm sure it is winter fairly.

The birds sit chittering in the thorn,
  A' day they fare but sparely;
And lang 's the night frae e'en to morn,
  I'm sure it 's winter fairly.
    Up in the morning 's, &c.

To daunton me

The blude-red rose at Yule may blaw,
The simmer lilies bloom in snaw,
The frost may freeze the deepest sea,
But an auld man shall never daunton me. –

CHORUS
To daunton me, to daunton me,
  An auld man shall never daunton me. –

2

To daunton me, and me sae young,
Wi' his fause heart and his flattering tongue,
That is the thing you shall never see
For an auld man shall never daunton me. –
  To daunton me, &c.

3

For a' his meal and a' his maut,
For a' his fresh beef and his saut,
For a' his gold and white monie,
An auld man shall never daunton me. –
  To daunton me, &c.

4

His gear may buy him kye and yowes,
His gear may buy him glens and knowes,
But me he shall not buy nor fee,
For an auld man shall never daunton me. –
  To daunton me, &c.

5

He hirples twa-fauld as he dow,
Wi' his teethless gab and his auld beld pow,

And the rain rins down frae his red-blear'd e'e,
That auld man shall never daunton me. –
  To daunton me, &c.

O'er the water to Charlie

Come boat me o'er, come row me o'er,
  Come boat me o'er to Charlie;
I'll gie John Ross anither bawbee
  To boat me o'er to Charlie. –

CHORUS
We'll o'er the water, we'll o'er the sea,
  We'll o'er the water to Charlie;
Come weal, come woe, we'll gather and go,
  And live or die wi' Charlie. –

I lo'e weel my Charlie's name,
  Tho' some there be abhor him:
But O, to see auld Nick gaun hame,
  And Charlie's faes before him!
    We'll o'er &c.

I swear and vow by moon and stars,
  And sun that shines so early!
If I had twenty thousand lives,
  I'd die as aft for Charlie. –
    We'll o'er &c.

Up and warn a' Willie

Up and warn a' Willie,
  Warn, warn a';
To hear my cantie Highland sang,
  Relate the thing I saw, Willie. –

When we gaed to the braes o' Mar,
  And to the wapon-shaw, Willie,
Wi' true design to serve the king
  And banish whigs awa, Willie. –
Up and warn a', Willie,
  Warn, warn a';
For Lords and lairds came there bedeen
  And wow but they were braw, Willie. –

But when the standard was set up
  Right fierce the wind did blaw, Willie;
The royal nit upon the tap
  Down to the ground did fa', Willie. –
Up and warn a', Willie,
  Warn, warn a';
Then second-sighted Sandie said
  We'd do nae gude at a', Willie. –

But when the army join'd at Perth,
  The bravest ere ye saw, Willie,
We didna doubt the rogues to rout,
  Restore our king and a', Willie.
Up and warn a' Willie,
  Warn, warn a';
The pipers play'd frae right to left
  O whirry whigs awa, Willie. –

But when we march'd to Sherramuir
  And there the rebels saw, Willie;

Brave Argyle attack'd our right,
    Our flank and front and a', Willie. –
Up and warn a', Willie,
    Warn, warn a';
Traitor Huntly soon gave way
    Seaforth, St Clair and a' Willie. –

But brave Glengary on our right,
    The rebel's left did claw, Willie,
He there the greatest slaughter made
    That ever Donald saw, Willie. –
Up and warn a', Willie,
    Warn, warn a',
And Whittam sh–t his breeks for fear
    And fast did rin awa', Willie. –

For he ca'd us a Highland mob
    And soon he'd slay us a', Willie;
But we chas'd him back to Stirling brig
    Dragoons and foot and a', Willie. –
Up and warn a' Willie,
    Warn, warn a',
At length we rallied on a hill
    And briskly up did draw, Willie. –

But when Argyle did view our line,
    And them in order saw, Willie,
He streight gaed to Dumblane again
    And back his left did draw, Willie. –
Up and warn a' Willie,
    Warn warn a',
Then we to Auchterairder march'd
    To wait a better fa' Willie. –

Now if ye spier wha wan the day,
    I've tell'd you what I saw, Willie,
We baith did fight and baith did beat
    And baith did rin awa, Willie.

Up and warn a', Willie,
Warn, warn a' Willie,
For second sighted Sandie said
We'd do nae gude at a', Willie. –

And I'll kiss thee yet, yet

Tune, Braes o' Balquhidder

An I'll kiss thee yet, yet,
An I'll kiss thee o'er again;
An I'll kiss thee yet, yet,
My bony Peggy Alison.
Ilk Care and Fear, when thou art near,
I ever mair defy them, O;
Young kings upon their hansel throne
Are no sae blest as I am, O!

When in my arms, wi' a' thy charms,
I clasp my countless treasure, O!
I seek nae mair o' Heav'n to share,
Than sic a moment's pleasure, O!

And by thy een sae bony blue,
I swear I'm thine forever O!
And on thy lips I seal my vow,
And break it shall I never O!

Rattlin, roarin Willie

O Rattlin, roarin Willie,
   O he held to the fair,
An' for to sell his fiddle
   And buy some other ware;
But parting wi' his fiddle,
   The saut tear blin't his e'e;
And Rattlin, roarin Willie,
   Ye're welcome hame to me.

O Willie, come sell your fiddle,
   O sell your fiddle sae fine;
O Willie, come sell your fiddle,
   And buy a pint o' wine;
If I should sell my fiddle,
   The warl' would think I was mad,
For mony a rantin day
   My fiddle and I hae had.

As I cam by Crochallan
   I cannily keekit ben,
Rattlin, roarin Willie
   Was sitting at yon boord-en',
Sitting at yon boord-en',
   And amang guid companie;
Rattlin, roarin Willie,
   Ye're welcome hame to me!

I love my Jean

Tune, Miss admiral Gordon's Strathspey

Of a' the airts the wind can blaw,
    I dearly like the West;
For there the bony Lassie lives,
    The Lassie I lo'e best:
There 's wild-woods grow, and rivers row,
    And mony a hill between;
But day and night my fancy's flight
    Is ever wi' my Jean. —

I see her in the dewy flowers,
    I see her sweet and fair;
I hear her in the tunefu' birds,
    I hear her charm the air:
There 's not a bony flower, that springs
    By fountain, shaw, or green;
There 's not a bony bird that sings
    But minds me o' my Jean. —

O, were I on Parnassus Hill

Tune, My love is lost to me

O were I on Parnassus hill;
Or had o' Helicon my fill;
That I might catch poetic skill,
   To sing how dear I love thee.
But Nith maun be my Muses well,
My Muse maun be thy bonie sell;
On Corsincon I'll glowr and spell,
   And write how dear I love thee.

Then come, sweet Muse, inspire my lay!
For a' the lee-lang simmer's day,
I couldna sing, I couldna say,
   How much, how dear, I love thee.
I see thee dancing o'er the green,
Thy waist sae jimp, thy limbs sae clean,
Thy tempting lips, thy roguish een –
   By Heaven and Earth I love thee.

By night, by day, a-field, at hame,
The thoughts o' thee my breast inflame;
And ay I muse and sing thy name,
   I only live to love thee.
Tho' I were doom'd to wander on,
Beyond the sea, beyond the sun,
Till my last, weary sand was run;
   Till then – and then I love thee.

Whistle o'er the lave o't

First when Maggy was my care,
Heaven, I thought, was in her air;
Now we're married – spier nae mair –
    Whistle o'er the lave o't. –

Meg was meek, and Meg was mild,
Sweet and harmless as a child –
Wiser men than me 's beguil'd;
    Whistle o'er the lave o't. –

How we live, my Meg and me,
How we love and how we gree;
I carena by how few may see,
    Whistle o'er the lave o't. –

Wha I wish were maggots' meat,
Dish'd up in her winding-sheet;
I could write – but Meg maun see 't –
    Whistle o'er the lave o't. –

Tam Glen

Tune, Merry beggars

My heart is a breaking, dear Tittie,
 Some counsel unto me come len';
To anger them a' is a pity,
 But what will I do wi' Tam Glen? –

I'm thinking, wi' sic a braw fellow,
 In poortith I might mak a fen':
What care I in riches to wallow,
 If I mauna marry Tam Glen. –

There 's Lowrie the laird o' Dumeller,
 'Gude day to you brute' he comes ben:
He brags and he blaws o' his siller,
 But when will he dance like Tam Glen. –

My Minnie does constantly deave me,
 And bids me beware o' young men;
They flatter, she says, to deceive me,
 But wha can think sae o' Tam Glen. –

My Daddie says, gin I'll forsake him,
 He'll gie me gude hunder marks ten:
But, if it 's ordain'd I maun take him,
 O wha will I get but Tam Glen?

Yestreen at the Valentines' dealing,
 My heart to my mou gied a sten;
For thrice I drew ane without failing,
 And thrice it was written, Tam Glen. –

The last Halloween I was waukin
 My droukit sark-sleeve, as ye ken;
His likeness cam up the house staukin,
 And the very grey breeks o' Tam Glen!

Come counsel, dear Tittie, don't tarry;
   I'll gie you my bonie black hen,
Gif ye will advise me to Marry
   The lad I lo'e dearly, Tam Glen. —

Auld lang syne

Should auld acquaintance be forgot
  And never brought to mind?
Should auld acquaintance be forgot,
  And auld lang syne!

For auld lang syne, my jo,
  For auld lang syne,
We'll tak a *cup o' kindness yet
  For auld lang syne.

And surely ye'll be your pint stowp!
  And surely I'll be mine!
And we'll tak a cup o' kindness yet,
  For auld lang syne.
      For auld, &c.

We twa hae run about the braes,
  And pou'd the gowans fine;
But we've wander'd mony a weary fitt,
  Sin auld lang syne.
      For auld, &c.

We twa hae paidl'd in the burn,
  Frae morning sun till dine;
But seas between us braid hae roar'd,
  Sin auld lang syne.
      For auld, &c.

And there 's a hand, my trusty fiere!
  And gie 's a hand o' thine!
And we'll tak a right gude-willie-waught,
  For auld lang sine.
      For auld, &c.

* Some sing, Kiss, in place of Cup.

33

My bony Mary

Go fetch to me a pint o' wine,
    And fill it in a silver tassie;
That I may drink, before I go,
    A service to my bonie lassie:
The boat rocks at the Pier o' Lieth,
    Fu' loud the wind blaws frae the Ferry,
The ship rides by the Berwick-law,
    And I maun leave my bony Mary.

The trumpets sound, the banners fly,
    The glittering spears are ranked ready,
The shouts o' war are heard afar,
    The battle closes deep and bloody.
It 's not the roar o' sea or shore,
    Wad make me langer wish to tarry;
Nor shouts o' war that 's heard afar –
    It 's leaving thee, my bony Mary!

Louis what reck I by thee

Louis, what reck I by thee,
   Or Geordie on his ocean:
Dyvor, beggar louns to me,
   I reign in Jeanie's bosom.

Let her crown my love her law,
   And in her breast enthrone me:
Kings and nations, swith awa!
   Reif randies I disown ye! –

Robin shure in hairst

CHORUS

Robin shure in hairst,
   I shure wi' him;
Fint a heuk had I,
   Yet I stack by him.

SONG

I gaed up to Dunse,
   To warp a wab o' plaiden;
At his daddie's yet,
   Wha met me but Robin.
     Robin shure &c.

Was na Robin bauld,
   Tho' I was a cotter,
Play'd me sic a trick
   And me the Eller's dochter!
     Robin shure &c.

Robin promis'd me
   A' my winter vittle;
Fient haet he had but three
   Goos feathers and a whittle.
     Robin shure &c.

Afton Water

Flow gently, sweet Afton, among thy green braes,
Flow gently, I'll sing thee a song in thy praise;
My Mary's asleep by thy murmuring stream,
Flow gently, sweet Afton, disturb not her dream.

Thou stock dove whose echo resounds thro' the glen,
Ye wild whistling blackbirds in yon thorny den,
Thou green crested lapwing thy screaming forbear,
I charge you disturb not my slumbering Fair.

How lofty, sweet Afton, thy neighbouring hills,
Far mark'd with the courses of clear, winding rills;
There daily I wander as noon rises high,
My flocks and my Mary's sweet Cot in my eye.

How pleasant thy banks and green vallies below,
Where wild in the woodlands the primroses blow;
There oft as mild ev'ning weeps over the lea,
The sweet scented birk shades my Mary and me.

Thy chrystal stream, Afton, how lovely it glides,
And winds by the cot where my Mary resides;
How wanton thy waters her snowy feet lave,
As gathering sweet flowerets she stems thy clear wave.

Flow gently, sweet Afton, among thy green braes,
Flow gently, sweet River, the theme of my lays;
My Mary's asleep by thy murmuring stream,
Flow gently, sweet Afton, disturb not her dream.

Willie brew'd a peck o' maut

O Willie brew'd a peck o' maut,
  And Rob and Allan cam to see;
Three blyther hearts, that lee lang night,
  Ye wad na found in Christendie.

CHORUS
We are na fou, we're nae that fou,
  But just a drappie in our e'e;
The cock may craw, the day may daw,
  And ay we'll taste the barley bree.

Here are we met, three merry boys,
  Three merry boys I trow are we;
And mony a night we've merry been,
  And mony mae we hope to be!
    Cho? We are na fou, &c.

It is the moon, I ken her horn,
  That 's blinkin in the lift sae hie;
She shines sae bright to wyle us hame,
  But by my sooth she'll wait a wee!
    Cho? We are na fou, &c.

Wha first shall rise to gang awa,
  A cuckold, coward loun is he!
Wha first beside his chair shall fa',
  He is the king amang us three!
    Cho? We are na fou, &c.

Ay waukin O

Simmer 's a pleasant time,
  Flowers of every colour;
The water rins o'er the heugh,
  And I long for my true lover!
CHORUS
  Ay waukin, Oh,
    Waukin still and weary:
  Sleep I can get nane,
    For thinking on my Dearie. –

When I sleep I dream,
  When I wauk I'm irie;
Sleep I can get nane,
  For thinking on my Dearie. –
            Ay waukin &c.

Lanely night comes on,
  A' the lave are sleepin:
I think on my bonie lad,
  And I bleer my een wi' greetin. –
            Ay waukin &c.

Lassie lie near me

Lang hae we parted been,
  Lassie my dearie;
Now we are met again,
  Lassie lie near me.
    Cho: Near me, near me,
      Lassie lie near me;
      Lang hast thou lien thy lane,
      Lassie lie near me.

A' that I hae endur'd,
  Lassie, my dearie,
Here in thy arms is cur'd,
  Lassie lie near me.
    Cho: Near me, &c.

My love she's but a lassie yet

My love she's but a lassie yet,
My love she's but a lassie yet;
We'll let her stand a year or twa,
    She'll no be half sae saucy yet. –

I rue the day I sought her O,
I rue the day I sought her O,
Wha gets her needs na say he's woo'd,
    But he may say he's bought her O. –

Come draw a drap o' the best o't yet,
Come draw a drap o' the best o't yet:
Gae seek for Pleasure whare ye will,
    But here I never misst it yet. –

We're a' dry wi' drinking o't,
We're a' dry wi' drinking o't:
The minister kisst the fidler's wife,
    He could na preach for thinkin o't. –

There 's a youth in this City

A Gaelic Air

1

There 's a youth in this city, it were a great pity
    That he from our lasses should wander awa;
For he 's bony and braw, weel-favour'd with a',
    And his hair has a natural buckle and a'. –
His coat is the hue of his bonnet sae blue;
    His facket is white as the new-driven snaw;
His hose they are blae, and his shoon like the slae;
    And his clear siller buckles they dazzle us a'. –

2

For beauty and fortune the laddie 's been courtin;
    Weel-featur'd, weel-tocher'd, weel-mounted and braw;
But chiefly the siller, that gars him gang till her;
    The Pennie 's the jewel that beautifies a'. –
There 's Meg wi' the mailin that fain wad a haen him;
    And Susie whase daddy was laird o' the Ha':
There 's lang-tocher'd Nancy maist fetters his fancy –
    But th' laddie's dear sel he lo'es dearest of a'. –

John Anderson my Jo

John Anderson my jo, John,
  When we were first acquent;
Your locks were like the raven,
  Your bony brow was brent;
But now your brow is beld, John,
  Your locks are like the snaw;
But blessings on your frosty pow,
  John Anderson my Jo.

John Anderson my jo, John,
  We clamb the hill the gither;
And mony a canty day, John,
  We've had wi' ane anither:
Now we maun totter down, John,
  And hand in hand we'll go;
And sleep the gither at the foot,
  John Anderson my Jo.

Awa whigs awa

Awa whigs awa,
Awa whigs awa,
Ye're but a pack o' traitor louns,
Ye'll do nae gude at a'.

Our thrissles flourish'd fresh and fair,
And bonie bloom'd our roses;
But whigs cam like a frost in June,
And wither'd a' our posies.
Cho: Awa whigs &c.

Our ancient crown 's fa'n in the dust;
Deil blin' them wi' the stoure o't,
And write their names in his black beuk
Wha gae the whigs the power o't!
Cho: Awa whigs &c.

Our sad decay in church and state
Surpasses my descriving:
The whigs cam o'er us for a curse,
And we hae done wi' thriving.
Cho: Awa whigs &c.

Grim Vengeance lang has taen a nap,
But we may see him wauken:
Gude help the day when royal heads
Are hunted like a maukin.
Cho: Awa whigs &c.

Merry hae I been teethin a heckle

❧❧❧

Tune, Boddich na' mbrigs, or Lord Breadalbine's March

O merry hae I been teethin a heckle,
   An' merry hae I been shapin a spoon:
O merry hae I been cloutin a kettle,
   An' kissin my Katie when a' was done.
O, a' the lang day I ca' at my hammer,
   An' a' the lang day I whistle and sing;
O, a' the lang night I cuddle my kimmer,
   An' a' the lang night as happy 's a king.

Bitter in dool I lickit my winnins
   O' marrying Bess, to gie her a slave:
Blest be the hour she cool'd in her linnens,
   And blythe be the bird that sings on her grave!
Come to my arms, my Katie, my Katie,
   An' come to my arms and kiss me again!
Druken or sober, here 's to thee, Katie!
   And blest be the day I did it again.

The Battle of Sherra-moor

Tune, Cameronian Rant

O cam ye here the fight to shun,
   Or herd the sheep wi' me, man,
Or were ye at the Sherra-moor,
   Or did the battle see, man.
I saw the battle sair and teugh,
And reekin-red ran mony a sheugh,
My heart for fear gae sough for sough,
To hear the thuds, and see the cluds
O' Clans frae woods, in tartan duds,
Wha glaum'd at kingdoms three, man.
        Cho: la la la, &c.

The red-coat lads wi' black cockauds
   To meet them were na slaw, man,
They rush'd, and push'd, and blude outgush'd,
   And mony a bouk did fa', man:
The great Argyle led on his files,
I wat they glanc'd for twenty miles,
They hough'd the Clans like nine-pin kyles,
They hack'd and hash'd while braid swords clash'd,
And thro' they dash'd, and hew'd and smash'd,
Till fey men di'd awa, man.
        Cho: la la la, &c.

But had ye seen the philibegs
   And skyrin tartan trews, man,
When in the teeth they dar'd our Whigs,
   And covenant Trueblues, man;
In lines extended lang and large,
When baiginets o'erpower'd the targe,
And thousands hasten'd to the charge;
Wi' Highland wrath they frae the sheath
Drew blades o' death, till out o' breath

They fled like frighted dows, man.
    Cho? la la la, &c.

O how deil Tam can that be true,
    The chace gaed frae the north, man;
I saw mysel, they did pursue
    The horse-men back to Forth, man;
And at Dunblane in my ain sight
They took the brig wi' a' their might,
And straught to Stirling wing'd their flight,
But, cursed lot! the gates were shut
And mony a huntit, poor Red-coat
For fear amaist did swarf, man.
        Cho? la la la, &c.

My sister Kate cam up the gate
    Wi' crowdie unto me, man;
She swoor she saw some rebels run
    To Perth and to Dundee, man:
Their left-hand General had nae skill;
The Angus lads had nae gude will,
That day their neebour's blude to spill;
For fear by foes that they should lose
Their cogs o' brose, they scar'd at blows
And hameward fast did flee, man.
        Cho? la la la, &c.

They've lost some gallant gentlemen
    Amang the Highland clans, man;
I fear my Lord Panmuir is slain,
    Or in his en'mies hands, man:
Now wad ye sing this double flight,
Some fell for wrang and some for right,
And mony bade the warld gudenight;
Say pell and mell, wi' muskets knell
How Tories fell, and Whigs to h–ll
Flew off in frighted bands, man.
        Cho? la la la, &c.

Ken ye ought o' Captain Grose?

Written in a wrapper inclosing a letter to Captn Grose, to be left with Mr Cardonnel Antiquarian –

Tune, Sir John Malcolm

Ken ye ought o' Captain Grose?
    Igo and ago –
If he 's amang his friends or foes?
    Iram coram dago. –

Is he South, or is he North?
    Igo and ago –
Or drowned in the river Forth?
    Iram coram dago. –

Is he slain by Highland bodies?
    Igo and ago –
And eaten like a wether-haggis?
    Iram coram dago. –

Is he to Abram's bosom gane?
    Igo and ago –
Or haudin Sarah by the wame?
    Iram coram dago. –

Whare'er he be, the Lord be near him!
    Igo and ago –
As for the deil, he daur na steer him,
    Iram coram dago. –

But please transmit th' inclosed letter,
    Igo and ago –
Which will oblidge your humble debtor,
    Iram coram dago. –

So may ye hae auld Stanes in store,
    Igo and ago –

The very Stanes that Adam bore;
    Iram coram dago. –

So may ye get in glad possession,
    Igo and ago –
The coins o' Satan's Coronation!
    Iram coram dago. –

There'll never be peace till Jamie comes hame

By yon castle wa' at the close of the day,
I heard a man sing tho' his head it was grey;
And as he was singing the tears down came,
There'll never be peace till Jamie comes hame. –
The Church is in ruins, the State is in jars,
Delusions, oppressions, and murderous wars:
We dare na weel say 't, but we ken wha 's to blame,
There'll never be peace till Jamie comes hame. –

My seven braw sons for Jamie drew sword,
And now I greet round their green beds in the yerd;
It brak the sweet heart of my faithfu' auld Dame,
There'll never be peace till Jamie comes hame. –
Now life is a burden that bows me down,
Sin I tint my bairns, and he tint his crown;
But till my last moments my words are the same,
There'll never be peace till Jamie comes hame. –

The Banks o' Doon (A)

Ye flowery banks o' bonie Doon,
  How can ye blume sae fair;
How can ye chant, ye little birds,
  And I sae fu' o' care!

Thou'll break my heart, thou bonie bird
  That sings upon the bough;
Thou minds me o' the happy days
  When my fause luve was true.

Thou'll break my heart, thou bonie bird
  That sings beside thy mate;
For sae I sat, and sae I sang,
  And wist na o' my fate.

Aft hae I rov'd by bonie Doon,
  To see the wood-bine twine,
And ilka bird sang o' its love,
  And sae did I o' mine.

Wi' lightsome heart I pu'd a rose
  Frae aff its thorny tree,
And my fause luver staw the rose,
  But left the thorn wi' me.

Wi' lightsome heart I pu'd a rose,
  Upon a morn in June:
And sae I flourish'd on the morn,
  And sae was pu'd or noon!

The Banks o' Doon (B)

Ye banks and braes o' bonie Doon,
    How can ye bloom sae fresh and fair;
How can ye chant, ye little birds,
    And I sae weary, fu' o' care!
Thou'll break my heart, thou warbling bird
    That wantons thro' the flowering thorn:
Thou minds me o' departed joys,
    Departed, never to return. –

Oft hae I rov'd by bonie Doon,
    To see the rose and woodbine twine;
And ilka bird sang o' its Luve,
    And fondly sae did I o' mine. –
Wi' lightsome heart I pu'd a rose,
    Fu' sweet upon its thorny tree;
And my fause Luver staw my rose,
    But, ah! he left the thorn wi' me. –

Ae fond kiss

Tune, Rory Dall's port

Ae fond kiss, and then we sever;
Ae fareweel, and then for ever!
Deep in heart-wrung tears I'll pledge thee,
Warring sighs and groans I'll wage thee. –

Who shall say that Fortune grieves him,
While the star of hope she leaves him:
Me, nae chearful twinkle lights me;
Dark despair around benights me. –

I'll ne'er blame my partial fancy,
Naething could resist my Nancy:
But to see her, was to love her;
Love but her, and love for ever. –

Had we never lov'd sae kindly,
Had we never lov'd sae blindly!
Never met – or never parted,
We had ne'er been broken-hearted. –

Fare-thee-weel, thou first and fairest!
Fare-thee-weel, thou best and dearest!
Thine be ilka joy and treasure,
Peace, Enjoyment, Love and Pleasure! –

Ae fond kiss, and then we sever!
Ae fareweel, Alas, for ever:
Deep in heart-wrung tears I'll pledge thee,
Warring sighs and groans I'll wage thee. –

O saw ye bonie Lesley

O saw ye bonie Lesley,
  As she gaed o'er the Border?
She 's gane, like Alexander,
  To spread her conquests farther.

To see her is to love her,
  And love but her for ever;
For Nature made her what she is
  And never made anither.

Thou art a queen, fair Lesley,
  Thy subjects we, before thee:
Thou art divine, fair Lesley,
  The hearts o' men adore thee.

The deil he could na scaith thee,
  Or aught that wad belang thee:
He'd look into thy bonie face,
  And say, 'I canna wrang thee!'

The Powers aboon will tent thee,
  Misfortune sha'na steer thee;
Thou'rt like themsels sae lovely,
  That ill they'll ne'er let near thee.

Return again, fair Lesley,
  Return to Caledonie!
That we may brag, we hae a lass
  There 's nane again sae bonie.

My Tochers the Jewel

O meikle thinks my Luve o' my beauty,
    And meikle thinks my Luve o' my kin;
But little thinks my Luve, I ken brawlie,
    My tocher 's the jewel has charms for him.
It 's a' for the apple he'll nourish the tree;
    It 's a' for the hiney he'll cherish the bee;
My laddie 's sae meikle in love wi' the siller,
    He canna hae luve to spare for me.

Your proffer o' luve 's an airle-penny,
    My tocher 's the bargain ye wad buy;
But an ye be crafty, I am cunnin,
    Sae ye wi' anither your fortune maun try.
Ye're like to the timmer o' yon rotten wood,
    Ye're like to the bark o' yon rotten tree,
Ye'll slip frae me like a knotless thread,
    And ye'll crack your credit wi' mae nor me.

I do confess thou art sae fair

I do confess thou art sae fair,
    I wad been o'er the lugs in luve;
Had I na found, the slightest prayer
    That lips could speak, thy heart could muve. –

I do confess thee sweet, but find,
    Thou art sae thriftless o' thy sweets,
Thy favors are the silly wind
    That kisseth ilka thing it meets. –

See yonder rose-bud, rich in dew,
    Amang its native briers sae coy,
How sune it tines its scent and hue,
    When pu'd and worn a common toy!

Sic fate ere lang shall thee betide;
    Tho' thou may gayly bloom a while,
Yet sune thou shalt be thrown aside,
    Like ony common weed and vile. –

It is na, Jean, thy bonie face

It is na, Jean, thy bonie face,
  Nor shape that I admire,
Altho' thy beauty and thy grace
  Might weel awauk desire. –

Something in ilka part o' thee
  To praise, to love, I find,
But dear as is thy form to me,
  Still dearer is thy mind. –

Nae mair ungen'rous wish I hae,
  Nor stronger in my breast,
Than, if I canna mak thee sae,
  At least to see thee blest.

Content am I, if Heaven shall give
  But happiness to thee:
And as wi' thee I'd wish to live,
  For thee I'd bear to die.

The bonny wee thing

Bonie wee thing, canie wee thing,
　　Lovely wee thing, was thou mine;
I wad wear thee in my bosom,
　　Least my Jewel I should tine. –

Wishfully I look and languish
　　In that bonie face o' thine;
And my heart it stounds wi' anguish,
　　Least my wee thing be na mine. –
　　　　Bonie wee &c.

Wit, and Grace, and Love, and Beauty,
　　In ae constellation shine;
To adore thee is my duty,
　　Goddess o' this soul o' mine!

The weary pund o' tow

The weary pund, the weary pund,
  The weary pund o' tow;
I think my wife will end her life,
  Before she spin her tow. –

I bought my wife a stane o' lint,
  As gude as e'er did grow;
And a' that she has made o' that
  Is ae poor pund o' tow. –
    The weary &c.

There sat a bottle in a bole,
  Beyont the ingle low;
And ay she took the tither souk,
  To drouk the stourie tow. –
    The weary &c.

Quoth I, for shame, ye dirty dame,
  Gae spin your tap o' tow!
She took the rock, and wi' a knock,
  She brak it o'er my pow. –
    The weary &c.

At last her feet, I sang to see 't,
  Gaed foremost o'er the knowe;
And or I wad anither jad,
  I'll wallop in a tow. –
    The weary &c.

I hae a wife o' my ain

I hae a wife o' my ain,
  I'll partake wi' naebody;
I'll tak Cuckold frae nane,
  I'll gie Cuckold to naebody. –

I hae a penny to spend,
  There, thanks to naebody;
I hae naething to lend,
  I'll borrow frae naebody. –

I am naebody's lord,
  I'll be slave to naebody;
I hae a gude braid sword,
  I'll tak dunts frae naebody. –

I'll be merry and free,
  I'll be sad for naebody;
Naebody cares for me,
  I care for naebody. –

When she cam ben she bobbed

O when she cam ben she bobbed fu' law,
O when she cam ben she bobbed fu' law;
And when she cam ben she kiss'd Cockpen,
  And syne deny'd she did it at a'. –

And was na Cockpen right saucy witha',
And was na Cockpen right saucy witha',
In leaving the dochter of a lord,
  And kissin a Collier-lassie an' a'. –

O never look down, my lassie at a',
O never look down, my lassie at a';
Thy lips are as sweet and thy figure compleat,
  As the finest dame in castle or ha'. –

Tho' thou has nae silk and holland sae sma,
Tho' thou has nae silk and holland sae sma,
Thy coat and thy sark are thy ain handywark
  And Lady Jean was never sae braw. –

O, for ane and twenty Tam

Tune, The Moudiewort

An O, for ane and twenty Tam!
   An hey, sweet ane and twenty, Tam!
I'll learn my kin a rattlin sang,
   An I saw ane and twenty, Tam.

They snool me sair, and haud me down,
   And gar me look like bluntie, Tam;
But three short years will soon wheel roun',
   And then comes ane and twenty, Tam.
      An O, for &c.

A gleib o' lan', a claut o' gear,
   Was left me by my Auntie, Tam;
At kith or kin I need na spier,
   An I saw ane and twenty, Tam.
      An O, for &c.

They'll hae me wed a wealthy coof,
   Tho' I mysel hae plenty, Tam;
But hearst thou, laddie, there 's my loof,
   I'm thine at ane and twenty, Tam!
      An O, for &c.

Bessy and her spinning wheel

O leeze me on my spinnin-wheel,
And leeze me on my rock and reel;
Frae tap to tae that cleeds me bien,
And haps me fiel and warm at e'en!
I'll set me down and sing and spin,
While laigh descends the simmer sun,
Blest wi' content, and milk and meal,
O leeze me on my spinnin-wheel. –

On ilka hand the burnies trot,
And meet below my theekit cot;
The scented birk and hawthorn white
Across the pool their arms unite,
Alike to screen the birdie's nest,
And little fishes' callor rest:
The sun blinks kindly in the biel'
Where, blythe I turn my spinnin wheel. –

On lofty aiks the cushats wail,
And Echo cons the doolfu' tale;
The lintwhites in the hazel braes,
Delighted, rival ithers lays:
The craik amang the claver hay,
The pairtrick whirrin o'er the ley,
The swallow jinkin round my shiel,
Amuse me at my spinnin wheel. –

Wi' sma' to sell, and less to buy,
Aboon distress, below envy,
O wha wad leave this humble state,
For a' the pride of a' the Great?
Amid their flairing, idle toys,
Amid their cumbrous, dinsome joys,
Can they the peace and pleasure feel
Of Bessy at her spinnin wheel!

Ye Jacobites by name

Ye Jacobites by name, give an ear, give an ear;
  Ye Jacobites by name, give an ear;
    Ye Jacobites by name
      Your fautes I will proclaim,
        Your doctrines I maun blame,
        You shall hear. –

What is Right, and what is Wrang, by the law, by the law?
  What is Right, and what is Wrang, by the law?
    What is Right, and what is Wrang?
      A short Sword, and a lang,
        A weak arm, and a strang
        For to draw. –

What makes heroic strife, fam'd afar, fam'd afar?
  What makes heroic strife, fam'd afar?
    What makes heroic strife?
      To whet th' Assassin's knife,
        Or hunt a Parent's life
        Wi' bludie war. –

Then let your schemes alone, in the State, in the State,
  Then let your schemes alone in the State,
    Then let your schemes alone,
      Adore the rising sun,
        And leave a Man undone
        To his fate. –

Song — Sic a wife as Willie's wife

Willie Wastle dwalls on Tweed,
  The spot they ca' it Linkumdoddie;
A creeshie wabster till his trade,
  Can steal a clue wi' ony body:
He has a wife that 's dour and din,
  Tinkler Madgie was her mither;
Sic a wife as Willie's wife,
  I wadna gie a button for her. —

She has an e'e, she has but ane,
  Our cat has twa, the very colour;
Five rusty teeth, forbye a stump,
  A clapper-tongue wad deave a miller:
A whiskin beard about her mou,
  Her nose and chin they threaten ither;
Sic a wife as Willie's wife,
  I wad na gie a button for her. —

She 's bow-hough'd, she 's hem-shin'd,
  Ae limpin leg a hand-bread shorter;
She 's twisted right, she 's twisted left,
  To balance fair in ilka quarter:
She has a hump upon her breast,
  The twin o' that upon her shouther;
Sic a wife as Willie's wife,
  I wad na gie a button for her. —

Auld baudrans by the ingle sits,
  And wi' her loof her face a washin;
But Willie's wife is nae sae trig,
  She dights her grunzie wi' a hushian:
Her waly nieves like midden-creels,
  Her feet wad fyle the Logan-water;
Sic a wife as Willie's wife,
  I wad na gie a button for her. —

Such a parcel of rogues in a nation

Fareweel to a' our Scotish fame,
    Fareweel our ancient glory;
Fareweel even to the Scotish name,
    Sae fam'd in martial story!
Now Sark rins o'er the Solway sands,
    And Tweed rins to the ocean,
To mark whare England's province stands,
    Such a parcel of rogues in a nation!

What force or guile could not subdue,
    Thro' many warlike ages,
Is wrought now by a coward few,
    For hireling traitors' wages.
The English steel we could disdain,
    Secure in valor's station;
But English gold has been our bane,
    Such a parcel of rogues in a nation!

O would, or I had seen the day
    That treason thus could sell us,
My auld grey head had lien in clay,
    Wi' BRUCE and loyal WALLACE!
But pith and power, till my last hour,
    I'll mak this declaration;
We're bought and sold for English gold,
    Such a parcel of rogues in a nation!

Hey Ca' thro'

Up wi' the carls of Dysart,
   And the lads o' Buckhiven,
And the Kimmers o' Largo,
   And the lasses o' Leven.
     Hey ca' thro' ca' thro'
      For we hae mickle a do,
     Hey ca' thro' ca' thro'
      For we hae mickle a do.

We hae tales to tell,
   And we hae sangs to sing;
We hae pennies to spend,
   And we hae pints to bring.
     Hey ca' thro' &c.

We'll live a' our days,
   And them that comes behin',
Let them do the like,
   And spend the gear they win.
     Hey ca' thro' &c.

The De'il's awa wi' th' Exciseman

The deil cam fiddlin thro' the town,
  And danc'd awa wi' th' Exciseman;
And ilka wife cries, auld Mahoun,
  I wish you luck o' the prize, man.

The deil 's awa the deil 's awa
  The deil 's awa wi' th' Exciseman,
He 's danc'd awa he 's danc'd awa
    He 's danc'd awa wi' th' Exciseman.

We'll mak our maut and we'll brew our drink,
  We'll laugh, sing, and rejoice, man;
And mony braw thanks to the meikle black deil,
  That danc'd awa wi' th' Exciseman.
    The deil 's awa &c.

There 's threesome reels, there 's foursome reels,
  There 's hornpipes and strathspeys, man,
But the ae best dance e'er cam to the Land
  Was, the deil 's awa wi' th' Exciseman.
    The deil 's awa &c.

The lea-rig

When o'er the hill the eastern star
   Tells bughtin-time is near, my jo,
And owsen frae the furrowed field
   Return sae dowf and weary O:
Down by the burn where scented birks
   Wi' dew are hanging clear, my jo,
I'll meet thee on the lea-rig,
   My ain kind Dearie O.

At midnight hour, in mirkest glen,
   I'd rove and ne'er be irie O,
If thro' that glen I gaed to thee,
   My ain kind Dearie O:
Altho' the night were ne'er sae wet,
   And I were ne'er sae weary O,
I'd meet thee on the lea-rig,
   My ain kind Dearie O.

The hunter lo'es the morning sun,
   To rouse the mountain deer, my jo,
At noon the fisher takes the glen,
   Adown the burn to steer, my jo;
Gie me the hour o' gloamin grey,
   It maks my heart sae cheary O
To meet thee on the lea-rig
   My ain kind Dearie O.

Duncan Gray

Duncan Gray cam here to woo,
    Ha, ha, the wooing o't,
On blythe Yule night when we were fu',
    Ha, ha, the wooing o't.
Maggie coost her head fu' high,
Look'd asklent and unco skiegh,
Gart poor Duncan stand abiegh;
    Ha, ha, the wooing o't.

Duncan fleech'd, and Duncan pray'd;
    Ha, ha, the wooing o't.
Meg was deaf as Ailsa craig,
    Ha, ha, the wooing o't.
Duncan sigh'd baith out and in,
Grat his een baith bleer't an' blin',
Spak o' lowpin o'er a linn;
    Ha, ha, the wooing o't.

Time and Chance are but a tide,
    Ha, ha, the wooing o't.
Slighted love is sair to bide,
    Ha, ha, the wooing o't.
Shall I, like a fool, quoth he,
For a haughty hizzie die?
She may gae to — France for me!
    Ha, ha, the wooing o't.

How it comes let Doctors tell,
    Ha, ha, the wooing o't.
Meg grew sick as he grew heal,
    Ha, ha, the wooing o't.
Something in her bosom wrings,
For relief a sigh she brings;

And O her een, they spak sic things!
　　Ha, ha, the wooing o't.

Duncan was a lad o' grace,
　　Ha, ha, the wooing o't.
Maggie's was a piteous case,
　　Ha, ha, the wooing o't.
Duncan could na be her death,
Swelling Pity smoor'd his Wrath;
Now they're crouse and canty baith,
　　Ha, ha, the wooing o't.

Here awa', there awa'

Here awa', there awa' wandering, Willie,
　　Here awa', there awa', haud awa' hame;
Come to my bosom, my ae only deary,
　　Tell me thou bring'st me my Willie the same.

Loud tho' the winter blew cauld on our parting,
　　'Twas na the blast brought the tear in my e'e:
Welcome now Simmer, and welcome my Willie;
　　The Simmer to Nature, my Willie to me.

Rest, ye wild storms, in the cave o' your slumbers,
　　How your dread howling a lover alarms!
Wauken, ye breezes! row gently, ye billows!
　　And waft my dear Laddie ance mair to my arms.

But oh, if he 's faithless, and minds na his Nanie,
　　Flow still between us, thou wide roaring main:
May I never see it, may I never trow it,
　　But, dying, believe that my Willie 's my ain!

O poortith cauld, and restless love

O poortith cauld, and restless love,
    Ye wrack my peace between ye;
Yet poortith a' I could forgive
    An 'twere na for my Jeanie.

CHORUS
    O why should Fate sic pleasure have,
        Life's dearest bands untwining?
    Or why sae sweet a flower as love,
        Depend on Fortune's shining?

This warld's wealth when I think on,
    Its pride, and a' the lave o't;
My curse on silly coward man,
    That he should be the slave o't.
        O why &c.

Her een sae bonie blue betray,
    How she repays my passion;
But Prudence is her o'erword ay,
    She talks o' rank and fashion.
        O why &c.

O wha can prudence think upon,
    And sic a lassie by him:
O wha can prudence think upon,
    And sae in love as I am?
        O why &c.

How blest the wild-wood Indian's fate,
    He wooes his simple Dearie:
The silly bogles, Wealth and State,
    Did never make them eerie.
        O why &c.

O, Logan, sweetly didst thou glide

Tune, Logan Water –

O, Logan, sweetly didst thou glide,
The day I was my Willie's bride;
And years sinsyne hae o'er us run,
Like Logan to the simmer sun.
But now thy flowery banks appear
Like drumlie Winter, dark and drear,
While my dear lad maun face his faes,
Far, far frae me and Logan braes. –

Again the merry month o' May
Has made our hills and vallies gay;
The birds rejoice in leafy bowers,
The bees hum round the breathing flowers:
Blythe Morning lifts his rosy eye,
And Evening's tears are tears of joy:
My soul, delightless, a' surveys,
While Willie 's far frae Logan braes. –

Within yon milkwhite hawthorn bush,
Amang her nestlings sits the thrush;
Her faithfu' Mate will share her toil,
Or wi' his song her cares beguile:
But, I wi' my sweet nurslings here,
Nae Mate to help, nae Mate to cheer,
Pass widowed nights and joyless days,
While Willie 's far frae Logan braes. –

O wae upon you, Men o' State,
That brethren rouse in deadly hate!
As ye make mony a fond heart mourn,
Sae may it on your heads return!

How can your flinty hearts enjoy
The widow's tears, the orphan's cry:
But soon may Peace bring happy days
And Willie, hame to Logan braes!

O whistle, and I'll come to ye, my lad

◦•◦•◦

O whistle, and I'll come to ye, my lad,
O whistle, and I'll come to ye, my lad;
Tho' father, and mother, and a' should gae mad,
    Thy JEANIE will venture wi' ye, my lad.

But warily tent, when ye come to court me,
And come nae unless the back-yett be a-jee;
Syne up the back-style and let naebody see,
    And come as ye were na comin to me –
    And come as ye were na comin to me. –
        O whistle &c.

At kirk, or at market whene'er ye meet me,
Gang by me as tho' that ye car'd nae a flie;
But steal me a blink o' your bonie black e'e,
    Yet look as ye were na lookin at me –
    Yet look as ye were na lookin at me. –
        O whistle &c.

Ay vow and protest that ye care na for me,
And whyles ye may lightly my beauty a wee;
But court nae anither, tho' jokin ye be,
    For fear that she wyle your fancy frae me –
    For fear that she wyle your fancy frae me. –

Robert Bruce's March to Bannockburn

Tune, Hey tutti taiti

Scots, wha hae wi' WALLACE bled,
Scots, wham BRUCE has aften led,
Welcome to your gory bed, –
    Or to victorie. –

Now 's the day, and now 's the hour;
See the front o' battle lour;
See approach proud EDWARD's power,
    Chains and Slaverie. –

Wha will be a traitor-knave?
Wha can fill a coward's grave?
Wha sae base as be a Slave?
    – Let him turn and flie: –

Wha for SCOTLAND's king and law,
Freedom's sword will strongly draw,
FREE-MAN stand, or FREE-MAN fa',
    Let him follow me. –

By Oppression's woes and pains!
By your Sons in servile chains!
We will drain our dearest veins,
    But they *shall* be free!

Lay the proud Usurpers low!
Tyrants fall in every foe!
LIBERTY's in every blow!
    Let us DO – OR DIE!!!

A red red Rose

O my Luve 's like a red, red rose,
　　That 's newly sprung in June;
O my Luve 's like the melodie
　　That 's sweetly play'd in tune. –

As fair art thou, my bonie lass,
　　So deep in luve am I;
And I will love thee still, my Dear,
　　Till a' the seas gang dry. –

Till a' the seas gang dry, my Dear,
　　And the rocks melt wi' the sun:
I will love thee still, my Dear,
　　While the sands o' life shall run. –

And fare thee weel, my only Luve!
　　And fare thee weel, a while!
And I will come again, my Luve,
　　Tho' it were ten thousand mile!

Ca' the yowes to the knowes (B)

CHORUS —
Ca' the yowes to the knowes,
    Ca' them whare the heather grows,
    Ca' them whare the burnie rowes,
        My bonie Dearie.

1

Hark, the mavis' evening sang
Sounding Clouden's woods amang;
Then a faulding let us gang,
        My bonie Dearie.
    Ca' the &c.

2

We'll gae down by Clouden side,
Through the hazels spreading wide
O'er the waves, that sweetly glide
        To the moon sae clearly.
    Ca' the &c.

3

Yonder Clouden's silent towers,
Where at moonshine midnight hours
O'er the dewy bending flowers
        Fairies dance sae cheary.
    Ca' the &c.

4

Ghaist nor bogle shalt thou fear;
Thou'rt to Love and Heaven sae dear,
Nocht of Ill may come thee near,
        My bonie Dearie.
    Ca' the &c.

5
Fair and lovely as thou art,
Thou hast stown my very heart;
I can die – but canna part,
        My bonie Dearie.
    Ca' the &c.

Contented wi' little

❦

Contented wi' little, and cantie wi' mair,
Whene'er I forgather wi' Sorrow and Care,
I gie them a skelp, as they're creeping alang,
Wi' a cog o' gude swats and an auld Scotish sang.

I whyles claw the elbow o' troublesome thought;
But Man is a soger, and Life is a faught:
My mirth and gude humour are coin in my pouch,
And my FREEDOM's my Lairdship nae monarch dare touch.

A towmond o' trouble, should that be my fa',
A night o' gude fellowship sowthers it a';
When at the blythe end of our journey at last,
Wha the deil ever thinks o' the road he has past.

Blind Chance, let her snapper and stoyte on her way;
Be 't to me, be 't frae me, e'en let the jade gae:
Come Ease, or come Travail; come Pleasure, or Pain;
My warst word is – 'Welcome and welcome again!'

For a' that and a' that

Is there, for honest Poverty
    That hings his head, and a' that;
The coward-slave, we pass him by,
    We dare be poor for a' that!
  For a' that, and a' that,
    Our toils obscure, and a' that,
  The rank is but the guinea's stamp,
    The Man 's the gowd for a' that. –

What though on hamely fare we dine,
    Wear hoddin grey, and a' that.
Gie fools their silks, and knaves their wine,
    A Man 's a Man for a' that.
  For a' that, and a' that,
    Their tinsel show, and a' that;
  The honest man, though e'er sae poor,
    Is king o' men for a' that. –

Ye see yon birkie ca'd, a lord,
    Wha struts, and stares, and a' that,
Though hundreds worship at his word,
    He 's but a coof for a' that.
  For a' that, and a' that,
    His ribband, star and a' that,
  The man of independant mind,
    He looks and laughs at a' that. –

A prince can mak a belted knight,
    A marquis, duke, and a' that;
But an honest man's aboon his might,
    Gude faith he mauna fa' that!
  For a' that, and a' that,
    Their dignities, and a' that,

The pith o' Sense, and pride o' Worth,
    Are higher rank than a' that. –

Then let us pray that come it may,
    As come it will for a' that,
That Sense and Worth, o'er a' the earth
    Shall bear the gree, and a' that.
    For a' that, and a' that,
      Its comin yet for a' that,
    That Man to Man the warld o'er,
      Shall brothers be for a' that. –

The Dumfries Volunteers

Tune, Push about the jorum

Does haughty Gaul invasion threat,
  Then let the louns bewaure, Sir,
There 's WOODEN WALLS upon our seas,
  And VOLUNTEERS on shore, Sir:
The *Nith* shall run to *Corsincon*,*
  And *Criffell*† sink in *Solway*,
E'er we permit a Foreign Foe
  On British ground to rally.

O, let us not, like snarling tykes,
  In wrangling be divided,
Till, slap! come in an *unco loun*,
  And wi' a rung decide it!
Be BRITAIN still to BRITAIN true,
  Amang oursels united;
For never but by British hands
  Must British wrongs be righted.

The *kettle* o' the Kirk and State,
  Perhaps a clout may fail in 't;
But deil a foreign tinkler-loun
  Shall ever ca' a nail in 't:
Our FATHERS' BLUDE the *kettle* bought,
  And wha wad dare to spoil it,
By Heavens, the sacreligious dog
  Shall fuel be to boil it!

The wretch that would a *Tyrant* own,
  And the wretch, his true-sworn brother,
Who'd set the *Mob* above the *Throne*,
  May they be damn'd together!

* A high hill at the source of the Nith.
† A high hill at the confluence of the Nith with Solway Frith.

Who will not sing, GOD SAVE THE KING,
　　Shall hang as high 's the steeple;
But while we sing, GOD SAVE THE KING,
　　We'll ne'er forget THE PEOPLE!
Fal de ral &c.

Scotish Ballad

Tune, the Lothian Lassie

Last May a braw wooer cam down the lang glen,
   And sair wi' his love he did deave me;
I said, there was naething I hated like men,
   The deuce gae wi'm, to believe me, believe me,
   The deuce gae wi'm, to believe me.

He spak o' the darts in my bonie black een,
   And vow'd for my love he was dying;
I said, he might die when he liked for JEAN —
   The Lord forgie me for lying, for lying,
   The Lord forgie me for lying!

A weel-stocked mailen, himsel for the laird,
   And marriage aff-hand, were his proffers:
I never loot on that I kend it, or car'd,
   But thought I might hae waur offers, waur offers,
   But thought I might hae waur offers.

But what wad ye think? in a fortnight or less,
   The deil tak his taste to gae near her!
He up the lang loan to my black cousin, Bess,
   Guess ye how, the jad! I could bear her, could bear her,
   Guess ye how, the jad! I could bear her.

But a' the niest week as I petted wi' care,
   I gaed to the tryste o' Dalgarnock;
And wha but my fine, fickle lover was there,
   I glowr'd as I'd seen a warlock, a warlock,
   I glowr'd as I'd seen a warlock.

But owre my left shouther I gae him a blink,
   Least neebors might say I was saucy:
My wooer he caper'd as he'd been in drink,
   And vow'd I was his dear lassie, dear lassie,
   And vow'd I was his dear lassie.

I spier'd for my cousin fu' couthy and sweet,
 Gin she had recover'd her hearin,
And how her new shoon fit her auld shachl't feet;
 But, heavens! how he fell a swearin, a swearin,
 But, heavens! how he fell a swearin.

He begged, for Gudesake! I wad be his wife,
 Or else I wad kill him wi' sorrow:
So e'en to preserve the poor body in life,
 I think I maun wed him tomorrow, tomorrow,
 I think I maun wed him tomorrow. –

Hey for a lass wi' a tocher

Tune, Balinamona and ora

Awa wi' your witchcraft o' beauty's alarms,
The slender bit beauty you grasp in your arms:
O, gie me the lass that has acres o' charms,
O, gie me the lass wi' the weel-stockit farms.

CHORUS

 Then hey, for a lass wi' a tocher, then hey, for a lass wi' a tocher,
 Then hey, for a lass wi' a tocher; the nice yellow guineas for me.

Your beauty 's a flower, in the morning that blows,
And withers the faster the faster it grows;
But the rapturous charm o' the bonie green knowes,
Ilk Spring they're new deckit wi' bonie white yowes.
 Then hey &c.

And e'en when this Beauty your bosom has blest,
The brightest o' beauty may cloy, when possest;
But the sweet yellow darlings wi' Geordie imprest,
The langer ye hae them, – the mair they're carest!
 Then hey &c.

The lovely lass o' Inverness

The luvely Lass o' Inverness,
    Nae joy nor pleasure can she see;
For e'en and morn she cries, Alas!
    And ay the saut tear blins her e'e:
Drumossie moor, Drumossie day,
    A waefu' day it was to me;
For there I lost my father dear,
    My father dear and brethren three!

Their winding-sheet the bludy clay,
    Their graves are growing green to see;
And by them lies the dearest lad
    That ever blest a woman's e'e!
Now wae to thee, thou cruel lord,
    A bludy man I trow thou be;
For mony a heart thou has made sair
    That ne'er did wrang to thine or thee!

As I stood by yon roofless tower

~◇~◇~◇~

Tune, Cumnock Psalms –

As I stood by yon roofless tower,
   Where the wa'-flower scents the dewy air,
Where the houlet mourns in her ivy bower,
   And tells the midnight moon her care:

CHORUS
A lassie all alone was making her moan,
   Lamenting our lads beyond the sea;
In the bluidy wars they fa', and our honor 's gane and a',
   And broken-hearted we maun die. –

The winds were laid, the air was still,
   The stars they shot alang the sky;
The tod was howling on the hill,
   And the distant-echoing glens reply. –
The lassie &c.

The burn, adown its hazelly path,
   Was rushing by the ruin'd wa',
Hasting to join the sweeping Nith
   Whase roarings seem'd to rise and fa'. –
The lassie &c.

The cauld, blae north was streaming forth
   Her lights, wi' hissing, eerie din;
Athort the lift they start and shift,
   Like Fortune's favors, tint as win. –
The lassie &c.

Now, looking over firth and fauld,
   Her horn the pale-fac'd Cynthia rear'd,
When, lo, in form of Minstrel auld,
   A stern and stalwart ghaist appear'd. –
The lassie &c.

And frae his harp sic strains did flow,
    Might rous'd the slumbering Dead to hear;
But Oh, it was a tale of woe,
    As ever met a Briton's ear. –
The lassie &c.

He sang wi' joy his former day,
    He weeping wail'd his latter times:
But what he said it was nae play,
    I winna ventur 't in my rhymes. –
The lassie &c.

Comin thro' the rye

❦

Comin thro' the rye, poor body,
    Comin thro' the rye,
She draigl't a' her petticoatie
    Comin thro' the rye.
      Oh Jenny 's a' weet, poor body,
       Jenny 's seldom dry;
      She draigl't a' her petticoatie
      Comin thro' the rye.

Gin a body meet a body
    Comin' thro' the rye,
Gin a body kiss a body
    Need a body cry.
      Cho: Oh Jenny 's a' weet, &c.

Gin a body meet a body
    Comin thro' the glen;
Gin a body kiss a body
    Need the warld ken!
      Cho: Oh Jenny 's a' weet, &c.

Charlie he's my darling

❦

'Twas on a monday morning,
   Right early in the year,
That Charlie cam to our town,
   The young Chevalier. –

CHORUS
An' Charlie he's my darling, my darling, my darling,
Charlie he's my darling, the young Chevalier. –

As he was walking up the street,
   The city for to view,
O there he spied a bonie lass
   The window looking thro'. –
     An Charlie &c.

Sae light 's he jimped up the stair,
   And tirled at the pin;
And wha sae ready as hersel
   To let the laddie in. –
     An Charlie &c.

He set his Jenny on his knee,
   All in his Highland dress;
For brawlie weel he ken'd the way
   To please a bonie lass. –
     An Charlie &c.

Its up yon hethery mountain,
   And down yon scroggy glen,
We daur na gang a milking,
   For Charlie and his men. –
     An Charlie &c.

For the sake o' Somebody

My heart is sair, I dare na tell,
  My heart is sair for Somebody;
I could wake a winter-night
  For the sake o' Somebody. –
    Oh-hon! for Somebody!
    Oh-hey! for Somebody!
I could range the warld round,
  For the sake o' Somebody. –

Ye Powers that smile on virtuous love,
  O, sweetly smile on Somebody!
Frae ilka danger keep him free,
  And send me safe my Somebody. –
    Ohon! for Somebody!
    Ohey! for Somebody!
I wad do – what wad I not –
  For the sake o' Somebody!

The cardin o't —

❧❧❧

I coft a stane o' haslock woo,
    To mak a wab to Johnie o't;
For Johnie is my onlie jo,
    I lo'e him best of onie yet. —

CHORUS —
    The cardin o't, the spinnin o't,
        The warpin o't, the winnin o't;
    When ilka ell cost me a groat,
        The taylor staw the lynin o't. —

For though his locks be lyart grey,
    And though his brow be beld aboon,
Yet I hae seen him on a day
    The pride of a' the parishon. —
        The cardin &c.

Tibbie Fowler

Tibbie Fowler o' the glen,
  There 's o'er mony wooin at her,
Tibbie Fowler o' the glen,
  There 's o'er mony wooin at her.

CHORUS
  Wooin at her, pu'in at her,
    Courtin at her, canna get her:
  Filthy elf, it 's for her pelf,
    That a' the lads are wooin at her.

Ten cam east, and ten cam west,
  Ten came rowin o'er the water;
Twa came down the lang dyke side,
  There 's twa and thirty wooin at her.
    Wooin at her, &c.

There 's seven but, and seven ben,
  Seven in the pantry wi' her;
Twenty head about the door,
  There 's ane and forty wooin at her.
    Wooin at her, &c.

She 's got pendles in her lugs,
  Cockle-shells wad set her better;
High-heel'd shoon and siller tags,
  And a' the lads are wooin at her.
    Wooin at her, &c.

Be a lassie e'er sae black,
  An she hae the name o' siller,
Set her upo' Tintock-tap,
  The wind will blaw a man till her.
    Wooin at her, &c.

Be a lassie e'er sae fair,
    An she want the pennie siller;
A flie may fell her in the air,
    Before a man be even till her.
        Wooin at her, &c.

I'll ay ca' in by yon town

CHORUS

I'll ay ca' in by yon town,
    And by yon garden green, again;
I'll ay ca' in by yon town,
    And see my bonie Jean again. –

There 's nane sall ken, there 's nane sall guess,
    What brings me back the gate again,
But she, my fairest faithfu' lass,
    And stownlins we sall meet again. –
        I'll ay ca' &c. –

She'll wander by the aiken tree,
    When trystin time draws near again;
And when her lovely form I see,
    O haith, she 's doubly dear again!
        I'll ay ca' &c. –

Bannocks o' bear-meal

❧❦❧

Bannocks o' bear meal,
Bannocks o' barley,
Here 's to the Highlandman's bannocks o' barley. –

Wha, in a brulzie, will first cry a parley?
Never the lads wi' the bannocks o' barley. –
    Bannocks o' &c.

Wha, in his wae days, were loyal to Charlie?
Wha but the lads wi' the bannocks o' Barley. –
    Bannocks o' &c. –

It was a' for our rightfu' king

❦

It was a' for our rightfu' king
    We left fair Scotland's strand;
It was a' for our rightfu' king,
    We e'er saw Irish land, my dear,
    We e'er saw Irish land. –

Now a' is done that men can do,
    And a' is done in vain:
My Love and Native Land fareweel,
    For I maun cross the main, my dear,
    For I maun cross the main.

He turn'd him right and round about,
    Upon the Irish shore,
And gae his bridle-reins a shake,
    With, Adieu for evermore, my dear,
    And adieu for evermore.

The soger frae the wars returns,
    The sailor frae the main,
But I hae parted frae my Love,
    Never to meet again, my dear,
    Never to meet again.

When day is gane, and night is come,
    And a' folk bound to sleep;
I think on him that 's far awa,
    The lee-lang night and weep, my dear,
    The lee-lang night and weep. –

My Lady's gown there's gairs upon't

CHORUS

My Lady's gown there's gairs upon 't,
And gowden flowers sae rare upon 't;
But Jenny's jimps and jirkinet
My Lord thinks meikle mair upon 't.

My Lord a hunting he is gane,
But hounds or hawks wi' him are nane;
By Colin's cottage lies his game,
If Colin's Jenny be at hame.
      My Lady's gown &c.

My Lady 's white, my Lady 's red
And kith and kin o' Cassillis' blude,
But her tenpund lands o' tocher gude
Were a' the charms his Lordship lo'ed.
      My Lady's gown &c.

Out o'er yon moor, out o'er yon moss,
Whare gor-cocks thro' the heather pass,
There wons auld Colin's bonie lass,
A lily in a wilderness.
      My Lady's gown &c.

Sae sweetly move her genty limbs,
Like music-notes o' Lovers hymns;
The diamond-dew in her een sae blue
Where laughing love sae wanton swims.
      My Lady's gown &c.

My Lady 's dink, my Lady 's drest,
The flower and fancy o' the west;
But the Lassie that a man loes best,
O that 's the Lass to mak him blest.
      My Lady's gown &c.

Oh wert thou in the cauld blast

Oh wert thou in the cauld blast,
   On yonder lea, on yonder lea;
My plaidie to the angry airt,
   I'd shelter thee, I'd shelter thee:
Or did misfortune's bitter storms
   Around thee blaw, around thee blaw,
Thy bield should be my bosom,
   To share it a', to share it a'.

Or were I in the wildest waste,
   Sae black and bare, sae black and bare,
The desart were a paradise,
   If thou wert there, if thou wert there.
Or were I monarch o' the globe,
   Wi' thee to reign, wi' thee to reign;
The brightest jewel in my crown,
   Wad be my queen, wad be my queen.

PART TWO

POEMS, EPISTLES, EPIGRAMS

BEFORE 1784
LOCHLIE AND MOUNT OLIPHANT
❦❦

Winter, A Dirge
❦❦

I

The Wintry West extends his blast,
    And hail and rain does blaw;
Or, the stormy North sends driving forth,
    The blinding sleet and snaw:
While, tumbling brown, the Burn comes down,
    And roars frae bank to brae;
And bird and beast, in covert, rest,
    And pass the heartless day.

II

'The sweeping blast, the sky o'ercast,'*
    The joyless *winter-day*,
Let others fear, to me more dear,
    Than all the pride of May:
The Tempest's howl, it *soothes* my soul,
    My *griefs* it seems to join;
The leafless trees my fancy please,
    Their *fate* resembles mine!

III

Thou Pow'r Supreme, whose mighty Scheme,
    These *woes* of mine fulfil;

* Dr Young.

Here, firm, I rest, they *must* be best,
    Because they are *Thy* Will!
Then all I want (Oh, do thou grant
    This one request of mine!)
Since to *enjoy* Thou dost deny,
    Assist me to *resign*!

Extempore

O why the deuce should I repine,
    And be an ill foreboder;
I'm twenty-tree, and five feet nine,
    I'll go and be a sodger.

I gat some gear wi' meikle care,
    I held it weel thegither;
But now its gane, and something mair,
    I'll go and be a sodger.

The Death and Dying Words of Poor Mailie, The Author's only Pet Yowe, An Unco Mournfu' Tale

As Mailie, an' her lambs thegither,
Was ae day nibbling on the tether,
Upon her cloot she coost a hitch,
An' owre she warsl'd in the ditch:
There, groaning, dying, she did ly,
When *Hughoc he cam doytan by.

Wi' glowrin een, an' lifted han's,
Poor *Hughoc* like a statue stan's;
He saw her days were near hand ended,
But, waes my heart! he could na mend it!
He gaped wide, but naething spak,
At length poor *Mailie* silence brak.

'O thou, whase lamentable face
Appears to mourn my woefu' case!
My *dying words* attentive hear,
An' bear them to my *Master* dear.

Tell him, if e'er again he keep
As muckle gear as buy a *sheep*,
O, bid him never tye them mair,
Wi' wicked strings o' hemp or hair!
But ca' them out to park or hill,
An' let them wander at their will:
So, may his flock increase an' grow
To *scores* o' lambs, an' *packs* of woo'!

Tell him, he was a Master kin',
An' ay was guid to me an' mine;

---

* A neibor herd-callan.

An' now my *dying* charge I gie him,
My helpless *lambs*, I trust them wi' him.

O, bid him save their harmless lives,
Frae dogs an' tods, an' butchers' knives!
But gie them guid *cow-milk* their fill,
Till they be fit to fend themsel;
An' tent them duely, e'en an' morn,
Wi' taets o' *hay* an' ripps o' *corn*.

An' may they never learn the gaets,
Of ither vile, wanrestfu' *Pets*!
To slink thro' slaps, an' reave an' steal,
At stacks o' pease, or stocks o' kail.
So may they, like their great *forbears*,
For monie a year come thro' the sheers:
So *wives* will gie them bits o' bread,
An' *bairns* greet for them when they're dead.

My poor *toop-lamb*, my son an' heir,
O, bid him breed him up wi' care!
An' if he live to be a beast,
To pit some havins in his breast!
An' warn him, what I winna name,
To stay content wi' *yowes* at hame;
An' no to rin an' wear his cloots,
Like ither menseless, graceless brutes.

An' niest my *yowie*, silly thing,
Gude keep thee frae a *tether string*!
O, may thou ne'er forgather up,
Wi' onie blastet, moorlan *toop*;
But ay keep mind to moop an' mell,
Wi' sheep o' credit like thysel!

And now, *my bairns*, wi' my last breath,
I lea'e my blessin wi' you baith:
An' when you think upo' your Mither,
Mind to be kind to ane anither.

Now, honest *Hughoc*, dinna fail,
To tell my Master a' my tale;
An' bid him burn this cursed *tether*,
An' for thy pains thou 'se get my blather.'

This said, poor *Mailie* turn'd her head,
An' clos'd her een amang the dead!

Poor Mailie's Elegy

Lament in rhyme, lament in prose,
Wi' saut tears trickling down your nose;
Our *Bardie*'s fate is at a close,
        Past a' remead!
The last, sad cape-stane of his woes;
        Poor Mailie 's dead!

It 's no the loss o' warl's gear,
That could sae bitter draw the tear,
Or make our *Bardie*, dowie, wear
        The mourning weed:
He 's lost a friend and neebor dear,
        In *Mailie* dead.

Thro' a' the town she trotted by him;
A lang half-mile she could descry him;
Wi' kindly bleat, when she did spy him,
        She ran wi' speed:
A friend mair faithfu' ne'er came nigh him,
        Than *Mailie* dead.

I wat she was a *sheep* o' sense,
An' could behave hersel wi' mense:
I'll say 't, she never brak a fence,
        Thro' thievish greed.
Our *Bardie*, lanely, keeps the spence
        Sin' *Mailie* 's dead.

Or, if he wanders up the howe,
Her living image in *her yowe*,
Comes bleating to him, owre the knowe,
        For bits o' bread;
An' down the briny pearls rowe
        For *Mailie* dead.

She was nae get o' moorlan tips,
Wi' tauted ket, an' hairy hips;
For her forbears were brought in ships,
          Frae 'yont the TWEED:
A bonier *fleesh* ne'er cross'd the clips
          Than *Mailie*'s dead.

Wae worth that man wha first did shape,
That vile, wanchancie thing – *a raep*!
It maks guid fellows girn an' gape,
          Wi' chokin dread;
An' *Robin*'s bonnet wave wi' crape
          For *Mailie* dead.

O, a' ye *Bards* on bonie DOON!
An' wha on AIRE your chanters tune!
Come, join the melancholious croon
          O' *Robin*'s reed!
His heart will never get aboon!
          His *Mailie* 's dead!

1784–5

MOSSGIEL

❦

Mock Epitaphs

On Wee Johnie

❦

Hic jacet *wee* Johnie

Whoe'er thou art, O reader, know,
    That Death has murder'd Johnie;
An' here his *body* lies fu' low –
    For *saul* he ne'er had ony.

For G. H. Esq;

❦

The poor man weeps – here Gavin sleeps,
    Whom canting wretches blam'd:
But with *such as he*, where'er he be,
    May I be *sav'd* or *d—'d*!

Address to the Unco Guid, or the Rigidly Righteous

❦

My Son, these maxims make a rule,
  And lump them ay thegither;
The Rigid Righteous *is a fool,*
  The Rigid Wise *anither:*
The cleanest corn that e'er was dight
  May hae some pyles o' caff in;
So ne'er a fellow-creature slight
  For random fits o' daffin.

SOLOMON. — Eccles. ch. vii. vers. 16.

I

O ye wha are sae guid yoursel,
  Sae pious and sae holy,
Ye've nought to do but mark and tell
  Your Neebours' fauts and folly!
Whase life is like a weel-gaun mill,
  Supply'd wi' store o' water,
The heaped happer 's ebbing still,
  And still the clap plays clatter.

II

Hear me, ye venerable Core,
  As counsel for poor mortals,
That frequent pass douce Wisdom's door
  For glaikit Folly's portals;
I, for their thoughtless, careless sakes
  Would here propone defences,
Their donsie tricks, their black mistakes,
  Their failings and mischances.

III

Ye see your state wi' theirs compar'd,
   And shudder at the niffer,
But cast a moment's fair regard
   What maks the mighty differ;
Discount what scant occasion gave,
   That purity ye pride in,
And (what's aft mair than a' the lave)
   Your better art o' hiding.

IV

Think, when your castigated pulse
   Gies now and then a wallop,
What ragings must his veins convulse,
   That still eternal gallop:
Wi' wind and tide fair i' your tail,
   Right on ye scud your sea-way;
But, in the teeth o' baith to sail,
   It maks an unco leeway.

V

See Social-life and Glee sit down,
   All joyous and unthinking,
Till, quite transmugrify'd, they're grown
   Debauchery and Drinking:
O would they stay to calculate
   Th' eternal consequences;
Or your more dreaded h—ll to state,
   D—mnation of expences!

VI

Ye high, exalted, virtuous Dames,
   Ty'd up in godly laces,
Before ye gie poor *Frailty* names,
   Suppose a change o' cases;
A dear-lov'd lad, convenience snug,
   A treacherous inclination –

But, let me whisper i' your lug,
   Ye're aiblins nae temptation.

VII

Then gently scan your brother Man,
   Still gentler sister Woman;
Tho' they may gang a kennin wrang,
   To step aside is human:
One point must still be greatly dark,
   The moving *Why* they do it;
And just as lamely can ye mark,
   How far perhaps they rue it.

VIII

Who made the heart, 'tis *He* alone
   Decidedly can try us,
He knows each chord its various tone,
   Each spring its various bias:
Then at the balance let 's be mute,
   We never can adjust it;
What 's *done* we partly may compute,
   But know not what 's *resisted*.

Epistle to J. Ranken

O rough, rude, ready-witted Ranken,
The wale o' cocks for fun an' drinkin!
There 's monie godly folks are thinkin,
                    Your *dreams** an' tricks
Will send you, Korah-like, a sinkin,
                    Straught to auld Nick's.

Ye hae sae monie cracks an' cants,
And in your wicked, druken rants,
Ye mak a devil o' the *Saunts*,
                    An' fill them fou;
And then their failings, flaws an' wants,
                    Are a' seen thro'.

Hypocrisy, in mercy spare it!
That *holy robe*, O dinna tear it!
Spare 't for their sakes wha aften wear it,
                    The lads in *black*;
But your curst wit, when it comes near it,
                    Rives 't aff their back.

Think, wicked Sinner, wha ye're skaithing:
It 's just the *Blue-gown* badge an' claithing,
O' Saunts; tak that, ye lea'e them naething,
                    To ken them by,
Frae ony unregenerate Heathen,
                    Like you or I.

I've sent you here, some rhymin ware,
A' that I bargain'd for, an' mair;
Sae when ye hae an hour to spare,
                    I will expect,

* A certain humorous *dream* of his was then making a noise in the country-side.

Yon *Sang** ye'll sen 't, wi' cannie care,
      And no neglect.

Tho' faith, sma' heart hae I to sing!
My Muse dow scarcely spread her wing:
I've play'd mysel a bonie *spring*,
      An' *danc'd* my fill!
I'd better gaen an' sair't the king,
      At Bunker's hill.

'Twas ae night lately, in my fun,
I gaed a rovin wi' the gun,
An' brought a *Paitrick* to the *grun*',
      A bonie *hen*,
And, as the twilight was begun,
      Thought nane wad ken.

The poor, wee thing was *little hurt*;
I *straiket* it a wee for sport,
Ne'er thinkan they wad fash me for 't;
      But, Deil-ma-care!
Somebody tells the *Poacher-Court*,
      The hale affair.

Some auld, us'd hands had taen a note,
That *sic a hen* had got a *shot*;
I was suspected for the plot;
      I scorn'd to lie;
So gat the whissle o' my groat,
      An' pay't the *fee*.

But by my *gun*, o' guns the wale,
An' by my *pouther* an' my *hail*,
An' by my *hen*, an' by her *tail*,
      I vow an' swear!
The *Game* shall Pay, owre moor an' *dail*,
      For this, niest year.

---

* A *Song* he had promised the Author.

As soon 's the *clockin-time* is by,
An' the *wee powts* begun to cry,
L—d, I 'se hae sportin by an' by,
      For my *gowd guinea*;
Tho' I should herd the *buckskin* kye
      For 't, in Virginia!

Trowth, they had muckle for to blame!
'Twas neither broken wing nor limb,
But twa-three *draps* about the *wame*
      Scarce thro' the *feathers*;
An' baith a *yellow George* to claim,
      An' *thole* their *blethers*!

It pits me ay as mad 's a hare;
So I can rhyme nor write nae mair;
But *pennyworths* again is fair,
      When time 's expedient:
Meanwhile I am, respected Sir,
      Your most obedient.

Verses

Addressed to the above J. Ranken, on his writing to the Poet, that a girl in that part of the country was with child by him.

I am a keeper of the law
In some sma' points, altho' not a';
Some people tell gin I fa',
      Ae way or ither,
The breaking of ae point, tho' sma',
      Breaks a' thegither.

I hae been in for 't ance or twice,
And winna say o'er far for thrice,
Yet never met with that surprise
      That broke my rest,
But now a rumour 's like to rise,
      A whaup 's i' the nest.

Epistle to Davie, a Brother Poet

I

While winds frae off BEN-LOMOND blaw,
And bar the doors wi' driving snaw,
   And hing us owre the ingle,
I set me down, to pass the time,
And spin a verse or twa o' rhyme,
   In hamely, *westlin* jingle.
While frosty winds blaw in the drift,
   Ben to the chimla lug,
I grudge a wee the *Great-folk*'s gift,
   That live sae bien an' snug:
     I tent less, and want less
      Their roomy fire-side;
     But hanker, and canker,
      To see their cursed pride.

II

It 's hardly in a body's pow'r,
To keep, at times, frae being sour,
   To see how things are shar'd;
How *best o' chiels* are whyles in want,
While *Coofs* on countless thousands rant,
   And ken na how to wair 't:
But DAVIE lad, ne'er fash your head,
   Tho' we hae little gear,
We're fit to win our daily bread,
   As lang 's we're hale and fier:
     'Mair spier na, nor fear na,'*
      Auld age ne'er mind a feg;

* Ramsay.

The last o't, the warst o't,
    Is only but to beg.

III

To lye in kilns and barns at e'en,
When banes are craz'd, and bluid is thin,
    Is, doubtless, great distress!
Yet then *content* could make us blest;
Ev'n then, sometimes we'd snatch a taste
    Of truest happiness.
The honest heart that 's free frae a'
    Intended fraud or guile,
However Fortune kick the ba',
    Has ay some cause to smile:
        And mind still, you'll find still,
            A comfort this nae sma';
        Nae mair then, we'll care then,
            Nae *farther* we can *fa'*.

IV

What tho', like Commoners of air,
We wander out, we know not where,
    But either house or hal'?
Yet *Nature*'s charms, the hills and woods,
The sweeping vales, and foaming floods,
    Are free alike to all.
In days when Daisies deck the ground,
    And Blackbirds whistle clear,
With honest joy, our hearts will bound,
    To see the *coming* year:
        On braes when we please then,
            We'll sit and *sowth* a tune;
        Syne *rhyme* till 't, we'll time till 't,
            And sing 't when we hae done.

V

It 's no in titles nor in rank;
It 's no in wealth like *Lon'on Bank*,

To purchase peace and rest;
It 's no in makin muckle, *mair*:
It 's no in books; it 's no in Lear,
    To make us truly blest:
If Happiness hae not her seat
    And center in the breast,
We may be *wise*, or *rich*, or *great*,
    But never can be *blest*:
        Nae treasures, nor pleasures
            Could make us happy lang;
        The *heart* ay 's the part ay,
            That makes us right or wrang.

VI

Think ye, that sic as *you* and *I*,
Wha drudge and drive thro' wet and dry,
    Wi' never-ceasing toil;
Think ye, are we less blest than they,
Wha scarcely tent us in their way,
    As hardly worth their while?
Alas! how aft, in haughty mood,
    GOD's creatures they oppress!
Or else, neglecting a' that 's guid,
    They riot in excess!
        Baith careless, and fearless,
            Of either Heaven or Hell:
        Esteeming, and deeming,
            It 's a' an idle tale!

VII

Then let us chearfu' acquiesce;
Nor make our scanty Pleasures less,
    By pining at our state:
And, ev'n should Misfortunes come,
I, here wha sit, hae met wi' some,
    An 's thankfu' for them yet.
They gie the wit of *Age to Youth*;
    They let us ken oursel;

They make us see the naked truth,
   The *real* guid and ill.
     Tho' losses, and crosses,
      Be lessons right severe,
     There 's *wit* there, ye'll get there,
      Ye'll find nae other where.

VIII

But tent me, DAVIE, *Ace o' Hearts*!
(To say aught less wad wrang the *cartes*,
   And flatt'ry I detest)
This life has joys for you and I;
And joys that riches ne'er could buy;
   And joys the very best.
There 's a' the *Pleasures o' the Heart*,
   The *Lover* and the *Frien'*;
Ye hae your MEG, your dearest part,
   And I my darling JEAN!
     It warms me, it charms me,
      To mention but her *name*:
     It heats me, it beets me,
      And sets me a' on flame!

IX

O, all ye *Pow'rs* who rule above!
O THOU, whose very self art *love*!
   THOU know'st my words sincere!
The *life blood* streaming thro' my heart,
Or my more dear *Immortal part*,
   Is not more fondly dear!
When heart-corroding care and grief
   Deprive my soul of rest,
Her dear idea brings relief,
   And solace to my breast.
     Thou BEING, Allseeing,
      O hear my fervent pray'r!
     Still take her, and make her,
      THY most peculiar care!

X

All hail! ye tender feelings dear!
The smile of love, the friendly tear,
   The sympathetic glow!
Long since, this world's thorny ways
Had number'd out my weary days,
   Had it not been for you!
Fate still has blest me with a friend,
   In ev'ry care and ill;
And oft a more *endearing* band,
   A *tye* more tender still.
     It lightens, it brightens,
      The tenebrific scene,
     To meet with, and greet with,
      My DAVIE or my JEAN!

XI

O, how that *name* inspires my style!
The words come skelpan, rank and file,
   Amaist before I ken!
The ready measure rins as fine,
As *Phoebus* and the famous *Nine*
   Were glowran owre my pen.
My spavet *Pegasus* will limp,
   Till ance he 's fairly het;
And then he'll hilch, and stilt, and jimp,
   And rin an unco fit:
     But least then, the beast then,
      Should rue this hasty ride,
     I'll light now, and dight now,
      His sweaty, wizen'd hide.

The Holy Tulzie

Blockheads with reason wicked Wits abhor,
But Fool with Fool is barbarous civil war. –

POPE –

O a' ye pious, godly Flocks
Weel fed in pastures orthodox,
Wha now will keep you frae the fox,
      Or worryin tykes?
Or wha will tent the waifs and crocks
      About the dykes?

The twa best Herds in a' the west
That e'er gae gospel horns a blast
This five and fifty simmers past,
      O dool to tell!
Hae had a bitter, black outcast
      Atween themsel. –

O Moodie man, and wordy Russel,
How could ye breed sae vile a bustle?
Ye'll see how New-light Herds will whistle,
      And think it fine!
The L——d's cause gat na sic a twissle
      Since I hae min'. –

O Sirs! wha ever wad expeckit
Your duty ye wad sae negleckit?
You wha was ne'er by Lairds respeckit,
      To wear the Plaid;
But by the vera Brutes eleckit
      To be their Guide. –

What Flock wi' Moodie's Flock could rank,
Sae hale and hearty every shank?
Nae poison'd Ariminian stank
      He loot them taste;

119

But Calvin's fountain-head they drank,
   That was a feast!

The Fulmart, Wil-cat, Brock and Tod
Weel kend his voice thro' a' the wood;
He knew their ilka hole and road,
   Baith out and in:
And liked weel to shed their blood,
   And sell their skin. –

And wha like Russel tell'd his tale;
His voice was heard o'er moor and dale:
He kend the L——d's sheep ilka tail,
   O'er a' the height;
And tell'd gin they were sick or hale
   At the first sight. –

He fine a maingie sheep could scrub,
And nobly swing the Gospel-club;
Or New-light Herds could nicely drub,
   And pay their skin;
Or hing them o'er the burning dub,
   Or shute them in. –

Sic twa — O, do I live to see 't,
Sic famous twa sud disagree't
And names like, 'Villain, Hypocrite,'
   Each other giein;
While enemies wi' laughin spite
   Say, 'Neither 's liein.' –

O ye wha tent the Gospel-fauld,
Thee, Duncan deep, and Peebles shaul,
And chiefly great Apostle Auld,
   We trust in thee,
That thou wilt work them het and cauld
   To gar them gree. –

Consider, Sirs, how we're beset;
There 's scarce a new Herd that we get

But comes frae 'mang that cursed Set,
        I winna name:
I trust in Heaven, to see them het
        Yet in a flame. —

There 's D'rymple has been lang our fae;
Mcgill has wrought us meikle wae;
And that curst rascal ca'd Mcquhey;
        And baith the Shaws,
Wha aft hae made us black and blae
        Wi' vengefu' paws. —

Auld Wodrow lang has wrought mischief,
We trusted death wad bring relief;
But he has gotten, to our grief,
        Ane to succeed him;
A chap will soundly buff our beef
        I meikle dread him. —

And mony mae that I could tell
Wha fair and openly rebel;
Forby Turn-coats amang oursel,
        There 's Smith for ane;
I doubt he 's but a Gray-neck still
        And that ye'll fin'. —

O a' ye flocks o'er a' the hills,
By mosses, meadows, moors and fells,
Come join your counsels and your skills
        To cowe the Lairds,
And get the Brutes the power themsels
        To chuse their Herds. —

Then Orthodoxy yet may prance,
And Learning in a woody dance;
And that curst cur ca'd Common Sense
        Wha bites sae sair,
Be banish'd o'er the seas to France,
        Let him bark there. —

Then Shaw's and Dalrymple's eloquence,
Mcgill's close nervous excellence,
Mcquhey's pathetic manly sense,
                    And guid M'Math
Wi' Smith wha thro' the heart can glance,
                    May a' pack aff.

Holy Willie's Prayer

And send the Godly in a pet to pray –

Argument.

Holy Willie was a rather oldish batchelor Elder in the parish of Mauchline,
and much and justly famed for that polemical chattering which ends in
tippling Orthodoxy, and for that Spiritualized Bawdry which refines to
Liquorish Devotion. – In a Sessional process with a gentleman in Mauchline,
a Mr Gavin Hamilton, Holy Willie, and his priest, father Auld, after full
hearing in the Presbytry of Ayr, came off but second best; owing partly to the
oratorical powers of Mr Robt Aiken, Mr Hamilton's Counsel; but chiefly to
Mr Hamilton's being one of the most irreproachable and truly respectable
characters in the country. – On losing his Process, the Muse overheard him at
his devotions as follows –

> O thou that in the heavens does dwell!
> Wha, as it pleases best thysel,
> Sends ane to heaven and ten to h–ll,
>> A' for thy glory!
> And no for ony gude or ill
>> They've done before thee. –

> I bless and praise thy matchless might,
> When thousands thou has left in night,
> That I am here before thy sight,
>> For gifts and grace,
> A burning and a shining light
>> To a' this place. –

> What was I, or my generation,
> That I should get such exaltation?
> I, wha deserv'd most just damnation,
>> For broken laws
> Sax thousand years ere my creation,
>> Thro' Adam's cause!

When from my mother's womb I fell,
Thou might hae plunged me deep in hell,
To gnash my gooms, and weep, and wail,
                    In burning lakes,
Where damned devils roar and yell
                    Chain'd to their stakes. –

Yet I am here, a chosen sample,
To shew thy grace is great and ample:
I'm here, a pillar o' thy temple
                    Strong as a rock,
A guide, a ruler and example
                    To a' thy flock. –

O L—d thou kens what zeal I bear,
When drinkers drink, and swearers swear,
And singin' there, and dancin' here,
                    Wi' great an' sma';
For I am keepet by thy fear,
                    Free frae them a'. –

But yet – O L—d – confess I must –
At times I'm fash'd wi' fleshly lust;
And sometimes too, in warldly trust
                    Vile Self gets in;
But thou remembers we are dust,
                    Defil'd wi' sin. –

O L—d – yestreen – thou kens – wi' Meg –
Thy pardon I sincerely beg!
O may't ne'er be a living plague,
                    To my dishonor!
And I'll ne'er lift a lawless leg
                    Again upon her. –

Besides, I farther maun avow,
Wi' Leezie's lass, three times – I trow –
But L—d, that friday I was fou
                    When I cam near her;

Or else, thou kens, thy servant true
        Wad never steer her. –

Maybe thou lets this fleshly thorn
Buffet thy servant e'en and morn,
Lest he o'er proud and high should turn,
        That he's sae gifted;
If sae, thy hand maun e'en be borne
        Untill thou lift it. –

L—d bless thy Chosen in this place,
For here thou has a chosen race:
But G–d, confound their stubborn face,
        And blast their name,
Wha bring thy rulers to disgrace
        And open shame. –

L—d mind Gaun Hamilton's deserts!
He drinks, and swears, and plays at cartes,
Yet has sae mony taking arts
        Wi' Great and Sma',
Frae G–d's ain priest the people's hearts
        He steals awa. –

And when we chasten'd him therefore,
Thou kens how he bred sic a splore,
And set the warld in a roar
        O' laughin at us:
Curse thou his basket and his store,
        Kail and potatoes. –

L—d hear my earnest cry and prayer
Against that Presbytry of Ayr!
Thy strong right hand, L—d, make it bare
        Upon their heads!
L—d visit them, and dinna spare,
        For their misdeeds!

O L—d my G–d, that glib-tongu'd Aiken!
My very heart and flesh are quaking

To think how I sat, sweating, shaking,
          And p—ss'd wi' dread,
While Auld wi' hingin lip gaed sneaking
          And hid his head!

L—d, in thy day o' vengeance try him!
L—d visit him that did employ him!
And pass not in thy mercy by them,
          Nor hear their prayer;
But for thy people's sake destroy them,
          And dinna spare!

But L—d, remember me and mine
Wi' mercies temporal and divine!
That I for grace and gear may shine,
          Excell'd by nane!
And a' the glory shall be thine!
          AMEN! AMEN!

Epitaph on Holy Willie

Here Holy Willie's sair worn clay
    Taks up its last abode;
His saul has ta'en some other way,
    I fear, the left-hand road.

Stop! there he is as sure 's a gun,
    Poor silly body see him;
Nae wonder he 's as black 's the grun,
    Observe wha 's standing wi' him.

Your brunstane devilship I see
    Has got him there before ye;
But ha'd your nine-tail cat a wee,
    Till ance you've heard my story.

Your pity I will not implore,
    For pity ye have nane;
Justice, alas! has gi'en him o'er,
    And mercy's day is gaen.

But hear me, Sir, de'il as ye are,
    Look something to your credit;
A coof like him wou'd stain your name,
    If it were kent ye did it.

Death and Doctor Hornbook. A True Story

Some books are lies frae end to end,
And some great lies were never penn'd:
Ev'n Ministers they hae been kenn'd,
      In holy rapture,
A rousing whid, at times, to vend,
      And nail 't wi' Scripture.

But this that I am gaun to tell,
Which lately on a night befel,
Is just as true 's the Deil 's in h–ll,
      Or Dublin city:
That e'er he nearer comes oursel
      'S a muckle pity.

The Clachan yill had made me canty,
I was na fou, but just had plenty;
I stacher'd whyles, but yet took tent ay
      To free the ditches;
An' hillocks, stanes, an' bushes kenn'd ay
      Frae ghaists an' witches.

The rising Moon began to glowr
The distant *Cumnock* hills out-owre;
To count her horns, wi' a' my pow'r,
      I set mysel,
But whether she had three or four,
      I cou'd na tell.

I was come round about the hill,
And todlin down on *Willie's mill*,
Setting my staff wi' a' my skill,
      To keep me sicker;
Tho' leeward whyles, against my will,
      I took a bicker.

I there wi' *Something* does forgather,
That pat me in an eerie swither;
An awfu' scythe, out-owre ae shouther,
        Clear-dangling, hang;
A three-tae'd leister on the ither
        Lay, large an' lang.

Its stature seem'd lang Scotch ells twa,
The queerest shape that e'er I saw,
For fient a wame it had ava,
        And then its shanks,
They were as thin, as sharp an' sma'
        As cheeks o' branks.

'Guid-een,' quo' I; 'Friend! hae ye been mawin,
'When ither folk are busy sawin*?'
It seem'd to mak a kind o' stan',
        But naething spak;
At length, says I, 'Friend, whare ye gaun,
        'Will ye go back?'

It spak right howe – 'My name is *Death*,
'But be na' fley'd.' – Quoth I, 'Guid faith,
'Ye're maybe come to stap my breath;
        'But tent me, billie;
'I red ye weel, tak care o' skaith,
        'See, there 's a gully!'

'Gudeman,' quo' he, 'put up your whittle,
'I'm no design'd to try its mettle;
'But if I did, I wad be kittle
        'To be mislear'd,
'I wad na' mind it, no that spittle
        'Out-owre my beard.'

'Weel, weel!' says I, 'a bargain be 't;
'Come, gies your hand, an' sae we're gree't;
'We'll ease our shanks an' tak a seat,
        'Come, gies your news!

* The rencounter happened in seed-time 1785.

'This while* ye hae been mony a gate,
   'At mony a house.'

'Ay, ay!' quo' he, an' shook his head,
'It 's e'en a lang, lang time indeed
'Sin' I began to nick the thread,
   'An' choke the breath:
'Folk maun do something for their bread,
   'An' sae maun *Death*.

'Sax thousand years are near hand fled
'Sin' I was to the butching bred,
'And mony a scheme in vain 's been laid,
   'To stap or scar me;
'Till ane Hornbook 's† ta'en up the trade,
   'And faith, he'll waur me.

'Ye ken *Jock Hornbook* i' the Clachan,
'Deil mak his king's-hood in a spleuchan!
'He 's grown sae weel acquaint wi' *Buchan*‡,
   'And ither chaps,
'The weans haud out their fingers laughin,
   'And pouk my hips.

'See, here 's a scythe, and there 's a dart,
'They hae pierc'd mony a gallant heart;
'But Doctor *Hornbook*, wi' his art
   'And cursed skill,
'Has made them baith no worth a f—t,
   'D—n'd haet they'll kill!

''Twas but yestreen, nae farther gaen,
'I threw a noble throw at ane;
'Wi' less, I'm sure, I've hundreds slain;
   'But deil-ma-care!

---

* An epidemical fever was then raging in that country.

† This gentleman, Dr Hornbook, is professionally, a brother of the sovereign Order of the Ferula; but, by intuition and inspiration, is at once an Apothecary, Surgeon, and Physician.

‡ Buchan's Domestic Medicine.

'It just play'd dirl on the bane,
   'But did nae mair.

'*Hornbook* was by, wi' ready art,
'And had sae fortify'd the part,
'That when I looked to my dart,
   'It was sae blunt,
'Fient haet o't wad hae pierc'd the heart
   'Of a kail-runt.

'I drew my scythe in sic a fury,
'I nearhand cowpit wi' my hurry,
'But yet the bauld *Apothecary*
   'Withstood the shock;
'I might as weel hae try'd a quarry
   'O' hard whin-rock.

'Ev'n them he canna get attended,
'Altho' their face he ne'er had kend it,
'Just sh— in a kail-blade and send it,
   'As soon 's he smells 't,
'Baith their disease, and what will mend it,
   'At once he tells 't.

'And then a' doctor's saws and whittles,
'Of a' dimensions, shapes, an' mettles,
'A' kinds o' boxes, mugs, an' bottles,
   'He 's sure to hae;
'Their Latin names as fast he rattles
   'As A B C.

'Calces o' fossils, earths, and trees;
'True Sal-marinum o' the seas;
'The Farina of beans and pease,
   'He has 't in plenty;
'Aqua-fontis, what you please,
   'He can content ye.

'Forbye some new, uncommon weapons,
'Urinus Spiritus of capons;

'Or Mite-horn shavings, filings, scrapings,
   'Distill'd *per se*;
'Sal-alkali o' Midge-tail clippings,
   'And mony mae.'

'Waes me for *Johnny Ged's-Hole** now,'
Quoth I, 'if that thae news be true!
'His braw calf-ward whare gowans grew,
   'Sae white an' bonie,
'Nae doubt they'll rive it wi' the plew;
   'They'll ruin *Johnie*!'

The creature grain'd an eldritch laugh,
And says, 'Ye needna yoke the pleugh,
'Kirk-yards will soon be till'd eneugh,
   'Tak ye nae fear:
'They'll a' be trench'd wi' mony a sheugh,
   'In twa-three year.

'Whare I kill'd ane, a fair strae-death,
'By loss o' blood, or want o' breath,
'This night I'm free to tak my aith,
   'That *Hornbook*'s skill
'Has clad a score i' their last claith,
   'By drap and pill.

'An honest Wabster to his trade,
'Whase wife's twa nieves were scarce weel-bred,
'Gat tippence-worth to mend her head,
   'When it was sair;
'The wife slade cannie to her bed,
   'But ne'er spak mair.

'A countra Laird had ta'en the batts,
'Or some curmurring in his guts,
'His only son for *Hornbook* sets,
   'And pays him well,
'The lad, for twa guid gimmer-pets,
   'Was Laird himsel.

---

* The grave-digger.

'A bonie lass, ye kend her name,
'Some ill-brewn drink had hov'd her wame,
'She trusts hersel, to hide the shame,
            'In *Hornbook*'s care;
'*Horn* sent her aff to her lang hame,
            'To hide it there.

'That's just a swatch o' *Hornbook*'s way,
'Thus goes he on from day to day,
'Thus does he poison, kill, an' slay,
            'An's weel pay'd for 't;
'Yet stops me o' my lawfu' prey,
            'Wi' his d—mn'd dirt!

'But hark! I'll tell you of a plot,
'Tho' dinna ye be speakin o't;
'I'll nail the self-conceited Sot,
            'As dead's a herrin:
'Niest time we meet, I'll wad a groat,
            'He gets his fairin!'

But just as he began to tell,
The auld kirk-hammer strak the bell
Some wee, short hour ayont the *twal*,
            Which rais'd us baith:
I took the way that pleas'd mysel,
            And sae did *Death*.

1784-5

On Tam the Chapman

As Tam the chapman on a day
Wi' Death forgather'd by the way,
Weel pleased, he greets a wight sae famous,
And Death was nae less pleas'd wi' Thomas,
Wha cheerfully lays down his pack,
And there blaws up a hearty crack:
His social, friendly, honest heart
Sae tickled Death, they could na part;
Sae after viewing knives and garters,
Death taks him hame to gie him quarters.

Epistle to J. Lapraik, An Old Scotch Bard

April 1st, 1785.

While briers an' woodbines budding green,
An' Paitricks scraichan loud at e'en,
And morning Poossie whiddan seen,
      Inspire my Muse,
This freedom, in an *unknown* frien',
      I pray excuse.

On Fasteneen we had a rockin,
To ca' the crack and weave our stockin;
And there was muckle fun and jokin,
      Ye need na doubt;
At length we had a hearty yokin,
      At *sang about*.

There was ae *sang*, amang the rest,
Aboon them a' it pleas'd me best,
That some kind husband had addrest,
      To some sweet wife:
It thirl'd the heart-strings thro' the breast,
      A' to the life.

I've scarce heard ought describ'd sae weel,
What gen'rous, manly bosoms feel;
Thought I, 'Can this be *Pope*, or *Steele*,
      Or *Beattie*'s wark;'
They tald me 'twas an odd kind chiel
      About *Muirkirk*.

It pat me fidgean-fain to hear 't,
An' sae about him there I spier't;
Then a' that kent him round declar'd,
      He had *ingine*,
That nane excell'd it, few cam near 't,
      It was sae fine.

That set him to a pint of ale,
An' either douse or merry tale,
Or rhymes an' sangs he'd made himsel,
   Or witty catches,
'Tween Inverness and Tiviotdale,
   He had few matches.

Then up I gat, an' swoor an aith,
Tho' I should pawn my pleugh an' graith,
Or die a cadger pownie's death,
   At some dyke-back,
A *pint* an' *gill* I'd gie them *baith*,
   To hear your crack.

But first an' foremost, I should tell,
Amaist as soon as I could spell,
I to the *crambo-jingle* fell,
   Tho' rude an' rough,
Yet crooning to a body's sel,
   Does weel eneugh.

I am nae *Poet*, in a sense,
But just a *Rhymer* like by chance,
An' hae to Learning nae pretence,
   Yet, what the matter?
Whene'er my Muse does on me glance,
   I jingle at her.

Your Critic-folk may cock their nose,
And say, 'How can you e'er propose,
'You wha ken hardly *verse* frae *prose*,
   'To mak a *sang*?'
But by your leaves, my learned foes,
   Ye're maybe wrang.

What 's a' your jargon o' your Schools,
Your Latin names for horns an' stools;
If honest Nature made you *fools*,
   What sairs your Grammars?

Ye'd better taen up *spades* and *shools*,
        Or *knappin-hammers*.

A set o' dull, conceited Hashes,
Confuse their brains in *Colledge-classes*!
They *gang in* Stirks, and *come out* Asses,
        Plain truth to speak;
An' syne they think to climb Parnassus
        By dint o' Greek!

Gie me ae spark o' Nature's fire,
That 's a' the learning I desire;
Then tho' I drudge thro' dub an' mire
        At pleugh or cart,
My Muse, tho' hamely in attire,
        May touch the heart.

O for a spunk o' ALLAN's glee,
Or FERGUSON's, the bauld an' slee,
Or bright LAPRAIK's, my friend to be,
        If I can hit it!
That would be *lear* eneugh for me,
        If I could get it.

Now, Sir, if ye hae friends enow,
Tho' *real friends* I b'lieve are few,
Yet, if your catalogue be fow,
        I'se no insist;
But gif ye want ae friend that 's true,
        I'm on your list.

I winna blaw about *mysel*,
As ill I like my fauts to tell;
But friends an' folk that wish me well,
        They sometimes roose me;
Tho' I maun own, as monie still,
        As far abuse me.

There 's ae *wee faut* they whiles lay to me,
I like the lasses – Gude forgie me!

For monie a Plack they wheedle frae me,
      At dance or fair:
Maybe some *ither thing* they gie me
      They weel can spare.

But MAUCHLINE Race or MAUCHLINE Fair,
I should be proud to meet you there;
We'se gie ae night's discharge to *care*,
      If we forgather,
An' hae a swap o' *rhymin-ware*,
      Wi' ane anither.

The *four-gill chap*, we'se gar him clatter,
An' kirs'n him wi' reekin water;
Syne we'll sit down an' tak our whitter,
      To chear our heart;
An' faith, we'se be *acquainted* better
      Before we part.

Awa ye selfish, warly race,
Wha think that havins, sense an' grace
Ev'n love an' friendship should give place
      To *catch-the-plack*!
I dinna like to see your face,
      Nor hear your crack.

But ye whom social pleasure charms,
Whose hearts the *tide of kindness* warms,
Who hold your *being* on the terms,
      'Each aid the others,'
Come to my bowl, come to my arms,
      My friends, my brothers!

But to conclude my lang epistle,
As my auld pen 's worn to the grissle;
Twa lines frae you wad gar me fissle,
      Who am, most fervent,
While I can either sing, or whissle,
      Your friend and servant.

To the Same

April 21st, 1785.

While new-ca'd kye rowte at the stake,
An' pownies reek in pleugh or braik,
This hour on e'enin's edge I take,
    To own I'm debtor,
To honest-hearted, auld Lapraik,
    For his kind *letter*.

Forjesket sair, with weary legs,
Rattlin the corn out-owre the rigs,
Or dealing thro' amang the naigs
    Their ten-hours bite,
My awkart Muse sair pleads and begs,
    I would na write.

The tapetless, ramfeezl'd hizzie,
She 's saft at best an' something lazy,
Quo' she, 'Ye ken we've been sae busy
    'This month an' mair,
'That trouth, my head is grown right dizzie,
    'An' something sair.'

Her dowf excuses pat me mad;
'Conscience,' says I, 'ye thowless jad!
'I'll write, an' that a hearty blaud,
    'This vera night;
'So dinna ye affront your trade,
    'But rhyme it right.

'Shall bauld Lapraik, the *king o' hearts*,
'Tho' mankind were a *pack o' cartes*,
'Roose you sae weel for your deserts,
    'In terms sae friendly,
'Yet ye'll neglect to shaw your parts
    'An' thank him kindly?'

Sae I gat paper in a blink,
An' down gaed *stumpie* in the ink:
Quoth I, 'Before I sleep a wink,
　　　　　'I vow I'll close it;
'An' if ye winna mak it clink,
　　　　　'By Jove I'll prose it!'

Sae I've begun to scrawl, but whether
In rhyme, or prose, or baith thegither,
Or some hotch-potch that 's rightly neither,
　　　　　Let time mak proof;
But I shall scribble down some blether
　　　　　Just clean aff-loof.

My worthy friend, ne'er grudge an' carp,
Tho' Fortune use you hard an' sharp;
Come, kittle up your *moorlan harp*
　　　　　Wi' gleesome touch!
Ne'er mind how Fortune *waft* an' *warp*;
　　　　　She 's but a b—tch.

She 's gien me monie a jirt an' fleg,
Sin' I could striddle owre a rig;
But by the L—d, tho' I should beg
　　　　　Wi' lyart pow,
I'll laugh, an' sing, an' shake my leg,
　　　　　As lang 's I dow!

Now comes the *sax an' twentieth* simmer,
I've seen the bud upo' the timmer,
Still persecuted by the limmer
　　　　　Frae year to year;
But yet, despite the kittle kimmer,
　　　　　I, Rob, am here.

Do ye envy the *city-gent*,
Behint a kist to lie an' sklent,
Or purse-proud, big wi' cent per cent,
　　　　　An' muckle wame,

In some bit *Brugh* to represent
    A *Baillie*'s name?

Or is 't the paughty, feudal *Thane*,
Wi' ruffl'd sark an' glancin cane,
Wha thinks himsel nae *sheep-shank bane*,
    But lordly stalks,
While caps an' bonnets aff are taen,
    As by he walks?

'O *Thou* wha gies us each guid gift!
'Gie me o' *wit* an' *sense* a lift,
'Then turn me, if *Thou* please, *adrift*,
    'Thro' Scotland wide;
'Wi' *cits* nor *lairds* I wadna shift,
    'In a' their pride!'

Were this the *charter* of our state,
'On pain o' *hell* be rich an' great,'
Damnation then would be our fate,
    Beyond remead;
But, thanks to *Heav'n*, that 's no the gate
    We learn our *creed*.

For thus the royal *Mandate* ran,
When first the human race began,
'The social, friendly, honest man,
    'Whate'er he be,
''Tis *he* fulfils *great Nature's plan*,
    'And none but *he*.'

O *Mandate*, glorious and divine!
The followers o' the ragged Nine,
Poor, thoughtless devils! yet may shine
    In glorious light,
While sordid sons o' Mammon's line
    Are dark as night!

Tho' here they scrape, an' squeeze, an' growl,
Their worthless nievefu' of a *soul*,

May in some *future carcase* howl,
   The forest's fright;
Or in some day-detesting *owl*
   May shun the light.

Then may Lapraik and Burns arise,
To reach their native, kindred skies,
And *sing* their pleasures, hopes an' joys,
   In some mild sphere,
Still closer knit in friendship's ties
   Each passing year!

To W. Simpson, Ochiltree

May – 1785.

I gat your letter, winsome Willie;
Wi' gratefu' heart I thank you brawlie;
Tho' I maun say 't, I wad be silly,
      An' unco vain,
Should I believe, my coaxin billie,
      Your flatterin strain.

But I'se believe ye kindly meant it,
I sud be laith to think ye hinted
Ironic satire, sidelins sklented,
      On my poor Musie;
Tho' in sic phraisin terms ye've penn'd it,
      I scarce excuse ye.

My senses wad be in a creel,
Should I but dare a *hope* to speel,
Wi' *Allan*, or wi' *Gilbertfield*,
      The braes o' fame;
Or *Ferguson*, the writer-chiel,
      A deathless name.

(O *Ferguson*! thy glorious *parts*,
Ill-suited *law*'s dry, musty arts!
My curse upon your whunstane hearts,
      Ye Enbrugh Gentry!
The tythe o' what ye waste at *cartes*
      Wad stow'd his pantry!)

Yet when a tale comes i' my head,
Or lasses gie my heart a screed,
As whiles they're like to be my dead,
      (O sad disease!)
I kittle up my *rustic reed*;
      It gies me ease.

Auld COILA, now, may fidge fu' fain,
She 's gotten *Bardies* o' her ain,
Chiels wha their chanters winna hain,
   But tune their lays,
Till echoes a' resound again
   Her weel-sung praise.

Nae *Poet* thought her worth his while,
To set her name in measur'd style;
She lay like some unkend-of isle
   Beside *New Holland*,
Or whare wild-meeting oceans *boil*
   Besouth *Magellan*.

Ramsay an' famous *Ferguson*
Gied *Forth* an' *Tay* a lift aboon;
Yarrow an' *Tweed*, to monie a tune,
   Owre Scotland rings,
While *Irwin, Lugar, Aire* an' *Doon*,
   Naebody sings.

Th' *Illissus, Tiber, Thames* an' *Seine*,
Glide sweet in monie a tunefu' line;
But *Willie* set your fit to mine,
   An' cock your crest,
We'll gar our streams an' burnies shine
   Up wi' the best.

We'll sing auld COILA's plains an' fells,
Her moors red-brown wi' heather bells,
Her banks an' braes, her dens an' dells,
   Where glorious WALLACE
Aft bure the gree, as story tells,
   Frae Suthron billies.

At WALLACE' name, what Scottish blood,
But boils up in a spring-tide flood!
Oft have our fearless fathers strode
   By WALLACE' side,

Still pressing onward, red-wat-shod,
  Or glorious dy'd!

O sweet are COILA's haughs an' woods,
When lintwhites chant amang the buds,
And jinkin hares, in amorous whids,
  Their loves enjoy,
While thro' the braes the cushat croods
  With wailfu' cry!

Ev'n winter bleak has charms to me,
When winds rave thro' the naked tree;
Or frosts on hills of *Ochiltree*
  Are hoary gray;
Or blinding drifts wild-furious flee,
  Dark'ning the day!

O NATURE! a' thy shews an' forms
To feeling, pensive hearts hae charms!
Whether the Summer kindly warms,
  Wi' life an' light,
Or Winter howls, in gusty storms,
  The lang, dark night!

The *Muse*, nae *Poet* ever fand her,
Till by himsel he learn'd to wander,
Adown some trottin burn's meander,
  An' no think lang;
O sweet, to stray an' pensive ponder
  A heart-felt sang!

The warly race may drudge an' drive,
Hog-shouther, jundie, stretch an' strive,
Let me fair NATURE's face descrive,
  And I, wi' pleasure,
Shall let the busy, grumbling hive
  Bum owre their treasure.

Fareweel, 'my rhyme-composing brither!'
We've been owre lang unkenn'd to ither:

Now let us lay our heads thegither,
    In love fraternal:
May *Envy* wallop in a tether,
    Black fiend, infernal!

While Highlandmen hate tolls an' taxes;
While moorlan herds like guid, fat braxies;
While Terra firma, on her axis,
    Diurnal turns,
Count on a friend, in faith an' practice,
    In ROBERT BURNS.

Postscript

My memory 's no worth a preen;
I had amaist forgotten clean,
Ye bad me write you what they mean
    By this *new-light,**
'Bout which our *herds* sae aft hae been
    Maist like to fight.

In days when mankind were but callans,
At *Grammar, Logic,* an' sic talents,
They took nae pains their speech to balance,
    Or rules to gie,
But spak their thoughts in plain, braid lallans,
    Like you or me.

In thae auld times, they thought the *Moon,*
Just like a sark, or pair o' shoon,
Woor by degrees, till her last roon
    Gaed past their viewin,
An' shortly after she was done
    They gat a new ane.

This past for certain, undisputed;
It ne'er cam i' their heads to doubt it,
Till chiels gat up an' wad confute it,
    An' ca'd it wrang;

* A cant-term for those religious opinions, which DR TAYLOR of Norwich has defended so strenuously.

An' muckle din there was about it,
         Baith loud an' lang.

Some *herds,* weel learn'd upo' the beuk,
Wad threap auld folk the thing misteuk;
For 'twas the *auld moon* turn'd a newk
         An' out o' sight,
An' backlins-comin, to the leuk,
         She grew mair bright.

This was deny'd, it was affirm'd;
The *herds* an' *hissels* were alarm'd;
The rev'rend gray-beards rav'd an' storm'd,
         That beardless laddies
Should think they better were inform'd,
         Than their auld dadies.

Frae less to mair it gaed to sticks;
Frae words an' aiths to clours an' nicks;
An' monie a fallow gat his licks,
         Wi' hearty crunt;
An' some, to learn them for their tricks,
         Were hang'd an' brunt.

This game was play'd in monie lands,
An' *auld-light* caddies bure sic hands,
That faith, the *youngsters* took the sands
         Wi' nimble shanks,
Till *Lairds* forbad, by strict commands,
         Sic bluidy pranks.

But *new-light herds* gat sic a cowe,
Folk thought them ruin'd stick-an-stowe,
Till now amaist on ev'ry *knowe*
         Ye'll find ane plac'd;
An' some, their *New-light* fair avow,
         Just quite barefac'd.

Nae doubt the *auld-light flocks* are bleatan;
Their zealous *herds* are vex'd an' sweatan;

Mysel, I've ev'n seen them greetan
        Wi' girnan spite,
To hear the *Moon* sae sadly lie'd on
        By word an' write.

But shortly they will cowe the louns!
Some *auld-light herds* in neebor towns
Are mind't, in things they ca' *balloons*,
        To tak a flight,
An' stay ae month amang the *Moons*
        An' see them right.

Guid observation they will gie them;
An' when the *auld Moon* 's gaun to lea'e them,
The hindmost *shaird*, they'll fetch it wi' them,
        Just i' their pouch,
An' when the *new-light* billies see them,
        I think they'll crouch!

Sae, ye observe that a' this clatter
Is naething but a 'moonshine matter;'
But tho' dull *prose-folk* Latin splatter
        In logic tulzie,
I hope we, *Bardies*, ken some better
        Than mind sic brulzie.

A Poet's Welcome to his love-begotten Daughter; the first instance that entitled him to the venerable appellation of Father

Thou 's welcome, Wean! Mischanter fa' me,
If thoughts o' thee, or yet thy Mamie,
Shall ever daunton me or awe me,
      My bonie lady;
Or if I blush when thou shalt name me
      Tyta, or Daddie. –

Tho' now they ca' me, Fornicator,
And tease my name in kintra clatter,
The mair they talk, I'm kend the better;
      E'en let them clash!
An auld wife's tongue 's a feckless matter
      To gie ane fash. –

Welcome! My bonie, sweet, wee Dochter!
Tho' ye come here a wee unsought for;
And tho' your comin I hae fought for,
      Baith Kirk and Queir;
Yet by my faith, ye're no unwrought for,
      That I shall swear!

Wee image o' my bonie Betty,
As fatherly I kiss and daut thee,
As dear and near my heart I set thee,
      Wi' as gude will,
As a' the Priests had seen me get thee
      That 's out o' h—. –

Sweet fruit o' monie a merry dint,
My funny toil is no a' tint;
Tho' ye come to the warld asklent,
      Which fools may scoff at,

149

In my last plack your part 's be in 't,
   The better half o't. –

Tho' I should be the waur bestead,
Tho 's be as braw and bienly clad,
And thy young years as nicely bred
   Wi' education,
As any brat o' Wedlock's bed,
   In a' thy station. –

Lord grant that thou may ay inherit
Thy Mither's looks an' gracefu' merit;
An' thy poor, worthless Daddie's spirit,
   Without his failins!
'Twad please me mair to see thee heir it
   Than stocked mailins!

For if thou be, what I wad hae thee,
And tak the counsel I shall gie thee,
I'll never rue my trouble wi' thee,
   The cost nor shame o't,
But be a loving Father to thee,
   And brag the name o't. –

The Vision.
Duan First*

❧❧❧

The sun had clos'd the *winter-day*,
The Curlers quat their roaring play,
And hunger'd Maukin taen her way
        To kail-yards green,
While faithless snaws ilk step betray
        Whare she has been.

The Thresher's weary *flingin-tree*,
The lee-lang day had tir'd me;
And when the Day had clos'd his e'e,
        Far i' the West,
Ben i' the *Spence*, right pensivelie,
        I gaed to rest.

There, lanely, by the ingle-cheek,
I sat and ey'd the spewing reek,
That fill'd, wi' hoast-provoking smeek,
        The auld, clay biggin;
And heard the restless rattons squeak
        About the riggin.

All in this mottie, misty clime,
I backward mus'd on wasted time,
How I had spent my *youthfu' prime*,
        An' done nae-thing,
But stringing blethers up in rhyme
        For fools to sing.

* Duan, a term of Ossian's for the different divisions of a digressive Poem. See his Cath-Loda, Vol. 2, of McPherson's Translation.

Had I to guid advice but harket,
I might, by this, hae led a market,
Or strutted in a Bank and clarket
   My *Cash-Account*;
While here, half-mad, half-fed, half-sarket,
   Is a' th' amount.

I started, mutt'ring blockhead! coof!
And heav'd on high my wauket loof,
To swear by a' yon starry roof,
   Or some rash aith,
That I, henceforth, would be *rhyme-proof*
   Till my last breath –

When click! the *string* the *snick* did draw;
And jee! the door gaed to the wa';
And by my ingle-lowe I saw,
   Now bleezan bright,
A tight, outlandish *Hizzie*, braw,
   Come full in sight.

Ye need na doubt, I held my whisht;
The infant aith, half-form'd, was crusht;
I glowr'd as eerie 's I'd been dusht,
   In some wild glen;
When sweet, like *modest Worth*, she blusht,
   And stepped ben.

Green, slender, leaf-clad *Holly-boughs*
Were twisted, gracefu', round her brows,
I took her for some SCOTTISH MUSE,
   By that same token;
And come to stop those reckless vows,
   Would soon been broken.

A 'hare-brain'd, sentimental trace'
Was strongly marked in her face;
A wildly-witty, rustic grace
   Shone full upon her;

Her *eye*, ev'n turn'd on empty space,
          Beam'd keen with *Honor*.

Down flow'd her robe, a *tartan* sheen,
Till half a leg was scrimply seen;
And such a *leg*! my bonie JEAN
          Could only peer it;
Sae straught, sae taper, tight and clean,
          Nane else came near it.

Her *Mantle* large, of greenish hue,
My gazing wonder chiefly drew;
Deep *lights* and *shades*, bold-mingling, threw
          A lustre grand;
And seem'd, to my astonish'd view,
          A *well-known* Land.

Here, rivers in the sea were lost;
There, mountains to the skies were tost:
Here, tumbling billows mark'd the coast,
          With surging foam;
There, distant shone, *Art*'s lofty boast,
          The lordly dome.

Here, DOON pour'd down his far-fetch'd floods;
There, well-fed IRWINE stately thuds:
Auld, hermit AIRE staw thro' his woods,
          On to the shore;
And many a lesser torrent scuds,
          With seeming roar.

Low, in a sandy valley spread,
An ancient BOROUGH rear'd her head;
Still, as in *Scottish Story* read,
          She boasts a *Race*,
To ev'ry nobler virtue bred,
          And polish'd grace.

By stately tow'r, or palace fair,
Or ruins pendent in the air,

Bold stems of Heroes, here and there,
        I could discern;
Some seem'd to muse, some seem'd to dare,
        With feature stern.

My heart did glowing transport feel,
To see a Race* heroic wheel,
And brandish round the deep-dy'd steel
        In sturdy blows;
While back-recoiling seem'd to reel
        Their Suthron foes.

His COUNTRY's SAVIOUR†, mark him well!
Bold RICHARDTON's‡ heroic swell;
The Chief on *Sark*§ who glorious fell,
        In high command;
And *He* whom ruthless Fates expel
        His native land.

There, where a sceptr'd *Pictish*¶ shade
Stalk'd round his ashes lowly laid,
I mark'd a martial Race, pourtray'd
        In colours strong;
Bold, soldier-featur'd, undismay'd
        They strode along.

* The Wallaces.

† William Wallace.

‡ Adam Wallace of Richardton, cousin to the immortal Preserver of Scottish Independence.

§ Wallace Laird of Craigie, who was second in command, under Douglas Earl of Ormond, at the famous battle on the banks of Sark, fought *anno* 1448. That glorious victory was principally owing to the judicious conduct and intrepid valour of the gallant Laird of Craigie, who died of his wounds after the action.

¶ Coilus King of the Picts, from whom the district of Kyle is said to take its name, lies buried, as tradition says, near the family-seat of the Montgomeries of Coilsfield, where his burial place is still shown.

*Thro' many a wild, romantic grove,
Near many a hermit-fancy'd cove,
(Fit haunts for Friendship or for Love,
        In musing mood)
An *aged Judge*, I saw him rove,
        Dispensing good.

†With deep-struck, reverential awe,
The learned *Sire* and *Son* I saw,
To Nature's God and Nature's law
        They gave their lore,
This, all its source and end to draw,
        That, to adore.

BRYDON's brave Ward§ I well could spy,
Beneath old SCOTIA's smiling eye;
Who call'd on Fame, low standing by,
        To hand him on,
Where many a Patriot-name on high
        And Hero shone.

* Barskimming, the seat of the Lord Justice Clerk.
† Catrine, the seat of the late Doctor, and present Professor Stewart.
§ Colonel Fullarton.

Duan Second

With musing-deep, astonish'd stare,
I view'd the heavenly-seeming *Fair*;
A whisp'ring *throb* did witness bear
                    Of kindred sweet,
When with an elder Sister's air
                    She did me greet.

'All hail! *my own* inspired Bard!
'In me thy native Muse regard!
'Nor longer mourn thy fate is hard,
                    'Thus poorly low!
'I come to give thee such *reward*,
                    'As *we* bestow.

'Know, the great *Genius* of this Land,
'Has many a light, aerial band,
'Who, all beneath his high command,
                    'Harmoniously,
'As *Arts* or *Arms* they understand,
                    'Their labors ply.

'They SCOTIA's Race among them share;
'Some fire the *Sodger* on to dare;
'Some rouse the *Patriot* up to bare
                    'Corruption's heart:
'Some teach the *Bard*, a darling care,
                    'The tuneful Art.

''Mong swelling floods of reeking gore,
'They ardent, kindling spirits pour;
'Or, mid the venal Senate's roar,
                    'They, sightless, stand,
'To mend the honest *Patriot-lore*,
                    'And grace the hand.

'And when the Bard, or hoary Sage,
'Charm or instruct the future age,
'They bind the wild, Poetic rage
      'In energy,
'Or point the inconclusive page
      'Full on the eye.

'Hence, FULLARTON, the brave and young;
'Hence, DEMPSTER's truth-prevailing tongue;
'Hence, sweet harmonious BEATTIE sung
      'His "Minstrel lays;"
'Or tore, with noble ardour stung,
      'The *Sceptic*'s bays.

'To lower Orders are assign'd,
'The humbler ranks of Human-kind,
'The rustic Bard, the lab'ring Hind,
      'The Artisan;
'All chuse, as, various they're inclin'd,
      'The various man.

'When yellow waves the heavy grain,
'The threat'ning *Storm*, some, strongly, rein;
'Some teach to meliorate the plain,
      'With *tillage-skill*;
'And some instruct the Shepherd-train,
      'Blythe o'er the hill.

'Some hint the Lover's harmless wile;
'Some grace the Maiden's artless smile;
'Some soothe the Lab'rer's weary toil,
      'For humble gains,
'And make his *cottage-scenes* beguile
      'His cares and pains.

'Some, bounded to a district-space,
'Explore at large Man's *infant race*,
'To mark the embryotic trace,
      'Of *rustic Bard*;

'And careful note each op'ning grace,
          'A guide and guard.

'*Of these am I* – COILA my name;
'And this district as mine I claim,
'Where once the *Campbells*, chiefs of fame,
          'Held ruling pow'r:
'I mark'd thy embryo-tuneful flame,
          'Thy natal hour.

'With future hope, I oft would gaze,
'Fond, on thy little, early ways,
'Thy rudely-caroll'd, chiming phrase,
          'In uncouth rhymes,
'Fir'd at the simple, artless lays
          'Of other times.

'I saw thee seek the sounding shore,
'Delighted with the dashing roar;
'Or when the *North* his fleecy store
          'Drove thro' the sky,
'I saw grim Nature's visage hoar,
          'Struck thy young eye.

'Or when the deep-green-mantl'd Earth,
'Warm-cherish'd ev'ry floweret's birth,
'And joy and music pouring forth,
          'In ev'ry grove,
'I saw thee eye the gen'ral mirth
          'With boundless love.

'When ripen'd fields, and azure skies,
'Call'd forth the *Reaper*'s rustling noise,
'I saw thee leave their ev'ning joys,
          'And lonely stalk,
'To vent thy bosom's swelling rise,
          'In pensive walk.

'When *youthful Love*, warm-blushing, strong,
'Keen-shivering shot thy nerves along,

'Those accents, grateful to thy tongue,
                    'Th' adored *Name*,
'I taught thee how to pour in song,
                    'To soothe thy flame.

'I saw thy pulse's maddening play,
'Wild-send thee Pleasure's devious way,
'Misled by Fancy's *meteor-ray*,
                    'By Passion driven;
'But yet the *light* that led astray,
                    'Was *light* from Heaven.

'I taught thy manners-painting strains,
'The *loves*, the *ways* of simple swains,
'Till now, o'er all my wide domains,
                    'Thy fame extends;
'And some, the pride of *Coila*'s plains,
                    'Become thy friends.

'Thou canst not learn, nor I can show,
'To paint with *Thomson*'s landscape-glow;
'Or wake the bosom-melting throe,
                    'With *Shenstone*'s art;
'Or pour, with *Gray*, the moving flow,
                    'Warm on the heart.

'Yet all beneath th' unrivall'd Rose,
'The lowly Daisy sweetly blows;
'Tho' large the forest's Monarch throws
                    'His army shade,
'Yet green the juicy Hawthorn grows,
                    'Adown the glade.

'Then never murmur nor repine;
'Strive in thy *humble sphere* to shine;
'And trust me, not *Potosi*'s mine,
                    'Nor *King*'s regard,
'Can give a bliss o'ermatching thine,
                    'A *rustic Bard*.

'To give my counsels all in one,
'Thy *tuneful flame* still careful fan;
'Preserve *the dignity of Man*,
                'With Soul erect;
'And trust, the UNIVERSAL PLAN
                'Will all protect.

'*And wear thou this*' – She solemn said,
And bound the *Holly* round my head:
The polish'd leaves, and berries red,
                Did rustling play;
And, like a passing thought, she fled,
                In light away.

Epistle to John Goldie in Kilmarnock, Author of, The Gospel recovered

August – 1785

O Gowdie, terror o' the whigs,
Dread o' black coats and reverend wigs!
Sour Bigotry on his last legs
      Girns and looks back,
Wishing the ten Egyptian plagues
      May sieze you quick. –

Poor gapin, glowrin Superstition!
Waes me, she 's in a sad condition:
Fye! bring Black Jock* her state-physician,
      To see her water:
Alas! there 's ground for great suspicion,
      She'll ne'er get better. –

Enthusiasm 's past redemption,
Gane in a gallopin consumption:
Not a' her quacks wi' a' their gumption
      Can ever mend her;
Her feeble pulse gies strong presumption,
      She'll soon surrender. –

Auld Orthodoxy lang did grapple
For every hole to get a stapple;
But now, she fetches at the thrapple
      And fights for breath;
Haste, gie her name up in the Chapel†
      Near unto death. –

* The Revd J. R–ss–ll – Kilmck –.
† Chapel – Mr Russel's kirk –.

It 's you and Taylor* are the chief
To blame for a' this black mischief;
But could the L——d's ain folk get leave,
      A toom tar-barrel
And twa red peats wad bring relief
      And end the quarrel. –

For me, my skill 's but very sma',
And skill in Prose I've nane ava;
But quietlenswise, between us twa,
      Weel may ye speed;
And tho' they sud you sair misca',
      Ne'er fash your head. –

E'en swinge the dogs; and thresh them sicker!
The mair they squeel ay chap the thicker;
And still 'mang hands a hearty bicker
      O' something stout;
It gars an Owther's pulse beat quicker,
      And helps his wit. –

There 's naething like the honest nappy;
Whare'll ye e'er see men sae happy,
Or women sonsie, saft and sappy,
      'Tween morn and morn,
As them wha like to taste the drappie
      In glass or horn. –

I've seen me daez't upon a time,
I scarce could wink or see a styme;
Just ae hauf-mutchkin does me prime,
      (Ought less, is little)
Then back I rattle on the rhyme,
      As gleg 's a whittle. –
        I am &c.

---

* Taylor – Dr Taylor of Norwich –.

Man was Made to Mourn, A Dirge

•••

I

When chill November's surly blast
   Made fields and forests bare,
One ev'ning, as I wand'red forth,
   Along the banks of AIRE,
I spy'd a man, whose aged step
   Seem'd weary, worn with care;
His face was furrow'd o'er with years,
   And hoary was his hair.

II

Young stranger, whither wand'rest thou?
   Began the rev'rend Sage;
Does thirst of wealth thy step constrain,
   Or youthful Pleasure's rage?
Or haply, prest with cares and woes,
   Too soon thou hast began,
To wander forth, with me, to mourn
   The miseries of Man.

III

The Sun that overhangs yon moors,
   Out-spreading far and wide,
Where hundreds labour to support
   A haughty lordling's pride;
I've seen yon weary winter-sun
   Twice forty times return;
And ev'ry time has added proofs,
   That Man was made to mourn.

IV

O Man! while in thy early years,
   How prodigal of time!

Mispending all thy precious hours,
   Thy glorious, youthful prime!
Alternate Follies take the sway;
   Licentious Passions burn;
Which tenfold force gives Nature's law,
   That Man was made to mourn.

V

Look not alone on youthful Prime,
   Or Manhood's active might;
Man then is useful to his kind,
   Supported is his right:
But see him on the edge of life,
   With Cares and Sorrows worn,
Then Age and Want, Oh! ill-match'd pair!
   Show Man was made to mourn.

VI

A few seem favourites of Fate,
   In Pleasure's lap carest;
Yet, think not all the Rich and Great,
   Are likewise truly blest.
But Oh! what crouds in ev'ry land,
   All wretched and forlorn,
Thro' weary life this lesson learn,
   That Man was made to mourn!

VII

Many and sharp the num'rous Ills
   Inwoven with our frame!
More pointed still we make ourselves,
   Regret, Remorse and Shame!
And Man, whose heav'n-erected face,
   The smiles of love adorn,
Man's inhumanity to Man
   Makes countless thousands mourn!

VIII

See, yonder poor, o'erlabour'd wight,
    So abject, mean and vile,
Who begs a brother of the earth
    To give him leave to toil;
And see his lordly *fellow-worm*,
    The poor petition spurn,
Unmindful, tho' a weeping wife,
    And helpless offspring mourn.

IX

If I'm design'd yon lordling's slave,
    By Nature's law design'd,
Why was an independent wish
    E'er planted in my mind?
If not, why am I subject to
    His cruelty, or scorn?
Or why has Man the will and pow'r
    To make his fellow mourn?

X

Yet, let not this too much, my Son,
    Disturb thy youthful breast:
This partial view of human-kind
    Is surely not the *last*!
The poor, oppressed, honest man
    Had never, sure, been born,
Had there not been some recompence
    To comfort those that mourn!

XI

O Death! the poor man's dearest friend,
    The kindest and the best!
Welcome the hour, my aged limbs
    Are laid with thee at rest!

The Great, the Wealthy fear thy blow,
From pomp and pleasure torn;
But Oh! a blest relief to those
That weary-laden mourn!

Third Epistle to J. Lapraik

Sept. 13*th*, 1785.

Guid speed an' furder to you Johny,
  Guid health, hale han's, an' weather bony;
Now when ye're nickan down fu' cany
      The staff o' bread,
May ye ne'er want a stoup o' brany
      To clear your head.

May Boreas never thresh your rigs,
Nor kick your rickles aff their legs,
Sendin' the stuff o'er muirs an' haggs
      Like drivin' wrack;
But may the tapmast grain that wags
      Come to the sack.

I'm bizzie too, an' skelpin' at it,
But bitter, daudin showers hae wat it,
Sae my auld stumpie pen I gat it
      Wi' muckle wark,
An' took my jocteleg an' whatt it,
      Like ony clark.

It 's now twa month that I'm your debtor,
For your braw, nameless, dateless letter,
Abusin' me for harsh ill nature
      On holy men,
While deil a hair yoursel ye're better,
      But mair profane.

But let the kirk-folk ring their bells,
Let 's sing about our noble sels;
We'll cry nae jads frae heathen hills
      To help, or roose us,
But browster wives an' whiskie stills,
      They are the muses.

Your friendship sir, I winna quat it,
An' if ye mak' objections at it,
Then han' in nieve some day we'll knot it,
      An' witness take,
An' when wi' Usquabae we've wat it
      It winna break.

But if the beast and branks be spar'd
Till kye be gaun without the herd,
An' a' the vittel in the yard,
      An' theekit right,
I mean your ingle-side to guard
      Ae winter night.

Then muse-inspirin' aqua-vitae
Shall make us baith sae blythe an' witty,
Till ye forget ye're auld an' gutty,
      An' be as canty
As ye were nine year less than thretty,
      Sweet ane an' twenty!

But stooks are cowpet wi' the blast,
An' now the sinn keeks in the west,
Then I maun rin amang the rest
      An' quat my chanter;
Sae I subscribe mysel in haste,
      Yours, RAB THE RANTER.

To the Rev. John M'Math, Inclosing a copy of Holy Willie's Prayer, which he had requested

Sept. 17*th*, 1785.

While at the stook the shearers cow'r
To shun the bitter blaudin' show'r,
Or in gulravage rinnin scow'r
      To pass the time,
To you I dedicate the hour
      In idle rhyme.

My musie, tir'd wi' mony a sonnet
On gown, an' ban', an' douse black bonnet,
Is grown right eerie now she 's done it,
      Lest they shou'd blame her,
An' rouse their holy thunder on it
      And anathem her.

I own 'twas rash, an' rather hardy,
That I, a simple, countra bardie,
Shou'd meddle wi' a pack sae sturdy,
      Wha, if they ken me,
Can easy, wi' a single wordie,
      Louse h–ll upon me.

But I gae mad at their grimaces,
Their sighan, cantan, grace-proud faces,
Their three-mile prayers, an' hauf-mile graces,
      Their raxan conscience,
Whase greed, revenge, an' pride disgraces
      Waur nor their nonsense.

There 's *Gaun*, miska't waur than a beast,
Wha has mair honor in his breast

Than mony scores as guid 's the priest
      Wha sae abus't him:
An' may a bard no crack his jest
      What way they've use't him?

See him, the poor man's friend in need,
The gentleman in word an' deed,
An' shall his fame an' honor bleed
      By worthless skellums,
An' not a muse erect her head
      To cowe the blellums?

O Pope, had I thy satire's darts
To gie the rascals their deserts,
I'd rip their rotten, hollow hearts,
      An' tell aloud
Their jugglin' hocus pocus arts
      To cheat the crowd.

God knows, I'm no the thing I shou'd be,
Nor am I even the thing I cou'd be,
But twenty times, I rather wou'd be
      An atheist clean,
Than under gospel colors hid be
      Just for a screen.

An honest man may like a glass,
An honest man may like a lass,
But mean revenge, an' malice fause
      He'll still disdain,
An' then cry zeal for gospel laws,
      Like some we ken.

They take religion in their mouth;
They talk o' mercy, grace an' truth,
For what? – to gie their malice skouth
      On some puir wight,
An' hunt him down, o'er right an' ruth,
      To ruin streight.

All hail, Religion! maid divine!
Pardon a muse sae mean as mine,
Who in her rough imperfect line
        Thus daurs to name thee;
To stigmatize false friends of thine
        Can ne'er defame thee.

Tho' blotch't an' foul wi' mony a stain,
An' far unworthy of thy train,
With trembling voice I tune my strain
        To join with those,
Who boldly dare thy cause maintain
        In spite of foes:

In spite o' crowds, in spite o' mobs,
In spite of undermining jobs,
In spite o' dark banditti stabs
        At worth an' merit,
By scoundrels, even wi' holy robes,
        But hellish spirit.

O Ayr, my dear, my native ground,
Within thy presbytereal bound
A candid lib'ral band is found
        Of public teachers,
As men, as Christians too renown'd
        An' manly preachers.

Sir, in that circle you are nam'd;
Sir, in that circle you are fam'd;
An' some, by whom your doctrine 's blam'd
        (Which gies you honor)
Even Sir, by them your heart 's esteem'd,
        An' winning manner.

Pardon this freedom I have ta'en,
An' if impertinent I've been,
Impute it not, good Sir, in ane
        Whase heart ne'er wrang'd ye,
But to his utmost would befriend
        Ought that belang'd ye.

To a Mouse, On turning her up in her Nest, with the Plough, November, 1785.

Wee, sleeket, cowran, tim'rous *beastie*,
O, what a panic 's in thy breastie!
Thou need na start awa sae hasty,
   Wi' bickering brattle!
I wad be laith to ruin an' chase thee,
   Wi' murd'ring *pattle*!

I'm truly sorry Man's dominion
Has broken Nature's social union,
An' justifies that ill opinion,
   Which makes thee startle,
At me, thy poor, earth-born companion,
   An' *fellow-mortal*!

I doubt na, whyles, but thou may *thieve*;
What then? poor beastie, thou maun live!
A *daimen-icker* in a *thrave*
   'S a sma' request:
I'll get a blessin wi' the lave,
   An' never miss 't!

Thy wee-bit *housie*, too, in ruin!
It's silly wa's the win's are strewin!
An' naething, now, to big a new ane,
   O' foggage green!
An' bleak *December's winds* ensuin,
   Baith snell an' keen!

Thou saw the fields laid bare an' wast,
An' weary *Winter* comin fast,
An' cozie here, beneath the blast,
   Thou thought to dwell,

Till crash! the cruel *coulter* past
       Out thro' thy cell.

That wee-bit heap o' leaves an' stibble,
Has cost thee monie a weary nibble!
Now thou 's turn'd out, for a' thy trouble,
       But house or hald,
To thole the Winter's *sleety dribble*,
       An' *cranreuch* cauld!

But Mousie, thou art no thy-lane,
In proving *foresight* may be vain:
The best laid schemes o' *Mice* an' *Men*,
       Gang aft agley,
An' lea'e us nought but grief an' pain,
       For promis'd joy!

Still, thou art blest, compar'd wi' *me*!
The *present* only toucheth thee:
But Och! I *backward* cast my e'e,
       On prospects drear!
An' *forward*, tho' I canna *see*,
       I *guess* an' *fear*!

The Holy Fair*

A robe of seeming truth and trust
   Hid crafty Observation;
And secret hung, with poison'd crust,
   The dirk of Defamation:
A mask that like the gorget show'd,
   Dye-varying, on the pigeon;
And for a mantle large and broad,
   He wrapt him in Religion. –

                    Hypocrisy a-la-Mode.

I

Upon a simmer *Sunday morn*,
   When Nature's face is fair,
I walked forth to view the corn,
   An' snuff the callor air:
The rising sun, owre GALSTON muirs,
   Wi' glorious light was glintan;
The hares were hirplan down the furrs,
   The lav'rocks they were chantan
               Fu' sweet that day.

II

As lightsomely I glowr'd abroad,
   To see a scene sae gay,
Three *hizzies*, early at the road,
   Cam skelpan up the way.
Twa had manteeles o' dolefu' black,
   But ane wi' lyart lining;
The *third*, that gaed a wee aback,
   Was in the fashion shining
               Fu' gay that day.

* *Holy Fair* is a common phrase in the West of Scotland for a sacramental occasion.

174

III

The *twa* appear'd like sisters twin,
   In feature, form an' claes;
Their visage – wither'd, lang an' thin,
   An' sour as onie slaes:
The *third* cam up, hap-step-an'-loup,
   As light as onie lambie, –
An' wi' a curchie low did stoop,
   As soon as e'er she saw me,
            Fu' kind that day.

IV

Wi' bonnet aff, quoth I, 'Sweet lass,
   'I think ye seem to ken me:
'I'm sure I've seen that bonie face,
   'But yet I canna name ye. – '
Quo' she, an' laughan as she spak,
   An' taks me by the hands,
'Ye, for my sake, hae gien the feck
   'Of a' the *ten commands*
            A screed some day.

V

'My name is FUN – your cronie dear,
   'The nearest friend ye hae;
'An' this is SUPERSTITION here,
   'An' that 's HYPOCRISY:
'I'm gaun to Mauchline *holy fair*,
   'To spend an hour in daffin;
'Gin ye'll go there, yon runkl'd pair,
   'We will get famous laughin
            At them this day.'

VI

Quoth I, 'With a' my heart, I'll do 't;
   'I'll get my Sunday's sark on,
'An' meet you on the holy spot;
   Faith we'se hae fine remarkin!'

Then I gaed hame, at crowdie-time,
    An' soon I made me ready;
For roads were clad, frae side to side,
    Wi' monie a weary body,
            In droves that day.

VII

Here, farmers gash, in ridin graith,
    Gaed hoddan by their cotters;
There, swankies young, in braw braid-claith,
    Are springan owre the gutters.
The lasses, skelpan barefit, thrang,
    In silks an' scarlets glitter;
Wi' *sweet-milk cheese*, in mony a whang,
    An' *farls*, bak'd wi' butter,
            Fu' crump that day.

VIII

When by the *plate* we set our nose,
    Weel heaped up wi' ha'pence,
A greedy glowr *Black-bonnet* throws,
    An' we maun draw our tippence.
Then in we go to see the show,
    On ev'ry side they're gath'ran;
Some carryan dails, some chairs an' stools,
    An' some are busy bleth'ran
            Right loud that day.

IX

Here, stands a shed to fend the show'rs,
    An' screen our countra Gentry;
There, *Racer-Jess*, an' twathree wh–res,
    Are blinkan at the entry:
Here sits a raw o' tittlan jads,
    Wi' heaving breasts an' bare neck;
An' there, a batch o' *Wabster lads*,
    Blackguarding frae Kilmarnock
            For *fun* this day.

X

Here, some are thinkan on their sins,
    An' some upo' their claes;
Ane curses feet that fyl'd his shins,
    Anither sighs an' pray's:
On this hand sits a Chosen swatch,
    Wi' screw'd-up, grace-proud faces;
On that, a set o' chaps, at watch,
    Thrang winkan on the lasses
              To *chairs* that day.

XI

O happy is that man, an' blest!
    Nae wonder that it pride him!
Whase ain dear lass, that he likes best,
    Comes clinkan down beside him!
Wi' arm repos'd on the *chair back*,
    He sweetly does compose him;
Which, by degrees, slips round her *neck*,
    An 's loof upon her *bosom*
              Unkend that day.

XII

Now a' the congregation o'er,
    Is silent expectation;
For Sawnie speels the holy door,
    Wi' tidings o' d–mn–t—n:
Should *Hornie*, as in ancient days,
    'Mang sons o' G— present him,
The vera sight o' Sawnie's face,
    To 's ain *het hame* had sent him
              Wi' fright that day.

XIII

Hear how he clears the points o' Faith
    Wi' rattlin an' thumpin!
Now meekly calm, now wild in wrath,
    He 's stampan, an' he 's jumpan!

His lengthen'd chin, his turn'd up snout,
   His eldritch squeel an' gestures,
O how they fire the heart devout,
   Like cantharidian plaisters
       On sic a day!

XIV

But hark! the *tent* has chang'd it's voice;
   There 's peace an' rest nae langer;
For a' the *real judges* rise,
   They canna sit for anger.
Smith opens out his cauld harangues,
   On *practice* and on *morals*;
An' aff the godly pour in thrangs,
   To gie the jars an' barrels
       A lift that day.

XV

What signifies his barren shine,
   Of *moral pow'rs* an' *reason*;
His English style, an' gesture fine,
   Are a' clean out o' season.
Like SOCRATES or ANTONINE,
   Or some auld pagan heathen,
The *moral man* he does define,
   But ne'er a word o' *faith* in
       That 's right that day.

XVI

In guid time comes an antidote
   Against sic poosion'd nostrum;
For Peebles, frae the water-fit,
   Ascends the *holy rostrum*:
See, up he 's got the Word o' G—,
   An' meek an' mim has view'd it,
While COMMON-SENSE has taen the road,

An' aff, an' up the *Cowgate**
  Fast, fast that day.

XVII

Wee Miller niest, the Guard relieves,
 An' Orthodoxy raibles,
Tho' in his heart he weel believes,
 An' thinks it auld wives' fables:
But faith! the birkie wants a *Manse*,
 So, cannilie he hums them;
Altho' his *carnal* Wit an' Sense
 Like hafflins-wise o'ercomes him
  At times that day.

XVIII

Now, butt an' ben, the Change-house fills,
 Wi' *yill-caup* Commentators:
Here 's crying out for bakes an' gills,
 An' there, the pint-stowp clatters;
While thick an' thrang, an' loud an' lang,
 Wi' *Logic*, an' wi' *Scripture*,
They raise a din, that, in the end,
 Is like to breed a rupture
  O' wrath that day.

XIX

Leeze me on Drink! it gies us mair
 Than either School or Colledge:
It kindles Wit, it waukens Lear,
 It pangs us fou o' Knowledge.
Be 't *whisky-gill* or *penny-wheep*,
 Or onie stronger potion,
It never fails, on drinkin deep,
 To kittle up our *notion*,
  By night or day.

---

* A street so called, which faces the *tent* in [Mauchline].

XX

The lads an' lasses, blythely bent
  To mind baith *saul* an' *body*,
Sit round the table, weel content,
  An' steer about the *Toddy*.
On this ane's dress, an' that ane's leuk,
  They're makin observations;
While some are cozie i' the neuk,
  An' forming *assignations*
        To meet some day.

XXI

But now the L——'s ain trumpet touts,
  Till a' the hills are rairan,
An' echos back return the shouts,
  Black Russel is na spairan:
His piercin words, like highlan swords,
  Divide the joints an' marrow;
His talk o' H—ll, whare devils dwell,
  Our vera 'Sauls does harrow'*
        Wi' fright that day.

XXII

A vast, unbottom'd, boundless *Pit*,
  Fill'd fou o' *lowan brunstane*,
Whase raging flame, an' scorching heat,
  Wad melt the hardest whunstane!
The *half-asleep* start up wi' fear,
  An' think they hear it roaran,
When presently it does appear,
  'Twas but some neebor *snoran*
        Asleep that day.

XXIII

'Twad be owre lang a tale to tell,
  How monie stories past,

* Shakespeare's Hamlet.

An' how they crouded to the yill,
　　When they were a' dismist:
How drink gaed round, in cogs an' caups,
　　Amang the furms an' benches;
An' cheese an' *bread*, frae women's laps,
　　Was dealt about in lunches,
　　　　　　An' dawds that day.

XXIV

In comes a gausie, gash *Guidwife*,
　　An' sits down by the fire,
Syn draws her *kebbuck* an' her knife;
　　The lasses they are shyer.
The auld *Guidmen*, about the *grace*,
　　Frae side to side they bother,
Till some ane by his bonnet lays,
　　An' gies them 't, like a *tether*,
　　　　　　Fu' lang that day.

XXV

Wae sucks! for him that gets nae lass,
　　Or lasses that hae naething!
Sma' need has he to say a grace,
　　Or melvie his braw claething!
O *Wives* be mindfu', ance yoursel,
　　How bonie lads ye wanted,
An' dinna, for a *kebbuck-heel*,
　　Let lasses be affronted
　　　　　　On sic a day!

XXVI

Now *Clinkumbell*, wi' rattlan tow,
　　Begins to jow an' croon;
Some swagger hame, the best they dow,
　　Some wait the afternoon.
At slaps the billies halt a blink,
　　Till lasses strip their shoon:

Wi' *faith* an' *hope*, an' *love* an' *drink*,
    They're a' in famous tune
          For crack that day.

XXVII

How monie hearts this day converts,
    O' Sinners and o' Lasses!
Their hearts o' stane, gin night are gane
    As saft as ony flesh is.
There 's some are fou o' *love divine*;
    There 's some are fou o' *brandy*;
An' monie jobs that day begin,
    May end in *Houghmagandie*
          Some ither day.

The Twa Dogs. A Tale

⟨∘∾∘∾∘⟩

'Twas in that place o' *Scotland*'s isle,
That bears the name o' auld king COIL,
Upon a bonie day in June,
When wearing thro' the afternoon,
Twa Dogs, that were na thrang at hame,
Forgather'd ance upon a time.

The first I'll name, they ca'd him *Ceasar*,
Was keepet for his Honor's pleasure;
His hair, his size, his mouth, his lugs,
Show'd he was nane o' Scotland's dogs;
But whalpet some place far abroad,
Whare sailors gang to fish for Cod.

His locked, letter'd, braw brass-collar,
Show'd him the *gentleman* an' *scholar*;
But tho' he was o' high degree,
The fient a pride na pride had he,
But wad hae spent an hour caressan,
Ev'n wi' a Tinkler-gipsey's *messan*:
At *Kirk* or *Market*, *Mill* or *Smiddie*,
Nae tawtied *tyke*, tho' e'er sae duddie,
But he wad stan't, as glad to see him,
An' stroan't on stanes an' hillocks wi' him.

The tither was a *ploughman's collie*,
A rhyming, ranting, raving billie,
Wha for his friend an' comrade had him,
And in his freaks had *Luath* ca'd him;
After some dog in * *Highlan Sang*,
    Wi' never-ceasing toil;
Was made lang syne, lord knows how lang.

* Cuchullin's dog in Ossian's Fingal.

183

He was a gash an' faithfu' *tyke*,
As ever lap a sheugh, or dyke!
His honest sonsie, baws'nt *face*,
Ay gat him friends in ilka place;
His *breast* was white, his towzie *back*,
Weel clad wi' coat o' glossy black;
His gawsie tail, wi' upward curl,
Hung owre his hurdies wi' a swirl.

Nae doubt but they were fain o' ither,
An' unco pack an' thick the gither;
Wi' social *nose* whyles snuff'd an' snowcket;
Whyles mice an' modewurks they howcket;
Whyles scour'd awa in lang excursion,
An' worry'd ither in *diversion*;
Untill wi' daffin weary grown,
Upon a knowe they sat them down,
An' there began a lang digression
About the *lords o' the creation*.

CEASAR

I've aften wonder'd, honest *Luath*,
What sort o' life poor dogs like you have;
An' when the *gentry*'s life I saw,
What way *poor bodies* liv'd ava.

Our *Laird* gets in his racked rents,
His coals, his kane, an' a' his stents;
He rises when he likes himsel;
His flunkies answer at the bell;
He ca's his coach; he ca's his horse;
He draws a bonie, silken purse
As lang 's my *tail*, whare thro' the steeks,
The yellow, letter'd *Geordie* keeks.

Frae morn to een it 's nought but toiling,
At baking, roasting, frying, boiling:
An' tho' the gentry first are steghan,
Yet ev'n the *ha' folk* fill their peghan

Wi' sauce, ragouts, an' sic like trashtrie,
That 's little short o' downright wastrie.
Our *Whipper-in*, wee, blastiet wonner,
Poor, worthless elf, it eats a dinner,
Better than ony *Tenant-man*
His Honor has in a' the lan':
An' what poor *Cot-folk* pit their painch in,
I own it 's past my comprehension. –

LUATH

Trowth, *Ceasar*, whyles they're fash'd eneugh;
A *Cotter* howckan in a sheugh,
Wi' dirty stanes biggan an dyke,
Bairan a quarry, an' sic like,
Himsel, a wife, he thus sustains,
A smytrie o' wee, duddie weans,
An' nought but his han'-daurk, to keep
Them right an' tight in *thack an' raep*.

An' when they meet wi' sair disasters,
Like loss o' health, or want o' masters,
Ye maist wad think, a wee touch langer,
An' they maun starve o' cauld an' hunger:
But how it comes, I never kent yet,
They're maistly wonderfu' contented;
An' buirdly chiels, an' clever hizzies,
Are bred in sic a way as this is.

CEASAR

But then, to see how ye're negleket,
How huff'd, an' cuff'd, an' disrespeket!
L—d man, our gentry care as little
For *delvers, ditchers*, an' sic cattle;
They gang as saucy by poor folk,
As I wad by a stinkan brock.

I've notic'd, on our Laird's *court-day*,
An' mony a time my heart 's been wae,
Poor *tenant-bodies*, scant o' cash,
How they maun thole a *factor*'s snash;

He'll stamp an' threaten, curse an' swear,
He'll *apprehend* them, *poind* their gear,
While they maun stand, wi' aspect humble,
An' hear it a', an' fear an' tremble!

I see how folk live that hae riches,
But surely poor-folk maun be *wretches*!

LUATH

They're no sae wretched 's ane wad think;
Tho' constantly on poortith's brink,
They're sae accustom'd wi' the sight,
The view o't gies them little fright.

Then chance an' fortune are sae guided,
They're ay in less or mair provided;
An' tho' fatigu'd wi' close employment,
A blink o' rest 's a sweet enjoyment.

The dearest comfort o' their lives,
Their grushie weans, an' faithfu' wives;
The *prattling things* are just their pride,
That sweetens a' their fire-side.

An' whyles, twalpennie-worth o' *nappy*
Can mak the bodies unco happy;
They lay aside their private cares,
To mind the Kirk an' State affairs;
They'll talk o' *patronage* an' *priests*,
Wi' kindling fury i' their breasts,
Or tell what new taxation 's comin,
An' ferlie at the folk in Lon'on.

As bleak-fac'd Hallowmass returns,
They get the jovial, rantan *Kirns*,
When *rural life*, of ev'ry station,
Unite in common recreation;
Love blinks, Wit slaps, an' social Mirth
Forgets there 's *care* upo' the earth.

That *merry day* the year begins,
They bar the door on frosty win's;
The nappy reeks wi' mantling ream,
An' sheds a heart-inspiring steam;
The luntan pipe, an' sneeshin mill,
Are handed round wi' right guid will;
The cantie, auld folks, crackan crouse,
The young anes rantan thro' the house –
My heart has been sae fain to see them,
That I for joy hae *barket* wi' them.

Still it 's owre true that ye hae said,
Sic game is now owre aften play'd;
There 's monie a creditable *stock*
O' decent, honest, fawsont folk,
Are riven out baith root an' branch,
Some rascal's pridefu' greed to quench,
Wha thinks to knit himsel the faster
In favor wi' some *gentle Master*,
Wha, aiblins, thrang a *parliamentin*,
For *Britain's guid* his saul indentin –

CEASAR

Haith lad, ye little ken about it;
For Britain's guid! guid faith! I doubt it.
Say rather, gaun as PREMIERS lead him,
An' saying *aye* or *no* 's they bid him:
At Operas an' Plays parading,
Mortgaging, gambling, masquerading:
Or maybe, in a frolic daft,
To HAGUE or CALAIS takes a waft,
To make a *tour* an' take a whirl,
To learn *bon ton* an' see the worl'.

There, at VIENNA or VERSAILLES,
He rives his father's auld entails;
Or by MADRID he takes the rout,
To thrum *guittarres* an' fecht wi' *nowt*;

Or down *Italian Vista* startles,
Wh—re-hunting amang groves o' myrtles
Then bowses drumlie *German-water*,
To make himsel look fair an' fatter,
An' clear the consequential sorrows,
Love-gifts of Carnival Signioras.
For Britain's guid! for her destruction!
Wi' dissipation, feud an' faction!

LUATH

Hech man! dear sirs! is that the gate,
They waste sae mony a braw estate!
Are we sae foughten an' harass'd
For gear to gang that gate at last!

O would they stay aback frae courts,
An' please themsels wi' countra sports,
It wad for ev'ry ane be better,
The *Laird*, the *Tenant*, an' the *Cotter*!
For thae frank, rantan, ramblan billies,
Fient haet o' them 's illhearted fellows;
Except for breakin o' their timmer,
Or speakin lightly o' their *Limmer*;
Or shootin of a hare or moorcock,
The ne'er-a-bit they're ill to poor folk.

But will ye tell me, master *Cesar*,
Sure *great folk*'s life 's a life o' pleasure?
Nae cauld nor hunger e'er can steer them,
The vera thought o't need na fear them.

CESAR

L—d man, were ye but whyles where I am,
The *gentles* ye wad ne'er envy them!

It 's true, they needna starve or sweat,
Thro' Winter's cauld, or Summer's heat;
They've nae sair-wark to craze their banes,
An' fill *auld-age* wi' grips an' granes:

But *human-bodies* are sic fools,
For a' their Colledges an' Schools,
That when nae *real* ills perplex them,
They *mak* enow themsels to vex them;
An' ay the less they hae to sturt them,
In like proportion, less will hurt them.

A countra fallow at the pleugh,
His *acre* 's till'd, he 's right eneugh;
A countra lassie at her wheel,
Her *dizzen* 's done, she 's unco weel;
But Gentlemen, an' Ladies warst,
Wi' ev'n down *want o' wark* they're curst.
They loiter, lounging, lank an lazy;
Tho' deil-haet ails them, yet uneasy;
Their days, insipid, dull an' tasteless,
Their nights, unquiet, lang an' restless.

An' ev'n their sports, their balls an' races,
Their galloping thro' public places,
There 's sic parade, sic pomp an' art,
The joy can scarcely reach the heart.

The *Men* cast out in *party-matches*,
Then sowther a' in deep debauches.
Ae night, they're mad wi' drink an' wh–ring,
Niest day their life is past enduring.

The *Ladies* arm-in-arm in clusters,
As great an' gracious a' as sisters;
But hear their *absent thoughts* o' ither,
They're a' run-deils an' jads the gither
Whyles, owre the wee bit cup an' platie,
They sip the *scandal-potion* pretty;
Or lee-lang nights, wi' crabbet leuks,
Pore owre the devil's *pictur'd beuks*;
Stake on a chance a farmer's stackyard,
An' cheat like ony *unhang'd blackguard*.

There 's some exceptions, man an' woman;
But this is Gentry's life in common.

By this, the sun was out o' sight,
An' darker gloamin brought the night:
The *bum-clock* humm'd wi' lazy drone,
The kye stood rowtan i' the loan;
When up they gat, an' shook their lugs,
Rejoic'd they were na *men* but *dogs*;
An' each took off his several way,
Resolv'd to meet some ither day.

The Cotter's Saturday Night. Inscribed to R. Aiken, Esq.

Let not Ambition mock their useful toil,
  Their homely joys, and destiny obscure;
Nor Grandeur hear, with a disdainful smile,
  The short and simple annals of the Poor.
                                    GRAY.

I

My lov'd, my honor'd, much respected friend,
  No mercenary Bard his homage pays;
With honest pride, I scorn each selfish end,
  My dearest meed, a friend's esteem and praise:
To you I sing, in simple Scottish lays,
  The *lowly train* in life's sequester'd scene;
The native feelings strong, the guileless ways,
  What Aiken in a *Cottage* would have been;
Ah! tho' his worth unknown, far happier there I ween!

II

November chill blaws loud wi' angry sugh;
  The short'ning winter-day is near a close;
The miry beasts retreating frae the pleugh;
  The black'ning trains o' craws to their repose:
The toil-worn COTTER frae his labor goes,
  This night his weekly moil is at an end,
Collects his *spades*, his *mattocks* and his *hoes*,
  Hoping the *morn* in ease and rest to spend,
And weary, o'er the muir, his course does hameward bend.

III

At length his lonely *Cot* appears in view,
  Beneath the shelter of an aged tree;

Th' expectant wee-things, toddlan, stacher thro'
　　To meet their *Dad*, wi' flichterin noise and glee.
His wee-bit ingle, blinkan bonilie,
　　His clean hearth-stane, his thrifty *Wifie*'s smile,
The *lisping infant*, prattling on his knee,
　　Does a' his weary carking cares beguile,
And makes him quite forget his labor and his toil.

IV

Belyve, the *elder bairns* come drapping in,
　　At *Service* out, amang the Farmers roun';
Some ca' the pleugh, some herd, some tentie rin
　　A cannie errand to a neebor toun:
Their eldest hope, their *Jenny*, woman-grown,
　　In youthfu' bloom, Love sparkling in her e'e,
Comes hame, perhaps to show a braw new gown,
　　Or deposite her sair-won penny-fee,
To help her *Parents* dear, if they in hardship be.

V

With joy unfeign'd, *brothers* and *sisters* meet,
　　And each for other's weelfare kindly spiers:
The social hours, swift-wing'd, unnotic'd, fleet;
　　Each tells the uncos that he sees or hears.
The *Parents partial* eye their hopeful years;
　　Anticipation forward points the view;
The *Mother* wi' her needle and her sheers
　　Gars auld claes look amaist as weel 's the new;
The *Father* mixes a', wi' admonition due.

VI

Their Master's and their Mistress's command,
　　The *youngkers* a' are warned to obey;
And mind their labors wi' an eydent hand,
　　And ne'er, tho' out o' sight, to jauk or play:
'And O! be sure to fear the Lord alway!
　　'And mind your *duty*, duely, morn and night!
'Lest in temptation's path ye gang astray,

'Implore His counsel and assisting might:
'They never sought in vain, that sought the LORD aright.'

VII

But hark! a rap comes gently to the door;
    Jenny, wha kens the meaning o' the same,
Tells how a neebor lad came o'er the muir,
    To do some errands, and convoy her hame.
The wily Mother sees the *conscious flame*
    Sparkle in *Jenny*'s e'e, and flush her cheek,
With heart-struck, anxious care enquires his name,
    While *Jenny* hafflins is afraid to speak;
Weel-pleas'd the Mother hears, it 's nae wild, worthless *Rake*.

VIII

With kindly welcome, *Jenny* brings him ben;
    A *strappan youth*, he takes the Mother's eye;
Blythe *Jenny* sees the *visit* 's no ill-taen;
    The Father cracks of horses, pleughs and kye.
The *youngster*'s artless heart o'erflows wi' joy,
    But blate and laithfu', scarce can weel behave;
The Mother, wi' a woman's wiles, can spy
    What makes the *youth* sae bashfu' and sae grave;
Weel-pleas'd to think her *bairn* 's respected like the lave.

IX

O happy love! where love like this is found!
    O heart-felt raptures! bliss beyond compare!
I've paced much this weary, *mortal round*,
    And sage EXPERIENCE bids me this declare –
'If Heaven a draught of heavenly pleasure spare,
    'One *cordial* in this melancholly *Vale*,
''Tis when a youthful, loving, *modest* Pair,
    'In other's arms, breathe out the tender tale,
'Beneath the milk-white thorn that scents the ev'ning gale.'

X

Is there, in human-form, that bears a heart –
    A wretch! a villain! lost to love and truth!

That can, with studied, sly, ensnaring art,
    Betray sweet *Jenny*'s unsuspecting youth?
Curse on his perjur'd arts! dissembling smoothe!
    Are *Honor, Virtue, Conscience*, all exil'd?
Is there no Pity, no relenting Ruth,
    Points to the Parents fondling o'er their Child?
Then paints the *ruin'd Maid*, and *their* distraction wild!

XI

But now the Supper crowns their simple board,
    The healsome *Porritch*, chief of SCOTIA's food:
The soupe their *only Hawkie* does afford,
    That 'yont the hallan snugly chows her cood:
The *Dame* brings forth, in complimental mood,
    To grace the lad, her weel-hain'd kebbuck, fell;
And aft he's prest, and aft he ca's it guid;
    The frugal *Wifie*, garrulous, will tell,
How 'twas a towmond auld, sin' Lint was i' the bell.

XII

The chearfu' Supper done, wi' serious face,
    They, round the ingle, form a circle wide;
The Sire turns o'er, with patriarchal grace,
    The big *ha'-Bible*, ance his *Father*'s pride:
His bonnet rev'rently is laid aside,
    His *lyart haffets* wearing thin and bare;
Those strains that once did sweet in ZION glide,
    He wales a portion with judicious care;
'*And let us worship God!*' he says with solemn air.

XIII

They chant their artless notes in simple guise;
    They tune their hearts, by far the noblest aim:
Perhaps *Dundee*'s wild-warbling measures rise,
    Or plaintive *Martyrs*, worthy of the name;
Or noble *Elgin* beets the heaven-ward flame,
    The sweetest far of SCOTIA's holy lays:
Compar'd with these, *Italian trills* are tame;

The tickl'd ears no heart-felt raptures raise;
Nae unison hae they, with our CREATOR's praise.

XIV

The priest-like Father reads the sacred page,
    How *Abram* was the Friend of GOD on high;
Or, *Moses* bade eternal warfare wage,
    With *Amalek*'s ungracious progeny;
Or how the *royal Bard* did groaning lye,
    Beneath the stroke of Heaven's avenging ire;
Or *Job*'s pathetic plaint, and wailing cry;
    Or rapt *Isiah*'s wild, seraphic fire;
Or other *Holy Seers* that tune the *sacred lyre*.

XV

Perhaps the *Christian Volume* is the theme;
    How *guiltless blood* for *guilty man* was shed;
How HE, who bore in Heaven the second name,
    Had not on Earth whereon to lay His head:
How His first *followers* and *servants* sped;
    The *Precepts sage* they wrote to many a land:
How *he*, who lone in *Patmos*, banished,
    Saw in the sun a mighty angel stand;
And heard great *Bab'lon*'s doom pronounc'd by Heaven's command.

XVI

Then kneeling down to HEAVEN'S ETERNAL KING,
    The *Saint*, the *Father*, and the *Husband* prays:
Hope 'springs exulting on triumphant wing,'*
    That *thus* they all shall meet in future days:
There, ever bask in *uncreated rays*,
    No more to sigh, or shed the bitter tear,
Together hymning their CREATOR's praise
    In *such society*, yet still more dear;
While circling Time moves round in an eternal sphere.

* Popes Windsor Forest.

XVII

Compar'd with this, how poor Religion's pride,
  In all the pomp of *method*, and of *art*,
When men display to congregations wide,
  Devotion's ev'ry grace, except the *heart*!
The POWER, incens'd, the Pageant will desert,
  The pompous strain, the sacredotal stole;
But haply, in some *Cottage* far apart,
  May hear, well pleas'd, the language of the *Soul*;
And in His *Book of Life* the Inmates poor enroll.

XVIII

Then homeward all take off their sev'ral way;
  The youngling *Cottagers* retire to rest:
The Parent-pair their *secret homage* pay,
  And proffer up to Heaven the warm request,
That 'HE who stills the *raven*'s clam'rous nest,
  'And decks the *lily* fair in flow'ry pride,
'Would, in the way His *Wisdom* sees the best,
  'For *them* and for their *little ones* provide;
'But chiefly, in their hearts with *Grace divine* preside.'

XIX

From Scenes like these, old SCOTIA's grandeur springs,
  That makes her lov'd at home, rever'd abroad:
Princes and lords are but the breath of kings,
  'An honest man 's the noble work of GOD:'
And *certes*, in fair Virtue's heavenly road,
  The *Cottage* leaves the *Palace* far behind:
What is a lordling's pomp? a cumbrous load,
  Disguising oft the *wretch* of human kind,
Studied in arts of Hell, in wickedness refin'd!

XX

O SCOTIA! my dear, my native soil!
  For whom my warmest wish to Heaven is sent!
Long may thy hardy sons of *rustic toil*
  Be blest with health and peace and sweet content!

And O may Heaven their simple lives prevent
 From *Luxury*'s contagion, weak and vile!
Then howe'er *crowns* and *coronets* be rent,
 A *virtuous Populace* may rise the while,
And stand a wall of fire, around their much-lov'd ISLE.

XXI

O THOU! who pour'd the *patriotic tide*,
 That stream'd thro' great, unhappy WALLACE' heart;
Who dar'd to, nobly, stem tyrannic pride,
 Or *nobly die*, the second glorious part:
(The Patriot's GOD, peculiarly thou art,
 His *friend, inspirer, guardian* and *reward*!)
O never, never SCOTIA's realm desert,
 But still the *Patriot*, and the *Patriot-bard*,
In bright succession raise, her *Ornament* and *Guard*!

THE following POEM will, by many Readers, be well enough understood; but, for the sake of those who are unacquainted with the manners and traditions of the country where the scene is cast, Notes are added, to give some account of the principal Charms and Spells of that Night, so big with Prophecy to the Peasantry in the West of Scotland. The passion of prying into Futurity makes a striking part of the history of Human-nature, in it's rude state, in all ages and nations; and it may be some entertainment to a philosophic mind, if any such should honor the Author with a perusal, to see the remains of it, among the more unenlightened in our own.

*Halloween**

❦❦❦

> *Yes! let the Rich deride, the Proud disdain,*
> *The simple pleasures of the lowly train;*
> *To me more dear, congenial to my heart,*
> *One native charm, than all the gloss of art.*
> GOLDSMITH.

I

Upon that *night*, when Fairies light,
　　On *Cassilis Downans*† dance,
Or owre the lays, in splendid blaze,
　　On sprightly coursers prance;
Or for *Colean*, the rout is taen,
　　Beneath the moon's pale beams;
There, up the *Cove*,‡ to stray an' rove,
　　Amang the rocks an' streams
　　　　To sport that night.

* Is thought to be a night when Witches, Devils, and other mischief-making beings, are all abroad on their baneful, midnight errands: particularly, those aerial people, the Fairies, are said, on that night, to hold a grand Anniversary.

† Certain little, romantic, rocky, green hills, in the neighbourhood of the ancient seat of the Earls of Cassilis.

‡ A noted cavern near Colean-house, called the Cove of Colean; which, as well as Cassilis Downans, is famed, in country story, for being a favourite haunt of Fairies.

II

Amang the bonie, winding banks,
  Where *Doon* rins, wimplin, clear,
Where Bruce* ance rul'd the martial ranks,
  An' shook his *Carrick* spear,
Some merry, friendly, countra folks,
  Together did convene,
To *burn* their nits, an' *pou* their stocks,
  An' haud their *Halloween*
              Fu' blythe that night.

III

The lasses feat, an' cleanly neat,
  Mair braw than when they're fine;
Their faces blythe, fu' sweetly kythe,
  Hearts leal, an' warm, an' kin':
The lads sae trig, wi' wooer-babs,
  Weel knotted on their garten,
Some unco blate, an' some wi' gabs,
  Gar lasses hearts gang startin
              Whyles fast at night.

IV

Then, first an' foremost, thro' the kail,
  Their *stocks*† maun a' be sought ance;
They steek their een, an' grape an' wale,
  For muckle anes, an' straught anes.

---

* The famous family of that name, the ancestors of ROBERT the great Deliverer of his country, were Earls of Carrick.

† The first ceremony of Halloween, is, pulling each a *Stock*, or plant of kail. They must go out, hand in hand, with eyes shut, and pull the first they meet with: its being big or little, straight or crooked, is prophetic of the size and shape of the grand object of all their Spells – the husband or wife. If any *yird*, or earth, stick to the root, that is *tocher*, or fortune; and the taste of the *custoc*, that is, the heart of the stem, is indicative of the natural temper and disposition. Lastly, the stems, or to give them their ordinary appellation, the *runts*, are placed somewhere above the head of the door; and the christian names of the people whom chance brings into the house, are, according to the priority of placing the *runts*, the names in question.

Poor hav'rel *Will* fell aff the drift,
 An' wander'd thro' the *Bow-kail*,
An' pow't, for want o' better shift,
 A *runt* was like a sow-tail
  Sae bow't that night.

V

Then, straught or crooked, yird or nane,
 They roar an' cry a' throw'ther;
The vera *wee-things*, toddlan, rin,
 Wi' stocks out owre their shouther:
An' gif the *custock*'s sweet or sour,
 Wi' joctelegs they taste them;
Syne coziely, aboon the door,
 Wi' cannie care, they've plac'd them
  To lye that night.

VI

The lasses staw frae 'mang them a',
 To pou their *stalks o' corn*;*
But *Rab* slips out, an' jinks about,
 Behint the muckle thorn:
He grippet *Nelly* hard an' fast;
 Loud skirl'd a' the lasses;
But her *tap-pickle* maist was lost,
 When kiutlan in the *Fause-house*†
  Wi' him that night.

VII

The auld Guidwife's weel-hoordet *nits*‡
 Are round an' round divided,

---

* They go to the barn-yard, and pull each, at three several times, a stalk of Oats. If the third stalk wants the *top-pickle*, that is, the grain at the top of the stalk, the party in question will come to the marriage-bed any thing but a Maid.

† When the corn is in a doubtful state, by being too green, or wet, the Stack-builder, by means of old timber, &c. makes a large apartment in his stack, with an opening in the side which is fairest exposed to the wind: this he calls a *Fause-house*.

‡ Burning the nuts is a favourite charm. They name the lad and lass to each particular nut, as they lay them in the fire; and according as they burn quietly together, or start from beside one another, the course and issue of the Courtship will be.

An' monie lads an' lasses fates
   Are there that night decided:
Some kindle, couthie, side by side,
   An' *burn* thegither trimly;
Some start awa, wi' saucy pride,
   An' jump out owre the chimlie
        Fu' high that night.

VIII

Jean slips in twa, wi' tentie e'e;
   Wha 'twas, she wadna tell;
But this is *Jock*, an' this is *me*,
   She says in to hersel:
He bleez'd owre her, an' she owre him,
   As they wad never mair part,
Till fuff! he started up the lum,
   An' *Jean* had e'en a sair heart
        To see 't that night.

IX

Poor *Willie*, wi' his *bow-kail runt*,
   Was *brunt* wi' primsie *Mallie*;
An' *Mary*, nae doubt, took the drunt,
   To be compar'd to *Willie*:
Mall's nit lap out, wi' pridefu' fling,
   An' her ain fit, it brunt it;
While *Willie* lap, an' swoor by *jing*,
   'Twas just the way he wanted
        To be that night.

X

Nell had the *Fause-house* in her min',
   She pits hersel an' *Rob* in;
In loving bleeze they sweetly join,
   Till white in ase they're sobbin:
Nell's heart was dancin at the view;
   She whisper'd *Rob* to leuk for't;
Rob, stownlins, prie'd her bonie mou,

Fu' cozie in the neuk for't,
      Unseen that night.

XI

But *Merran* sat behint their backs,
    Her thoughts on *Andrew Bell*;
She lea'es them gashan at their cracks,
    An' slips out by hersel:
She thro' the yard the nearest taks,
    An' for the *kiln* she goes then,
An' darklins grapet for the *bauks*,
    And in the *blue-clue** throws then,
        Right fear't that night.

XII

An' ay she *win't*, an' ay she swat,
    I wat she made nae jaukin;
Till something *held* within the *pat*,
    Guid L—d! but she was quaukin!
But whether 'twas the *Deil* himsel,
    Or whether 'twas a *bauk-en'*,
Or whether it was *Andrew Bell*,
    She did na wait on talkin
        To spier that night.

XIII

Wee Jenny to her Graunie says,
    'Will ye go wi' me Graunie?
'I'll *eat the apple†* at the *glass*,
    'I gat frae uncle Johnie:'

---

* Whoever would, with success, try this spell, must strictly observe these directions.
Steal out, all alone, to the *kiln*, and, darkling, throw into the *pot*, a clew of blue yarn:
wind it in a new clew off the old one; and towards the latter end, something will hold the
thread: demand, *wha hauds?* i.e. who holds? and answer will be returned from the kiln-
pot, by naming the christian and sirname of your future Spouse.

† Take a candle, and go, alone, to a looking glass: eat an apple before it, and some
traditions say you should comb your hair all the time: the face of your conjugal
companion, *to be*, will be seen in the glass, as if peeping over your shoulder.

She fuff't her pipe wi' sic a lunt,
   In wrath she was sae vap'rin,
She notic't na, an aizle brunt
   Her braw, new, worset apron
      Out thro' that night.

XIV

'Ye little Skelpie-limmer's-face!
   'I daur you try sic sportin,
'As seek the *foul Thief* onie place,
   'For him to spae your fortune:
'Nae doubt but ye may get a *sight*!
   'Great cause ye hae to fear it;
'For monie a ane has gotten a fright,
   'An' liv'd an' di'd deleeret,
      'On sic a night.

XV

'Ae Hairst afore the *Sherra-moor*,
   'I mind 't as weel 's yestreen,
'I was a gilpey then, I'm sure,
   'I was na past fyfteen:
'The Simmer had been cauld an' wat,
   'An' *Stuff* was unco green;
'An' ay a rantan *Kirn* we gat,
   'An' just on *Halloween*
      'It fell that night.

XVI

'Our *Stibble-rig* was *Rab M'Graen*,
   'A clever, sturdy fallow;
'His Sin gat *Eppie Sim* wi' wean,
   'That liv'd in Achmacalla:
'He gat *hemp-seed**, I mind it weel,

* Steal out, unperceived, and sow a handful of hemp seed; harrowing it with any thing you can conveniently draw after you. Repeat, now and then, 'Hemp seed I saw thee, Hemp seed I saw thee, and him (or her) that is to be my true-love, come after me and pou thee.' Look over your left shoulder, and you will see the appearance of the person

'An' he made unco light o't;
'But monie a day was *by himsel*,
'He was sae sairly frighted
'That vera night.'

XVII

Then up gat fechtan *Jamie Fleck*,
    An' he swoor by his conscience,
That he could *saw hemp-seed* a peck;
    For it was a' but nonsense:
The auld guidman raught down the pock,
    An' out a handfu' gied him;
Syne bad him slip frae 'mang the folk,
    Sometime when nae ane see'd him,
                An' try't that night.

XVIII

He marches thro' amang the stacks,
    Tho' he was something sturtan;
The *graip* he for a *harrow* taks,
    An' haurls at his curpan:
And ev'ry now an' then, he says,
    'Hemp-seed I saw thee,
'An' her that is to be my lass,
    'Come after me an' draw thee
                'As fast this night.'

XIX

He whistl'd up *lord Lenox' march*,
    To keep his courage cheary;
Altho' his hair began to arch,
    He was sae fley'd an' eerie:
Till presently he hears a squeak,
    An' then a grane an' gruntle;
He by his showther gae a keek,

---

invoked, in the attitude of pulling hemp. Some traditions say, 'come after me and shaw thee,' that is, show thyself; in which case it simply appears. Others omit the harrowing, and say, 'come after me and harrow thee.'

An' tumbl'd wi' a wintle
      Out owre that night.

XX

He roar'd a horrid murder-shout,
      In dreadfu' desperation!
An' young an' auld come rinnan out,
      An' hear the sad narration:
He swoor 'twas hilchan *Jean M'Craw*,
      Or crouchie *Merran Humphie*,
Till stop! she trotted thro' them a';
      An' wha was it but *Grumphie*
            Asteer that night?

XXI

Meg fain wad to the *Barn* gaen,
      To *winn three wechts o' naething*;*
But for to meet the Deil her lane,
      She pat but little faith in:
She gies the Herd a pickle nits,
      An' twa red cheeket apples,
To watch, while for the *Barn* she sets,
      In hopes to see *Tam Kipples*
            That vera night.

XXII

She turns the key, wi' cannie thraw,
      An' owre the threshold ventures;
But first on *Sawnie* gies a ca',
      Syne bauldly in she enters:

---

* This charm must likewise be performed, unperceived and alone. You go to the *barn*, and open both doors; taking them off the hinges, if possible; for there is danger, that the Being, about to appear, may shut the doors, and do you some mischief. Then take that instrument used in winnowing the corn, which, in our country-dialect, we call a *wecht*; and go thro' all the attitudes of letting down corn against the wind. Repeat it three times; and the third time, an apparition will pass thro' the barn, in at the windy door, and out at the other, having both the figure in question and the appearance or retinue, marking the employment or station in life.

A *ratton* rattl'd up the wa',
    An' she cry'd, L—d preserve her!
An' ran thro' midden-hole an' a',
    An' pray'd wi' zeal and fervour,
               Fu' fast that night.

XXIII

They hoy't out Will, wi' sair advice;
    They hecht him some fine braw ane;
It chanc'd the *Stack* he *faddom't thrice,**
    Was timmer-propt for thrawin:
He taks a swirlie, auld *moss-oak*,
    For some black, grousome *Carlin*;
An' loot a winze, an' drew a stroke,
    Till skin in blypes cam haurlin
               Aff 's nieves that night.

XXIV

A wanton widow *Leezie* was,
    As cantie as a kittlen;
But Och! that night, amang the shaws,
    She gat a fearfu' settlin!
She thro' the whins, an' by the cairn,
    An' owre the hill gaed scrievin,
Whare *three Lairds' lan's met at a burn,*†
    To dip her *left sark-sleeve* in,
               Was bent that night.

XXV

Whyles owre a linn the burnie plays,
    As thro' the glen it wimpl't;

---

* Take an opportunity of going, unnoticed, to a *Bear-stack*, and fathom it three times round. The last fathom of the last time, you will catch in your arms, the appearance of your future conjugal yoke-fellow.

† You go out, one or more, for this is a social spell, to a south-running spring or rivúlet, where 'three Lairds' lands meet,' and dip your left shirt-sleeve. Go to bed in sight of a fire, and hang your wet sleeve before it to dry. Ly awake; and sometime near midnight, an apparition, having the exact figure of the grand object in question, will come and turn the sleeve, as if to dry the other side of it.

Whyles round a rocky scar it strays;
  Whyles in a wiel it dimpl't;
Whyles glitter'd to the nightly rays,
  Wi' bickerin, dancin dazzle;
Whyles cooket underneath the braes,
  Below the spreading hazle
          Unseen that night.

XXVI

Amang the brachens, on the brae,
  Between her an' the moon,
The *Deil*, or else an outler Quey,
  Gat up an' gae a croon:
Poor *Leezie*'s heart maist lap the hool;
  Near lav'rock-height she jumpet,
But mist a fit, an' in the *pool*,
  Out owre the lugs she plumpet,
          Wi' a plunge that night.

XXVII

In order, on the clean hearth-stane,
  The *Luggies** three are ranged;
And ev'ry time great care is taen,
  To see them duely changed:
Auld, uncle *John*, wha *wedlock's joys*,
  Sin' *Mar's-year* did desire,
Because he gat the toom dish thrice,
  He heav'd them on the fire,
          In wrath that night.

XXVIII

Wi' merry sangs, an' friendly cracks,
  I wat they did na weary;

---

* Take three dishes; put clean water in one, foul water in another, and leave the third empty: blindfold a person, and lead him to the hearth where the dishes are ranged; he (or she) dips the left hand: if by chance in the clean water, the future husband or wife will come to the bar of Matrimony, a Maid; if in the foul, a widow; if in the empty dish, it foretells, with equal certainty, no marriage at all. It is repeated three times; and every time the arrangement of the dishes is altered.

And unco tales, an' funnie jokes,
　　Their sports were cheap an' cheary:
Till *buttr'd So'ns*,* wi' fragrant lunt,
　　Set a' their gabs a steerin;
Syne, wi' a social glass o' strunt,
　　They parted aff careerin
　　　　　　Fu' blythe that night.

* Sowens, with butter instead of milk to them, is always the *Halloween Supper*.

The Auld Farmer's New-year-morning Salutation to his Auld Mare, Maggie, on giving her the accustomed ripp of corn to hansel in the New-year

A *Guid New-year* I wish thee, Maggie!
Hae, there 's a ripp to thy auld baggie:
Tho' thou 's howe-backet, now, an' knaggie,
      I've seen the day,
Thou could hae gaen like ony staggie
      Out-owre the lay.

Tho' now thou 's dowie, stiff an' crazy,
An' thy auld hide as white 's a daisie,
I've seen thee dappl't, sleek an' glaizie,
      A bonie gray:
He should been tight that daur't to *raize* thee,
      Ance in a day.

Thou ance was i' the foremost rank,
A *filly* buirdly, steeve an' swank,
An' set weel down a shapely shank,
      As e'er tread yird;
An' could hae flown out-owre a stank,
      Like onie bird.

It 's now some nine-an'-twenty year,
Sin' thou was my *Guidfather's Meere*;
He gied me thee, o' tocher clear,
      An' fifty mark;
Tho' it was sma', 'twas *weel-won* gear,
      An' thou was stark.

When first I gaed to woo my *Jenny*,
Ye then was trottan wi' your Minnie:

Tho' ye was trickie, slee an' funnie,
      Ye ne'er was donsie;
But hamely, tawie, quiet an' cannie,
      An' unco sonsie.

That *day*, ye pranc'd wi' muckle pride,
When ye bure hame my bonie *Bride*:
An' sweet an' gracefu' she did ride
      Wi' maiden air!
KYLE-STEWART I could bragged wide,
      For sic a *pair*.

Tho' now ye dow but hoyte and hoble,
An' wintle like a saumont-coble,
That day, ye was a jinker noble,
      For heels an' win'!
An' ran them till they a' did wauble,
      Far, far behin'!

When thou an' I were young an' skiegh,
An' *Stable-meals* at Fairs were driegh,
How thou wad prance, an' snore, an' scriegh,
      An' tak the road!
Towns-bodies ran, an' stood abiegh,
      An' ca't thee mad.

When thou was corn't, an' I was mellow,
We took the road ay like a Swallow:
At *Brooses* thou had ne'er a fellow,
      For pith an' speed;
But ev'ry tail thou pay't them hollow,
      Whare'er thou gaed.

The sma', droop-rumpl't, hunter cattle,
Might aiblins waur't thee for a brattle;
But *sax Scotch mile*, thou try't their mettle,
      An' gart them whaizle:
Nae whip nor spur, but just a wattle
      O' saugh or hazle.

Thou was a noble *Fittie-lan'*,
As e'er in tug or tow was drawn!
Aft thee an' I, in aught hours gaun,
      On guid March-weather,
Hae turn'd *sax rood* beside our han',
      For days thegither.

Thou never braing't, an' fetch't, an' flisket,
But thy *auld tail* thou wad hae whisket,
An' spread abreed thy weel-fill'd *brisket*,
      Wi' pith an' pow'r,
Till sprittie knowes wad rair't an' risket,
      An' slypet owre.

When frosts lay lang, an' snaws were deep,
An' threaten'd *labor* back to keep,
I gied thy *cog* a wee-bit heap
      Aboon the timmer;
I ken'd my *Maggie* wad na sleep
      For that, or Simmer.

In *cart* or *car* thou never reestet;
The steyest brae thou wad hae fac't it;
Thou never lap, an' sten't, an' breastet,
      Then stood to blaw;
But just thy step a wee thing hastet,
      Thou snoov't awa.

My Pleugh is now thy *bairn-time* a';
Four gallant brutes, as e'er did draw;
Forby sax mae, I've sell't awa,
      That thou hast nurst:
They drew me thretteen pund an' twa,
      The vera warst.

Monie a sair daurk we twa hae wrought,
An' wi' the weary warl' fought!
An' monie an *anxious day*, I thought
      We wad be beat!

Yet here to *crazy Age* we're brought,
        Wi' something yet.

An' think na, my auld, trusty *Servan'*,
That now perhaps thou 's less deservin,
An' thy *auld days* may end in starvin',
        For my last fow,
A heapet *Stimpart*, I'll reserve ane
        Laid by for you.

We've worn to crazy years thegither;
We'll toyte about wi' ane anither;
Wi' tentie care I'll flit thy tether,
        To some hain'd rig,
Whare ye may nobly rax your leather,
        Wi' sma' fatigue.

Address to the Deil

O Prince, O chief of many throned pow'rs,
That led th' embattl'd Seraphim to war –

MILTON.

O thou, whatever title suit thee!
Auld Hornie, Satan, Nick, or Clootie,
Wha in yon cavern grim an' sooty
   Clos'd under hatches,
Spairges about the brunstane cootie,
   To scaud poor wretches!

Hear me, *auld Hangie*, for a wee,
An' let poor, *damned bodies* bee;
I'm sure sma' pleasure it can gie,
   Ev'n to a *deil*,
To skelp an' scaud poor dogs like me,
   An' hear us squeel!

Great is thy pow'r, an' great thy fame;
Far ken'd, an' noted is thy name;
An' tho' yon *lowan heugh*'s thy hame,
   Thou travels far;
An' faith! thou 's neither lag nor lame,
   Nor blate nor scaur.

Whyles, ranging like a roaring lion,
For prey, a' holes an' corners tryin;
Whyles, on the strong-wing'd Tempest flyin,
   Tirlan the *kirks*;
Whyles, in the human bosom pryin,
   Unseen thou lurks.

I've heard my rev'rend *Graunie* say,
In lanely glens ye like to stray;

213

Or where auld-ruin'd castles, gray,
          Nod to the moon,
Ye fright the nightly wand'rer's way,
          Wi' eldritch croon.

When twilight did my *Graunie* summon,
To say her pray'rs, douse, honest woman,
Aft 'yont the dyke she 's heard you bumman,
          Wi' eerie drone;
Or, rustling, thro' the boortries coman,
          Wi' heavy groan.

Ae dreary, windy, winter night,
The stars shot down wi' sklentan light,
Wi' you, *mysel*, I gat a fright
          Ayont the lough;
Ye, like a *rash-buss*, stood in sight,
          Wi' waving sugh:

The cudgel in my nieve did shake,
Each bristl'd hair stood like a stake,
When wi' an eldritch, stoor, *quaick, quaick*,
          Amang the springs,
Awa ye squatter'd like a *drake*,
          On whistling wings.

Let *Warlocks* grim, an' wither'd *Hags*,
Tell, how wi' you, on ragweed nags,
They skim the muirs an' dizzy crags,
          Wi' wicked speed;
And in kirk-yards renew their leagues,
          Owre howcket dead.

Thence, countra wives, wi' toil an' pain,
May plunge an' plunge the *kirn* in vain;
For Oh! the yellow treasure 's taen,
          By witching skill;
An' dawtit, twal-pint *Hawkie* 's gane
          As yell 's the Bill.

Thence, mystic knots mak great abuse,
On *Young-Guidmen*, fond, keen an' croose;
When the best *warklum* i' the house,
        By cantraip wit,
Is instant made no worth a louse,
        Just at the bit.

When thowes dissolve the snawy hoord,
An' float the jinglan icy-boord,
Then, *Water-kelpies* haunt the foord,
        By your direction,
An' nighted Trav'llers are allur'd
        To their destruction.

An' aft your moss-traversing *Spunkies*
Decoy the wight that late an' drunk is;
The bleezan, curst, mischievous monkies
        Delude his eyes,
Till in some miry slough he sunk is,
        Ne'er mair to rise.

When Masons' mystic *word* an' *grip*,
In storms an' tempests raise you up,
Some cock, or cat, your rage maun stop,
        Or, strange to tell!
The *youngest Brother* ye wad whip
        Aff straught to *H–ll*.

Lang syne in *Eden*'s bonie yard,
When youthfu' lovers first were pair'd,
An' all the Soul of Love they shar'd,
        The raptur'd hour,
Sweet on the fragrant, flow'ry swaird,
        In shady bow'r:

Then you, ye auld, snick-drawing dog!
Ye cam to Paradise incog,
An' play'd on a man a cursed brogue,
        (Black be your fa'!)

An' gied the infant warld a shog,
        'Maist ruin'd a'.

D'ye mind that day, when in a bizz,
Wi' reeket duds, an' reestet gizz,
Ye did present your smoutie phiz
        'Mang better folk,
An' sklented on the *man of Uz*
        Your spitefu' joke?

An' how ye gat him i' your thrall,
An' brak him out o' house an' hal',
While scabs an' botches did him gall,
        Wi' bitter claw,
An' lows'd his ill-tongu'd, wicked *Scawl*
        Was warst ava?

But a' your doings to rehearse,
Your wily snares an' fechtin fierce,
Sin' that day *MICHAEL did you pierce,
        Down to this time,
Wad ding a' *Lallan* tongue, or *Erse*,
        In Prose or Rhyme.

An' now, auld *Cloots*, I ken ye're thinkan,
A certain *Bardie*'s rantin, drinkin,
Some luckless hour will send him linkan,
        To your black pit;
But faith! he'll turn a corner jinkan,
        An' cheat you yet.

But fare you weel, auld *Nickie-ben*!
O wad ye tak a thought an' men'!
Ye aiblins might – I dinna ken –
        Still hae a *stake* –
I'm wae to think upo' yon den,
        Ev'n for your sake.

* Vide Milton, Book 6th.

Scotch Drink

❦❦❦

Gie him strong Drink *until he wink,*
That's sinking in despair;
An' liquor *guid, to fire his bluid,*
   That's prest wi' grief an' care:
There let him bowse an' deep carouse,
   Wi' bumpers flowing o'er,
Till he forgets his loves *or* debts,
   An' minds his griefs no more.
                    Solomon's Proverbs, Ch. 31st V. 6, 7.

Let other Poets raise a fracas
'Bout vines, an' wines, an' druken *Bacchus*,
An' crabbed names an' stories wrack us,
               An' grate our lug,
I sing the juice *Scotch bear* can mak us,
               In glass or jug.

O thou, my MUSE! guid, auld SCOTCH DRINK!
Whether thro' wimplin worms thou jink,
Or, richly brown, ream owre the brink,
               In glorious faem,
Inspire me, till I *lisp* an' *wink*,
               To sing thy name!

Let husky Wheat the haughs adorn,
And Aits set up their awnie horn,
An' Pease an' Beans, at een or morn,
               Perfume the plain,
Leeze me on thee *John Barleycorn*,
               Thou king o' grain!

On thee aft Scotland chows her cood,
In souple scones, the wale o' food!

217

Or tumbling in the boiling flood
   Wi' kail an' beef;
But when thou pours thy strong *heart's blood*,
    There thou shines chief.

Food fills the wame, an' keeps us livin:
Tho' life 's a gift no worth receivin,
When heavy-dragg'd wi' pine an' grievin;
    But oil'd by thee,
The wheels o' life gae down-hill, scrievin,
    Wi' rattlin glee.

Thou clears the head o' doited Lear;
Thou chears the heart o' drooping Care;
Thou strings the nerves o' Labor-sair,
   At 's weary toil;
Thou ev'n brightens dark Despair,
    Wi' gloomy smile.

Aft, clad in massy, siller weed,
Wi' Gentles thou erects thy head;
Yet, humbly kind, in time o' need,
    The *poorman*'s wine,
His wee drap parritch, or his bread,
    Thou kitchens fine.

Thou art the life o' public haunts;
But thee, what were our fairs an' rants?
Ev'n goodly meetings o' the saunts,
    By thee inspir'd,
When gaping they besiege the *tents*,
    Are doubly fir'd.

That *merry night* we get the corn in
O sweetly, then, thou reams the horn in!
Or reekan on a *New-year-mornin*
    In cog or bicker,
An' just a wee drap *sp'ritual burn* in,
    An' *gusty sucker!*

When Vulcan gies his bellys breath,
An' Ploughmen gather wi' their graith,
O rare! to see thee fizz an' fraeth
        I' the lugget caup!
Then *Burnewin* comes on like Death,
        At ev'ry chap.

Nae mercy, then, for airn *or* steel;
The brawnie, banie, Ploughman-chiel
Brings hard owrehip, wi' sturdy wheel,
        The strong forehammer,
Till block an' studdie ring an' reel
        Wi' dinsome clamour.

When skirlin weanies see the light,
Thou maks the gossips clatter bright,
How fumbling coofs their dearies slight,
        Wae worth the name!
Nae Howdie gets a social night,
        Or plack frae them.

When neebors anger at a plea,
An' just as wud as wud can be,
How easy can the *barley-bree*
        Cement the quarrel!
It 's ay the cheapest Lawyer's fee
        To taste the barrel.

Alake! that e'er my *Muse* has reason
To wyte her countrymen wi' treason!
But mony daily weet their weason
        Wi' liquors nice,
An' hardly, in a winter season,
        E'er spier her price.

Wae worth that *Brandy*, burnan trash!
Fell source o' monie a pain an' brash!
Twins mony a poor, doylt, druken hash
        O' half his days;
An' sends, beside, auld *Scotland*'s cash
        To her warst faes.

Ye Scots wha wish auld Scotland well,
Ye chief, to you my tale I tell,
Poor, plackless devils like *mysel*,
                    It sets you ill,
Wi' bitter, dearthfu' *wines* to mell,
                    Or *foreign gill*.

May *Gravels* round his blather wrench,
An' *Gouts* torment him, inch by inch,
Wha twists his gruntle wi' a glunch
                    O' sour disdain,
Out owre a glass o' *Whisky-punch*
                    Wi' honest men!

O *Whisky*! soul o' plays an' pranks!
Accept a *Bardie*'s humble thanks!
When wanting thee, what tuneless cranks
                    Are my poor Verses!
Thou comes – they rattle i' their ranks
                    At ither's arses!

Thee, *Ferintosh*! O sadly lost!
Scotland lament frae coast to coast!
Now colic-grips, an' barkin hoast,
                    May kill us a';
For loyal *Forbes' Charter'd boast*
                    Is taen awa!

Thae curst horse-leeches o' th' Excise,
Wha mak the *Whisky stills* their prize!
Haud up thy han' *Deil*! ance, twice, thrice!
                    There, sieze the blinkers!
An' bake them up in brunstane pies
                    For poor damn'd *Drinkers*.

Fortune, if thou'll but gie me still
Hale breeks, a scone, an' *Whisky gill*,
An' rowth o' *rhyme* to rave at will,
                    Tak a' the rest,
An' deal 't about as thy blind skill
                    Directs thee best.

To J. Smith

Friendship, mysterious cement of the soul!
Sweet'ner of Life, and solder of Society!
I owe thee much —

                            BLAIR.

Dear Smith, the sleest, pawkie thief,
That e'er attempted stealth or rief,
Ye surely hae some warlock-breef
                    Owre human hearts;
For ne'er a bosom yet was prief
                    Against your arts.

For me, I swear by sun an' moon,
And ev'ry star that blinks aboon,
Ye've cost me twenty pair o' shoon
                    Just gaun to see you;
And ev'ry ither pair that's done,
                    Mair taen I'm wi' you.

That auld, capricious carlin, *Nature*,
To mak amends for scrimpet stature,
She's turn'd you off, a human-creature
                    On her *first* plan,
And in her freaks, on ev'ry feature,
                    She's wrote, *the Man*.

Just now I've taen the fit o' rhyme,
My barmie noddle's working prime,
My fancy yerket up sublime
                    Wi' hasty summon:
Hae ye a leisure-moment's time
                    To hear what's comin?

Some rhyme a neebor's name to lash;
Some rhyme, (vain thought!) for needfu' cash;
Some rhyme to court the countra clash,
   An' raise a din;
For me, an *aim* I never fash;
   I rhyme for *fun*.

The star that rules my luckless lot,
Has fated me the russet coat,
An' damn'd my fortune to the groat;
   But, in requit,
Has blest me with a *random-shot*
   O' countra wit.

This while my notion 's taen a sklent,
To try my fate in guid, black *prent*;
But still the mair I'm that way bent,
   Something cries, 'Hoolie!
'I red you, honest man, tak tent!
   'Ye'll shaw your folly.

'There 's ither Poets, much your betters,
'Far seen in *Greek*, deep men o' *letters*,
'Hae thought they had ensur'd their debtors,
   'A' future ages;
'Now moths deform in shapeless tatters,
   'Their unknown pages.'

Then farewel hopes of Laurel-boughs,
To garland my poetic brows!
Henceforth, I'll rove where busy ploughs
   Are whistling thrang,
An' teach the lanely heights an' howes
   My rustic sang.

I'll wander on with tentless heed,
How never-halting moments speed,
Till fate shall snap the brittle thread;
   Then, all unknown,

I'll lay me with th' *inglorious dead*,
        Forgot and gone!

But why, o' Death, begin a tale?
Just now we 're living sound an' hale;
Then top and maintop croud the sail,
        Heave *Care* o'er-side!
And large, before Enjoyment's gale,
        Let 's tak the tide.

This life, sae far 's I understand,
Is a' enchanted fairy-land,
Where Pleasure is the Magic-wand,
        That, wielded right,
Maks Hours like Minutes, hand in hand,
        Dance by fu' light.

The *magic-wand* then let us wield;
For, ance that five an' forty 's speel'd,
See, crazy, weary, joyless Eild,
        Wi' wrinkl'd face,
Comes hostan, hirplan owre the field,
        Wi' creeping pace.

When ance *life's day* draws near the gloamin,
Then fareweel vacant, careless roamin;
An' fareweel chearfu' tankards foamin,
        An' social noise;
An' fareweel dear, deluding woman,
        The joy of joys!

O *Life*! how pleasant in thy morning,
Young Fancy's rays the hills adorning!
Cold-pausing Caution's lesson scorning,
        We frisk away,
Like school-boys, at th' expected warning,
        To joy and play.

We wander there, we wander here,
We eye the *rose* upon the brier,

Unmindful that the *thorn* is near,
   Among the leaves;
And tho' the puny wound appear,
   Short while it grieves.

Some, lucky, find a flow'ry spot,
For which they never toil'd nor swat;
They drink the *sweet* and eat the *fat*,
   But care or pain;
And haply, eye the barren hut,
   With high disdain.

With steady aim, some Fortune chase;
Keen hope does ev'ry sinew brace;
Thro' fair, thro' foul, they urge the race,
   And sieze the prey:
Then canie, in some cozie place,
   They close the *day*.

And others, like your humble servan',
Poor wights! nae rules nor roads observin;
To right or left, eternal swervin,
   They zig-zag on;
Till curst with Age, obscure an' starvin,
   They aften groan.

Alas! what bitter toil an' straining –
But truce with peevish, poor complaining!
Is Fortune's fickle *Luna* waning?
   E'en let her gang!
Beneath what light she has remaining,
   Let 's sing our Sang.

My pen I here fling to the door,
And kneel, Ye *Pow'rs!* and warm implore,
'Tho' I should wander *Terra* o'er,
   'In all her climes,
'Grant me but this, I ask no more,
   'Ay rowth o' rhymes.

'Gie dreeping roasts to *countra Lairds*,
'Till icicles hing frae their beards;
'Gie fine braw claes to fine *Life-guards*,
   'And *Maids of Honor*;
'And yill an' whisky gie to *Cairds*,
    'Until they sconner.

'A *Title*, DEMPSTER merits it;
'A *Garter* gie to WILLIE PIT;
'Gie Wealth to some be-ledger'd Cit,
   'In cent per cent;
'But give me real, sterling Wit,
    'And I'm content.

'While ye are pleas'd to keep me hale,
'I'll sit down o'er my scanty meal,
'Be 't *water-brose*, or *muslin-kail*,
   'Wi' chearfu' face,
'As lang 's the Muses dinna fail
    'To say the grace.'

An anxious e'e I never throws
Behint my lug, or by my nose;
I jouk beneath Misfortune's blows
   As weel 's I may;
Sworn foe to *sorrow*, *care*, and *prose*,
    I rhyme away.

O ye, douse folk, that live by rule,
Grave, tideless-blooded, calm and cool,
Compar'd wi' you – O fool! fool! fool!
   How much unlike!
Your hearts are just a standing pool,
    Your lives, a dyke!

Nae hare-brain'd, sentimental traces,
In your unletter'd, nameless faces!
In *arioso* trills and graces
   Ye never stray,

But *gravissimo*, solemn basses
      Ye hum away.

Ye are sae *grave*, nae doubt ye're *wise*;
Nae ferly tho' ye do despise
The hairum-scairum, ram-stam boys,
      The rattling squad:
I see ye upward cast your eyes –
      – Ye ken the road –

Whilst I – but I shall haud me there –
Wi' you I'll scarce gang *ony where* –
Then *Jamie*, I shall say nae mair,
      But quat my sang,
Content *with* YOU to mak a *pair*,
      Whare'er I gang.

The Author's Earnest Cry and Prayer*, to the Right Honorable and Honorable, the Scotch Representatives in the House of Commons

❧∞❧

> *Dearest of Distillation! last and best! –*
> *– How art thou lost! –*
>
> Parody on Milton.

Ye IRISH LORDS, ye *knights* an' *squires*,
Wha represent our BRUGHS an' SHIRES,
An' dousely manage our affairs
        In *Parliament*,
To you a simple Poet's pray'rs
        Are humbly sent.

Alas! my roupet *Muse* is haerse!
Your Honors' hearts wi' grief 'twad pierce,
To see her sittan on her arse
        Low i' the dust,
An' scriechan out prosaic verse,
        An' like to brust!

Tell them wha hae the chief direction,
Scotland and *me* 's in great affliction,
E'er sin' they laid that curst restriction
        On AQUAVITAE;
An' rouse them up to strong conviction,
        An' move their pity.

* This was wrote before the Act anent the Scotch Distilleries, of session 1786; for which Scotland and the Author return their most grateful thanks.

Stand forth and tell yon PREMIER YOUTH
The honest, open, naked truth;
Tell him o' mine an' Scotland's drouth,
            His servants humble:
The muckle devil blaw you south,
            If ye dissemble!

Does ony *great man* glunch an' gloom?
Speak out an' never fash your thumb!
Let *posts* an' *pensions* sink or swoom
            Wi' them wha grant them:
If honestly they canna come,
            Far better want them.

In gath'rin votes ye were na slack,
Now stand as tightly by your tack:
Ne'er claw your lug, an' fidge your back,
            An' hum an' haw,
But raise your arm, an' tell your crack
            Before them a'.

Paint Scotland greetan owre her thrissle;
Her *mutchkin stowp* as toom 's a whissle;
An' damn'd Excise-men in a bussle,
            Seizan a *Stell*,
Triumphant crushan 't like a muscle
            Or laimpet shell.

Then on the tither hand present her,
A blackguard *Smuggler*, right behint her,
An', cheek-for-chow, a chuffie *Vintner*,
            Colleaguing join, –
Picking her pouch as bare as Winter,
            Of a' kind coin.

Is there, that bears the name o' SCOT,
But feels his heart's bluid rising hot,
To see his poor, auld Mither's *pot*,
            Thus dung in staves;

An' plunder'd o' her hindmost groat,
          By gallows knaves?

Alas! I'm but a nameless wight,
Trode i' the mire out o' sight!
But could I like MONTGOMERIES fight,
          Or gab like BOSWEL,
There 's some *sark-necks* I wad *draw* tight,
          An' *tye* some *hose* well.

God bless your Honors, can ye see 't,
The kind, auld, cantie Carlin greet,
An' no get warmly to your feet,
          An' gar them hear it,
An' tell them, wi' a patriot-heat,
          Ye winna bear it?

Some o' you nicely ken the laws,
To round the period an' pause,
An' with rhetoric clause on clause
          To mak harangues;
Then echo thro' Saint Stephen's wa's
          Auld Scotland's wrangs.

Dempster, a true-blue Scot I'se warran;
Thee, aith-detesting, chaste *Kilkerran*;
An' that glib-gabbet Highlan Baron,
          The Laird o' *Graham*;
And ane, a chap that 's damn'd auldfarran,
          Dundass his name.

Erskine, a spunkie norland billie;
True Campbels, *Frederic* an' *Ilay*;
An' Livistone, the bauld *Sir Willie*;
          An' mony ithers,
Whom auld Demosthenes or Tully
          Might own for brithers.

Arouse my boys! exert your mettle,
To get auld Scotland back her *kettle*!

Or faith! I'll wad my new pleugh-pettle,
                Ye'll see 't or lang,
She'll teach you, wi' a reekan whittle,
                Anither sang.

This while she 's been in crankous mood,
Her *lost Militia* fir'd her bluid;
(Deil na they never mair do guid,
                Play'd her that pliskie!)
An' now she 's like to rin red-wud
                About her *Whisky*.

An' L——d! if ance they pit her till 't,
Her tartan petticoat she'll kilt
An' durk an' pistol at her belt,
                She'll tak the streets,
An' rin her whittle to the hilt,
                I' th' first she meets!

For G—d-sake, Sirs! then speak her fair,
An' straik her cannie wi' the hair,
An' to the *muckle house* repair,
                Wi' instant speed,
An' strive, wi' a' your Wit an' Lear,
                To get remead.

Yon ill-tongu'd tinkler, *Charlie Fox*,
May taunt you wi' his jeers an' mocks;
But gie him 't het, my hearty cocks!
                E'en cowe the cadie!
An' send him to his dicing box,
                An' sportin lady.

Tell yon guid bluid of auld *Boconnock*'s,
I'll be his debt twa mashlum bonnocks,
An' drink his health in auld * *Nanse Tinnock*'s
                Nine times a week,

---

* A worthy old Hostess of the Author's in *Mauchline*, where he sometimes studies Politics over a glass of guid auld *Scotch Drink*.

If he some scheme, like tea an' winnocks,
        Wad kindly seek.

Could he some *commutation* broach,
I'll pledge my aith in guid braid Scotch,
He need na fear their foul reproach
        Nor erudition,
Yon mixtie-maxtie, queer hotch-potch,
        The *Coalition*.

Auld Scotland has a raucle tongue;
She 's just a devil wi' a rung;
An' if she promise auld or young
        To tak their part,
Tho' by the neck she should be strung,
        She'll no desert.

And now, ye chosen FIVE AND FORTY,
May still your Mither's heart support ye;
Then tho' a *Minister* grow dorty,
        An' kick your place,
Ye'll snap your fingers, poor an' hearty,
        Before his face.

God bless your Honors, a' your days,
Wi' sowps o' kail an' brats o' claise,
In spite of a' the thievish kaes
        That haunt St *Jamie*'s!
Your humble Poet sings an' prays
        While *Rab* his name is.

POSTSCRIPT

Let half-starv'd slaves in warmer skies,
See future wines, rich-clust'ring, rise;
Their lot auld Scotland ne'er envies,
        But blyth an' frisky,
She eyes her freeborn, martial boys,
        Tak aff their Whisky.

What tho' their Phebus kinder warms,
While Fragrance blooms and Beauty charms!

When wretches range, in famish'd swarms,
              The scented groves,
Or hounded forth, *dishonor* arms,
              In hungry droves.

Their *gun*'s a burden on their shouther;
They downa bide the stink o' *powther*;
Their bauldest thought's a hank'ring swither,
              To stan' or rin,
Till skelp – a shot – they're aff, a' throu'ther,
              To save their skin.

But bring a SCOTCHMAN frae his hill,
Clap in his cheek a *highlan gill*,
Say, such is royal GEORGE's will,
              An' there's the foe,
He has nae thought but how to kill
              Twa at a blow.

Nae cauld, faint-hearted doubtings tease him;
Death comes, with fearless eye he sees him;
Wi' bluidy hand a welcome gies him;
              An' when he fa's,
His latest draught o' breathin lea'es him
              In faint huzzas.

Sages their solemn een may steek,
An' raise a philosophic reek,
An' physically causes seek,
              In *clime* an' *season*,
But tell me *Whisky*'s name in Greek,
              I'll tell the reason.

SCOTLAND, my auld, respected Mither!
Tho' whyles ye moistify your leather,
Till whare ye sit, on craps o' heather,
              Ye tine your dam;
FREEDOM and WHISKY gang thegither,
              Tak aff your dram!

Sketch

Hail, Poesie! thou nymph reserv'd!
In chase o' thee, what crowds hae swerv'd
Frae Common Sense, or sunk ennerv'd
    'Mang heaps o' clavers;
And Och! o'er aft thy joes hae starv'd
    'Mid a' thy favors!

Say, Lassie, why thy train amang,
While loud the trumps heroic clang,
And Sock and buskin skelp alang
    To death or marriage;
Scarce ane has tried the Shepherd-sang
    But wi' miscarriage?

In Homer's craft Jock Milton thrives;
Eschylus' pen Will Shakespeare drives;
Wee Pope, the knurlin, 'till him rives
    Horatian fame;
In thy sweet sang, Barbauld, survives
    E'en Sappho's flame.

But thee, Theocritus, wha matches?
They're no' Herd's ballats, Maro's catches;
Squire Pope but busks his skinklin patches
    O' Heathen tatters:
I pass by hunders, nameless wretches,
    That ape their betters.

In this braw age o' wit and lear,
Will nane the Shepherd's whistle mair
Blaw sweetly in his native air
    And rural grace;
And wi' the far-fam'd Grecian share
    A rival place?

Yes! there is ane; a Scotish callan!
There 's ane: come forrit, honest Allan!
Thou need na jouk behint the hallan,
    A chiel sae clever;
The teeth o' Time may gnaw Tamtallan,
    But thou 's for ever.

Thou paints auld Nature to the nines,
In thy sweet Caledonian lines;
Nae gowden stream thro' myrtles twines
    Where Philomel,
While nightly breezes sweep the vines,
    Her griefs will tell!

Thy rural loves are Nature's sel';
Nae bombast spates o' nonsense swell;
Nae snap conceits, but that sweet spell
    O' witchin' loove,
That charm that can the strongest quell,
    The sternest move.

In gowany glens thy burnie strays,
Where bonie lasses bleach their claes;
Or trots by hazelly shaws and braes
    Wi' hawthorns gray,
Where blackbirds join the shepherd's lays
    At close o' day.

To a Louse, On Seeing one on a Lady's Bonnet at Church

Ha! whare ye gaun, ye crowlan ferlie!
Your impudence protects you sairly:
I canna say but ye strunt rarely,
      Owre *gawze* and *lace*;
Tho' faith, I fear ye dine but sparely,
      On sic a place.

Ye ugly, creepan, blastet wonner,
Detested, shunn'd, by saunt an' sinner,
How daur ye set your fit upon her,
      Sae fine a *Lady*!
Gae somewhere else and seek your dinner,
      On some poor body.

Swith, in some beggar's haffet squattle;
There ye may creep, and sprawl, and sprattle,
Wi' ither kindred, jumping cattle,
      In shoals and nations;
Whare *horn* nor *bane* ne'er daur unsettle,
      Your thick plantations.

Now haud you there, ye're out o' sight,
Below the fatt'rels, snug and tight,.
Na faith ye yet! ye'll no be right,
      Till ye've got on it,
The vera tapmost, towrin height
      O' *Miss's bonnet*.

My sooth! right bauld ye set your nose out,
As plump an' gray as onie grozet:
O for some rank, mercurial rozet,
      Or fell, red smeddum,

I'd gie you sic a hearty dose o't,
       Wad dress your droddum!

I wad na been surpriz'd to spy
You on an auld wife's *flainen toy*;
Or aiblins some bit duddie boy,
       On 's *wylecoat*;
But Miss's fine *Lunardi*, fye!
       How daur ye do 't?

O *Jenny* dinna toss your head,
An' set your beauties a' abread!
Ye little ken what cursed speed
       The blastie 's makin!
Thae *winks* and *finger-ends*, I dread,
       Are notice takin!

O wad some Pow'r the giftie gie us
To see oursels as others see us!
It wad frae monie a blunder free us
       An' foolish notion:
What airs in dress an' gait wad lea'e us,
       And ev'n Devotion!

Love and Liberty – A Cantata

RECITATIVO –

When lyart leaves bestrow the yird,
Or wavering like the Bauckie-bird*,
  Bedim cauld Boreas' blast;
When hailstanes drive wi' bitter skyte,
And infant Frosts begin to bite,
  In hoary cranreuch drest;
Ae night at e'en a merry core
  O' randie, gangrel bodies,
In Poosie-Nansie's† held the splore,
  To drink their orra dudies:
    Wi' quaffing, and laughing,
      They ranted an' they sang;
    Wi' jumping, an' thumping,
      The vera girdle rang.

First, niest the fire, in auld, red rags,
Ane sat; weel brac'd wi' mealy bags,
  And knapsack a' in order;
His doxy lay within his arm;
Wi' USQEBAE an' blankets warm,
  She blinket on her Sodger:
An' ay he gies the tozie drab
  The tither skelpan kiss,
While she held up her greedy gab,
  Just like an aumous dish:
    Ilk smack still, did crack still,
      Just like a cadger's whip;
    Then staggering, an' swaggering,
      He roar'd this ditty up –

---

* The old Scotch name for the Bat.

† The Hostess of a noted Caravansary in M[auchline], well known to and much frequented by the lowest orders of Travellers and Pilgrims.

Tune, Soldier's Joy

I am a Son of Mars who have been in many wars,
    And show my cuts and scars wherever I come;
This here was for a wench, and that other in a trench,
    When welcoming the French at the sound of the drum.
                      Lal de daudle &c.

My Prenticeship I past where my LEADER breath'd his last,
    When the bloody die was cast on the heights of ABRAM;
And I served out my TRADE when the gallant *game* was play'd,
    And the MORO low was laid at the sound of the drum.

I lastly was with Curtis among the *floating batt'ries*;
    And there I left for witness, an arm and a limb;
Yet let my Country need me, with ELLIOT to head me,
    I'd clatter on my stumps at the sound of a drum.

And now tho' I must beg, with a wooden arm and leg,
    And many a tatter'd rag hanging over my bum,
I'm as happy with my wallet, my bottle and my Callet,
    As when I us'd in scarlet to follow a drum.

What tho', with hoary locks, I must stand the winter shocks,
    Beneath the woods and rocks oftentimes for a home,
When the tother bag I sell and the tother bottle tell,
    I could meet a troop of HELL at the sound of a drum.

RECITATIVO –
He ended; and the kebars sheuk,
    Aboon the chorus roar;
While frighted rattons backward leuk,
    An' seek the benmost bore:
A fairy FIDDLER frae the neuk,
    He skirl'd out, ENCORE.
But up arose the martial CHUCK,
    An' laid the loud uproar –

Tune, Sodger Laddie

I once was a Maid, tho' I cannot tell when,
And still my delight is in proper young men:
Some one of a troop of DRAGOONS was my dadie,
No wonder I'm fond of a SODGER LADDIE.
       Sing lal de dal &c.

The first of my LOVES was a swaggering blade,
To rattle the thundering drum was his trade;
His leg was so tight and his cheek was so ruddy,
Transported I was with my SODGER LADDIE.

But the godly old Chaplain left him in the lurch,
The sword I forsook for the sake of the church;
He ventur'd the SOUL, and I risked the BODY,
'Twas then I prov'd false to my SODGER LADDIE.

Full soon I grew sick of my sanctified *Sot*,
The Regiment AT LARGE for a HUSBAND I got;
From the gilded SPONTOON to the FIFE I was ready;
I asked no more but a SODGER LADDIE.

But the PEACE it reduc'd me to beg in despair,
Till I met my old boy in a CUNNINGHAM fair;
His RAGS REGIMENTAL they flutter'd so gaudy,
My heart it rejoic'd at a SODGER LADDIE.

And now I have lived – I know not how long,
And still I can join in a cup and a song;
But whilst with both hands I can hold the glass steady,
Here 's to thee, MY HERO, MY SODGER LADDIE.

RECITATIVO –
    Poor Merry-andrew, in the neuk,
      Sat guzzling wi' a Tinkler-hizzie;
    They mind't na wha the chorus teuk,
      Between themsels they were sae busy:
    At length wi' drink an' courting dizzy,
      He stoiter'd up an' made a face;

Then turn'd an' laid a smack on Grizzie,
 Syne tun'd his pipes wi' grave grimace.

Tune, Auld Sir Symon

Sir Wisdom 's a fool when he 's fou;
 Sir Knave is a fool in a Session,
He 's there but a prentice, I trow,
 But I am a fool by profession.

My Grannie she bought me a beuk,
 An' I held awa to the school;
I fear I my talent misteuk,
 But what will ye hae of a fool.

For drink I would venture my neck;
 A hizzie 's the half of my Craft:
But what could ye other expect
 Of ane that 's avowedly daft.

I, ance, was ty'd up like a stirk,
 For civilly swearing and quaffing;
I, ance, was abus'd i' the kirk,
 For towsing a lass i' my daffin.

Poor Andrew that tumbles for sport,
 Let nae body name wi' a jeer;
There 's even, I'm tauld, i' the Court
 A Tumbler ca'd the Premier.

Observ'd ye yon reverend lad
 Mak faces to tickle the Mob;
He rails at our mountebank squad,
 Its rivalship just i' the job.

And now my conclusion I'll tell,
 For faith I'm confoundedly dry:
The chiel that 's a fool for himsel,
 Guid L—d, he 's far dafter than I.

RECITATIVO–

Then niest outspak a raucle Carlin,
Wha ken't fu' weel to cleek the Sterlin;
For mony a pursie she had hooked,
An' had in mony a well been douked:
Her LOVE had been a HIGHLAND LADDIE,
But weary fa' the waefu' woodie!
Wi' sighs an' sobs she thus began
To wail her braw JOHN HIGHLANDMAN –

Tune, O an' ye were dead Gudeman

A HIGHLAND lad my Love was born,
The lalland laws he held in scorn;
But he still was faithfu' to his clan,
My gallant, braw JOHN HIGHLANDMAN.

CHORUS–

Sing hey my braw John Highlandman!
Sing ho my braw John Highlandman!
There 's not a lad in a' the lan'
Was match for my John Highlandman.

With his Philibeg, an' tartan Plaid,
An' guid Claymore down by his side,
The ladies' hearts he did trepan,
My gallant, braw John Highlandman.
Sing hey &c.

We ranged a' from Tweed to Spey,
An' liv'd like lords an' ladies gay:
For a lalland face he feared none,
My gallant, braw John Highlandman.
Sing hey &c.

They banish'd him beyond the sea,
But ere the bud was on the tree,

Adown my cheeks the pearls ran,
Embracing my John Highlandman.
　　　　Sing hey &c.

But Och! they catch'd him at the last,
And bound him in a dungeon fast,
My curse upon them every one,
They've hang'd my braw John Highlandman.
　　　　Sing hey &c.

And now a Widow I must mourn
The Pleasures that will ne'er return;
No comfort but a hearty can,
When I think on John Highlandman.
　　　　Sing hey &c.

　　　　RECITATIVO–
A pigmy Scraper wi' his Fiddle,
Wha us'd to trystes an' fairs to driddle,
Her strappan limb an' gausy middle,
　　　　(He reach'd nae higher)
Had hol'd his HEARTIE like a riddle,
　　　　An' blawn 't on fire.

Wi' hand on hainch, and upward e'e,
He croon'd his gamut, ONE, TWO, THREE,
Then in an ARIOSO key,
　　　　The wee Apollo
Set off wi' ALLEGRETTO glee
　　　　His GIGA SOLO –

　　　　Tune, Whistle owre the lave o't

　Let me ryke up to dight that tear,
　An' go wi' me an' be my DEAR;
　An' then your every CARE an' FEAR
　　　May whistle owre the lave o't.

CHORUS—
I am a Fiddler to my trade,
An' a' the tunes that e'er I play'd,
The sweetest still to WIFE or MAID,
Was whistle owre the lave o't.

At KIRNS an' WEDDINS we'se be there,
An' O sae nicely 's we will fare!
We'll bowse about till Dadie CARE
    Sing whistle owre the lave o't.
            I am &c.

Sae merrily 's the banes we'll pyke,
An' sun oursells about the dyke;
An' at our leisure when ye like
    We'll whistle owre the lave o't.
            I am &c.

But bless me wi' your heav'n o' charms,
An' while I kittle hair on thairms
HUNGER, CAULD, an' a' sic harms
    May whistle owre the lave o't.
            I am &c.

RECITATIVO—
Her charms had struck a sturdy CAIRD,
    As weel as poor GUTSCRAPER;
He taks the Fiddler by the beard,
    An' draws a roosty rapier –
He swoor by a' was swearing worth
    To speet him like a Pliver,
Unless he would from that time forth
    Relinquish her for ever:

Wi' ghastly e'e poor TWEEDLEDEE
    Upon his hunkers bended,
An' pray'd for grace wi' ruefu' face,
    An' so the quarrel ended;
But tho' his little heart did grieve,
    When round the TINKLER prest her,

He feign'd to snirtle in his sleeve
    When thus the CAIRD address'd her –

Tune, Clout the Caudron

My bonie lass I work in brass,
    A TINKLER is my station;
I've travell'd round all Christian ground
    In this my occupation;
I've ta'en the gold an' been enroll'd
    In many a noble squadron;
But vain they search'd when off I march'd
    To go an' clout the CAUDRON.
            I've ta'en the gold &c.

Despise that SHRIMP, that withered IMP,
    With a' his noise an' cap'rin;
An' take a share, with those that bear
    The *budget* and the *apron*!
And *by* that STOWP! my faith an' houpe,
    And *by* that dear KILBAIGIE*,
If e'er ye want, or meet with scant,
    May I ne'er weet my CRAIGIE!
            And by that Stowp, &c.

RECITATIVO–
The Caird prevail'd – th' unblushing fair
    In his embraces sunk;
Partly wi' LOVE o'ercome sae sair,
    An' partly she was drunk:
SIR VIOLINO with an air,
    That show'd a man o' spunk,
Wish'd UNISON between the PAIR,
    An' made the bottle clunk
            To their health that night.

---

* A peculiar sort of Whiskie so called: a great favorite with Poosie Nansie's Clubs.

But hurchin Cupid shot a shaft,
   That play'd a DAME a shavie –
The Fiddler RAK'D her, FORE AND AFT,
   Behint the Chicken cavie:
Her lord, a wight of HOMER's craft*,
   Tho' limpan wi' the Spavie,
He hirpl'd up an' lap like daft,
   An' shor'd them DAINTY DAVIE
          O' *boot* that night.

He was a care-defying blade,
   As ever BACCHUS listed!
Tho' Fortune sair upon him laid,
   His heart she ever miss'd it.
He had no WISH but – to be glad,
   Nor WANT but – when he thristed;
He hated nought but – to be sad,
   An' thus the Muse suggested
          His sang that night.

Tune, For a' that an' a' that

I am a BARD of no regard,
   Wi' gentle folks an' a' that;
But HOMER LIKE the glowran byke,
   Frae town to town I draw that.

CHORUS–
   For a' that an' a' that,
     An' twice as muckle 's a' that,
   I've lost but ANE, I've TWA behin',
   I've WIFE ENEUGH for a' that.

I never drank the Muses' STANK,
   Castalia's burn an' a' that,

---

* Homer is allowed to be the eldest Ballad singer on record.

But there it streams an' richly reams,
  My HELICON I ca' that.
            For a' that &c.

Great love I bear to all the FAIR,
  Their humble slave an' a' that;
But lordly WILL, I hold it still
  A mortal sin to thraw that.
            For a' that &c.

In raptures sweet this hour we meet,
  Wi' mutual love an' a' that;
But for how lang the FLIE MAY STANG,
  Let INCLINATION law that.
            For a' that &c.

Their tricks an' craft hae put me daft,
  They've ta'en me in, an' a' that,
But clear your decks an' here 's the SEX!
  I like the jads for a' that.
      For a' that an' a' that
        An' twice as muckle 's a' that,
      My DEAREST BLUID to do them guid,
        They're welcome till 't for a' that.

                RECITATIVO–
So sung the BARD – and Nansie's waws
Shook with a thunder of applause
  Re-echo'd from each mouth!
They toom'd their pocks, they pawn'd their duds,
They scarcely left to coor their fuds
  To quench their lowan drouth:
Then owre again the jovial thrang
  The Poet did request
To lowse his PACK an' wale a sang,
  A BALLAD o' the best.
      He, rising, rejoicing,
        Between his TWA DEBORAHS,
      Looks round him an' found them
        Impatient for the Chorus.

Tune, Jolly Mortals fill your glasses

See the smoking bowl before us,
    Mark our jovial, ragged ring!
Round and round take up the Chorus,
    And in raptures let us sing –

CHORUS–
    A fig for those by law protected!
    LIBERTY 's a glorious feast!
    Courts for Cowards were erected,
        Churches built to please the PRIEST.

What is TITLE, what is TREASURE,
    What is REPUTATION's care?
If we lead a life of pleasure,
    'Tis no matter HOW or WHERE.
        A fig, &c.

With the ready trick and fable
    Round we wander all the day;
And at night, in barn or stable,
    Hug our doxies on the hay.
        A fig for &c.

Does the train-attended CARRIAGE
    Thro' the country lighter rove?
Does the sober bed of MARRIAGE
    Witness brighter scenes of love?
        A fig for &c.

Life is all a VARIORUM,
    We regard not how it goes;
Let them cant about DECORUM,
    Who have character to lose.
        A fig for &c.

Here 's to BUDGETS, BAGS and WALLETS!
    Here 's to all the wandering train!
Here 's our ragged BRATS and CALLETS!
    One and all cry out, AMEN!

A fig for those by LAW protected,
    LIBERTY 's a glorious feast!
COURTS for Cowards were erected,
    CHURCHES built to please the Priest.

MOSSGIEL AND EDINBURGH

❧

The Inventory

❧

To Mr Robt Aiken in Ayr, in answer to his mandate requiring an account of
servants, carriages, carriage-horses, riding horses, wives, children, &c.

Sir, as your mandate did request,
I send you here a faithfu' list,
O' gudes an' gear, an' a' my graith,
To which I'm clear to gi'e my aith.

Imprimis then, for carriage cattle,
I have four brutes o' gallant mettle,
As ever drew afore a pettle.
My * *Lan' afore* 's a gude auld *has been*,
An' wight an' wilfu' a' his days been.
My † *Lan' ahin* 's a weel gaun fillie,
That aft has borne me hame frae Killie‡,
An' your auld burrough mony a time,
In days when riding was nae crime –
But ance whan in my wooing pride
I like a blockhead boost to ride,
The wilfu' creature sae I pat to,
(L—d pardon a' my sins an' that too!)

* The fore horse on the left-hand in the plough.
† The hindmost on the left-hand in the plough.
‡ Kilmarnock.

I play'd my fillie sic a shavie,
She 's a' bedevil'd wi' the spavie.
My § *Furr ahin* 's a wordy beast,
As e'er in tug or tow was trac'd. –
The fourth 's a Highland Donald hastie,
A d——n'd red wud Kilburnie blastie;
Foreby a *Cowt*, o' *Cowt's* the wale,
As ever ran afore a tail.
If he be spar'd to be a beast,
He'll draw me fifteen pun' at least. –
Wheel carriages I ha'e but few,
Three carts, an' twa are feckly new;
Ae auld wheelbarrow, mair for token,
Ae leg an' baith the trams are broken;
I made a poker o' the spin'le,
An' my auld mither brunt the trin'le. –
For men, I've three mischievous boys,
Run de'ils for rantin' an' for noise;
A gaudsman ane, a thrasher t'other,
Wee Davock hauds the nowt in fother.
I rule them as I ought, discreetly,
An' aften labour them compleatly.
An' ay on Sundays duly nightly,
I on the questions *targe* them tightly;
Till faith, wee Davock 's turn'd sae gleg,
Tho' scarcely langer than your leg,
He'll screed you aff Effectual Calling,
As fast as ony in the dwalling. –
I've nane in female servan' station,
(L——d keep me ay frae a' temptation!)
I ha'e nae wife; and that my bliss is,
An' ye have laid nae tax on misses;
An' then if kirk folks dinna clutch me,
I ken the devils dare na touch me.
Wi' weans I'm mair than weel contented,
Heav'n sent me ane mae than I wanted.

§ The same on the right-hand in the plough.

My sonsie smirking dear-bought Bess, ⎫
She stares the daddy in her face, ⎬
Enough of ought ye like but grace; ⎭
But her, my bonny sweet wee lady,
I've paid enough for her already,
An' gin ye tax her or her mither,
B' the L——d! ye'se get them a' thegither.

And now, remember Mr Aiken,
Nae kind of licence out I'm takin';
Frae this time forth, I do declare,
I'se ne'er ride horse nor hizzie mair;
Thro' dirt and dub for life I'll paidle,
Ere I sae dear pay for a saddle;
My travel a' on foot I'll shank it,
I've sturdy bearers, Gude be thankit. –
The Kirk an' you may tak' you that,
It puts but little in your pat;
Sae dinna put me in your buke,
Nor for my ten white shillings luke.

This list wi' my ain han' I wrote it,
Day an' date as under notit,
Then know all ye whom it concerns,
Subscripsi huic,

ROBERT BURNS.

Mossgiel, February 22d, 1786.

Letter to James Tennant of Glenconner

Auld com'rade dear and brither sinner,
How 's a' the folk about Glenconner;
How do ye this blae eastlin win',
That 's like to blaw a body blin':
For me my faculties are frozen,
My dearest member nearly dozen'd:
I've sent you here by Johnie Simson,
Twa sage Philosophers to glimpse on!
Smith, wi' his sympathetic feeling,
An' Reid, to common sense appealing.
Philosophers have fought an' wrangled,
An' meikle Greek an' Latin mangled,
Till with their Logic-jargon tir'd,
An' in the depth of science mir'd,
To common sense they now appeal,
What wives an' wabsters see an' feel;
But, hark ye, friend, I charge you strictly,
Peruse them an' return them quickly;
For now I'm grown sae cursed douse,
I pray an' ponder *butt* the house,
My shins, my lane, I there sit roastin,
Perusing Bunyan, Brown and Boston;
Till by an' by, if I haud on,
I'll grunt a real Gospel groan:
Already I begin to try it,
To cast my een up like a Pyet,
When by the gun she tumbles o'er,
Flutt'ring an' gasping in her gore:
Sae shortly you shall see me bright,
A burning an' a shining light.

My heart-warm love to guid auld Glen,
The ace an' wale of honest men;

When bending down with auld gray hairs,
Beneath the load of years and cares,
May he who made him still support him,
An' views beyond the grave comfort him.

His worthy fam'ly far and near,
God bless them a' wi' grace and gear.

My auld school-fellow, Preacher Willie,
The manly tar, my mason billie,
An' Auchenbay, I wish him joy;
If he 's a parent, lass or boy,
May he be dad, and Meg the mither,
Just five and forty years thegither!
An' no forgetting wabster Charlie,
I'm tauld he offers very fairly,
An' L——d, remember singing Sannock,
Wi' hale-breeks, saxpence an' a bannock;
An' next, my auld acquaintance, Nancy,
Since she is fitted to her fancy;
An' her kind stars hae airted till her,
A guid chiel wi' a pickle siller:
My kindest, best respects I sen' it,
To cousin Kate an' sister Janet,
Tell them frae me, wi' chiels be cautious;
For, faith, they'll ablins fin' them fashious:
To grant a heart is fairly civil,
But to grant a maidenhead 's the devil!
An' lastly, Jamie, for yoursel,
May guardian angels tak a spell,
An' steer you seven miles south o' hell;
But first, before you see heav'ns glory,
May ye get mony a merry story,
Mony a laugh and mony a drink,
An' ay aneugh o' needfu' clink.

Now fare ye well, an' joy be wi' you,
For my sake this I beg it o' you,

Assist poor Simson a' ye can,
Ye'll fin' him just an honest man:
Sae I conclude and quat my chanter,
Yours, saint or sinner,

RAB THE RANTER.

To a Mountain-Daisy, On turning one down, with the Plough, in April – 1786

Wee, modest, crimson-tipped flow'r,
Thou 's met me in an evil hour;
For I maun crush amang the stoure
      Thy slender stem:
To spare thee now is past my pow'r,
      Thou bonie gem.

Alas! it 's no thy neebor sweet,
The bonie *Lark*, companion meet!
Bending thee 'mang the dewy weet!
      Wi 's spreckl'd breast,
When upward-springing, blythe, to greet
      The purpling East.

Cauld blew the bitter-biting *North*
Upon thy early, humble birth;
Yet chearfully thou glinted forth
      Amid the storm,
Scarce rear'd above the *Parent-earth*
      Thy tender form.

The flaunting *flow'rs* our Gardens yield,
High-shelt'ring woods and wa's maun shield,
But thou, beneath the random bield
      O' clod or stane,
Adorns the histie *stibble-field*,
      Unseen, alane.

There, in thy scanty mantle clad,
Thy snawie bosom sun-ward spread,
Thou lifts thy unassuming head
      In humble guise;

But now the *share* uptears thy bed,
      And low thou lies!

Such is the fate of artless Maid,
Sweet *flow'ret* of the rural shade!
By Love's simplicity betray'd,
      And guileless trust,
Till she, like thee, all soil'd, is laid
      Low i' the dust.

Such is the fate of simple Bard,
On Life's rough ocean luckless starr'd!
Unskilful he to note the card
      Of *prudent Lore*,
Till billows rage, and gales blow hard,
      And whelm him o'er!

Such fate to *suffering worth* is giv'n,
Who long with wants and woes has striv'n,
By human pride or cunning driv'n
      To Mis'ry's brink,
Till wrench'd of ev'ry stay but HEAV'N,
      He, ruin'd, sink!

Ev'n thou who mourn'st the *Daisy*'s fate,
That fate is thine – no distant date;
Stern Ruin's *plough-share* drives, elate,
      Full on thy bloom,
Till crush'd beneath the *furrow*'s weight,
      Shall be thy doom!

Extempore – to Mr Gavin Hamilton

To you, Sir, this summons I've sent,
   Pray whip till the pownie is fraething;
But if you demand what I want,
   I honestly answer you, naething. –

Ne'er scorn a poor Poet like me,
   For idly just living and breathing,
While people of every degree
   Are busy employed about – naething. –

Poor Centum per centum may fast,
   And grumble his hurdies their claithing;
He'll find, when the balance is cast,
   He 's gane to the devil for – naething. –

The Courtier cringes and bows,
   Ambition has likewise its plaything;
A Coronet beams in his brows,
   And what is a Coronet? naething. –

Some quarrel the presbyter gown,
   Some quarrel Episcopal graithing,
But every good fellow will own
   Their quarrel is all about – naething. –

The lover may sparkle and glow,
   Approaching his bonie bit gay thing;
But marriage will soon let him know,
   He 's gotten a buskit up naething. –

The Poet may jingle and rhyme,
   In hopes of a laureate wreathing,
And when he has wasted his time,
   He 's kindly rewarded with naething. –

The thundering bully may rage,
   And swagger and swear like a heathen;
But collar him fast, I'll engage
   You'll find that his courage is naething. –

Last night with a feminine whig,
   A Poet she could na put faith in,
But soon we grew lovingly big,
   I taught her, her terrors were naething. –

Her whigship was wonderful pleased,
   But charmingly tickled wi' ae thing;
Her fingers I lovingly squeezed,
   And kissed her and promised her – naething. –

The Priest anathemas may threat,
   Predicament, Sir, that we 're baith in;
But when honor's reveillé is beat,
   The holy artillery 's naething. –

And now I must mount on the wave,
   My voyage perhaps there is death in;
But what of a watery grave!
   The drowning a Poet is naething. –

And now as grim death 's in my thought,
   To you, Sir, I make this bequeathing:
My service as lang as ye 've ought,
   And my friendship, by G—, when ye 've naething. –

On a Scotch Bard Gone to the West Indies

A' ye wha live by sowps o' drink,
A' ye wha live by crambo-clink,
A' ye wha live and never think,
    Come, mourn wi' me!
Our *billie* 's gien us a' a jink,
    An' owre the Sea.

Lament him a' ye rantan core,
Wha dearly like a random-splore;
Nae mair he 'll join the *merry roar*,
    In social key;
For now he 's taen anither shore,
    An' owre the Sea!

The bonie lasses weel may wiss him,
And in their dear *petitions* place him:
The widows, wives, an' a' may bless him,
    Wi' tearfu' e'e;
For weel I wat they 'll sairly miss him
    That 's owre the Sea!

O Fortune, they hae room to grumble!
Hadst thou taen aff some drowsy bummlé,
Wha can do nought but fyke an' fumble,
    'Twad been nae plea;
But he was gleg as onie wumble,
    That 's owre the Sea!

Auld, cantie KYLE may weepers wear,
An' stain them wi' the saut, saut tear:
'Twill mak her poor, auld heart, I fear,
    In flinders flee:
He was her *Laureat* monie a year,
    That 's owre the Sea!

He saw Misfortune's cauld *Nor-west*
Lang-mustering up a bitter blast;
A Jillet brak his heart at last,
        Ill may she be!
So, took a birth afore the mast,
        An' owre the Sea.

To tremble under Fortune's cummock,
On scarce a bellyfu' o' *drummock*,
Wi' his proud, independant stomach,
        Could ill agree;
So, row't his hurdies in a *hammock*,
        An' owre the Sea.

He ne'er was gien to great misguidin,
Yet coin his pouches wad na bide in;
Wi' him it ne'er was *under hidin*;
        He dealt it free:
The *Muse* was a' that he took pride in,
        That 's owre the Sea.

Jamaica bodies, use him weel,
An' hap him in a cozie biel:
Ye 'll find him ay a dainty chiel,
        An' fou o' glee:
He wad na wrang'd the vera *Diel*,
        That 's owre the Sea.

Fareweel, my *rhyme-composing billie*!
Your native soil was right ill-willie;
But may ye flourish like a lily,
        Now bonilie!
I'll toast ye in my hindmost *gillie*,
        Tho' owre the Sea!

Second Epistle to Davie

AULD NIBOR,

   I'm three times, doubly, o'er your debtor,
   For your auld-farrent, frien'ly letter;
   Tho' I maun say 't, I doubt ye flatter,
       Ye speak sae fair;
   For my puir, silly, rhymin' clatter
        Some less maun sair.

   Hale be your heart, hale be your fiddle;
   Lang may your elbuck jink an' diddle,
   Tae cheer you thro' the weary widdle
       O' war'ly cares,
   Till bairns' bairns kindly cuddle
        Your auld, gray hairs.

   But DAVIE, lad, I'm red ye're glaikit;
   I'm tauld the Muse ye hae negleckit;
   An' gif it 's sae, ye sud be licket
       Until ye fyke;
   Sic hauns as you sud ne'er be faikit,
       Be hain't wha like.

   For me, I'm on Parnassus brink,
   Rivan the words tae gar them clink;
   Whyles daez't wi' love, whyles daez't wi' drink,
       Wi' jads or masons;
   An' whyles, but ay owre late, I think
       Braw sober lessons.

   Of a' the thoughtless sons o' man,
   Commen' me to the Bardie clan;
   Except it be some idle plan
       O' rhymin clink,
   The devil-haet, that I sud ban,
       They never think.

Nae thought, nae view, nae scheme o' livin',
Nae cares tae gie us joy or grievin':
But just the pouchie put the nieve in,
   An' while ought 's there,
Then, hiltie, skiltie, we gae scrivin',
   An' fash nae mair.

Leeze me on rhyme! it 's ay a treasure,
My chief, amaist my only pleasure,
At hame, a-fiel, at wark or leisure,
   The Muse, poor hizzie!
Tho' rough an' raploch be her measure,
   She 's seldom lazy.

Haud tae the Muse, my dainty Davie:
The warl' may play you monie a shavie;
But for the Muse, she 'll never leave ye,
   Tho' e'er sae puir,
Na, even tho' limpan wi' the spavie
   Frae door tae door.

A Dedication to Gavin Hamilton Esq;

Expect na, Sir, in this narration,
A fleechan, fleth'ran *Dedication*,
To roose you up, an' ca' you guid,
An' sprung o' great an' noble bluid;
Because ye're sirnam'd like *His Grace*,
Perhaps related to the race:
Then when I'm tir'd – and sae are *ye*,
Wi' monie a fulsome, sinfu' lie,
Set up a face, how I stop short,
For fear your modesty be hurt.

This may do – maun do, Sir, wi' them wha
Maun please the Great-folk for a wamefou;
For me! sae laigh I need na bow,
For, LORD be thanket, *I can plough*;
And when I downa yoke a naig,
Then, LORD be thanket, *I can beg*;
Sae I shall say, an' that 's nae flatt'rin,
It 's just *sic Poet* an' *sic Patron*.

The Poet, some guid Angel help him,
Or else, I fear, some *ill ane* skelp him!
He may do weel for a' he 's done yet,
But only – he 's no just begun yet.

The Patron, (Sir, ye maun forgie me,
I winna lie, come what will o' me)
On ev'ry hand it will allow'd be,
He 's just – nae better than he should be.

I readily and freely grant,
He downa see a poor man want;
What 's no his ain, he winna tak it;
What ance he says, he winna break it;

Ought he can lend he'll no refus 't,
Till aft his guidness is abus'd;
And rascals whyles that do him wrang,
Ev'n *that*, he does na mind it lang:
As Master, Landlord, Husband, Father,
He does na fail his part in either.

But then, nae thanks to him for a' that;
Nae *godly symptom* ye can ca' that;
It 's naething but a milder feature,
Of our poor, sinfu', corrupt Nature:
Ye'll get the best o' moral works,
'Mang black *Gentoos*, and Pagan *Turks*,
Or Hunters wild on *Ponotaxi*,
Wha never heard of Orth–d–xy.
That he 's the poor man's friend in need,
The GENTLEMAN in word and deed,
It 's no through terror of D–mn–t—n;
It 's just a carnal inclination.

Morality, thou deadly bane,
Thy tens o' thousands thou hast slain!
Vain is his hope, whase stay an' trust is,
In *moral* Mercy, Truth and Justice!

No – stretch a point to catch a plack;
Abuse a Brother to his back;
Steal thro' the *winnock* frae a wh–re,
But point the Rake that taks the *door*;
Be to the Poor like onie whunstane,
And haud their noses to the grunstane;
Ply ev'ry art o' *legal* thieving;
No matter – stick to *sound believing*.

Learn three-mile pray'rs, an' half-mile graces,
Wi' weel spread looves, an' lang, wry faces;
Grunt up a solemn, lengthen'd groan,
And damn a' Parties but your own;
I'll warrant then, ye're nae Deceiver,
A steady, sturdy, staunch *Believer*.

O ye wha leave the springs o' C–lv–n,
For *gumlie dubs* of your ain delvin!
Ye sons of Heresy and Error,
Ye'll *some day* squeel in quaking terror!
When vengeance draws the sword in wrath,
And in the fire throws the *sheath*;
When Ruin, with his sweeping *besom*,
Just frets till Heav'n commission gies him;
While o'er the *Harp* pale Misery moans,
And strikes the ever-deep'ning tones,
Still louder shrieks, and heavier groans!

Your pardon, Sir, for this digression,
I maist forgat my *Dedication*;
But when Divinity comes cross me,
My readers still are sure to lose me.

So Sir, you see 'twas nae daft vapour,
But I maturely thought it proper,
When a' my works I did review,
To *dedicate* them, Sir, to YOU:
Because (ye need na tak it ill)
I thought them something like *yoursel*.

Then patronize them wi' your favor,
And your Petitioner shall ever –
I had amaist said, *ever pray*,
But that's a word I need na say:
For prayin I hae little skill o't;
I'm baith dead-sweer, an' wretched ill o't;
But I'se repeat each poor man's *pray'r*,
That kens or hears about you, Sir –

'May ne'er Misfortune's gowling bark,
'Howl thro' the dwelling o' the CLERK!
'May ne'er his gen'rous, honest heart,
'For that same gen'rous spirit smart!
'May Kennedy's far-honor'd name
'Lang beet his hymeneal flame,

'Till Hamilton's, at least a diz'n,
'Are frae their nuptial labors risen:
'Five bonie Lasses round their table,
'And sev'n braw fellows, stout an' able,
'To serve their King an' Country weel,
'By word, or pen, or pointed steel!
'May Health and Peace, with mutual rays,
'Shine on the ev'ning o' his days;
'Till his wee, curlie *John*'s ier-oe,
'When ebbing life nae mair shall flow,
'The last, sad, mournful rites bestow!'

  I will not wind a lang conclusion,
With complimentary effusion:
But whilst your wishes and endeavours,
Are blest with Fortune's smiles and favours,
I am, Dear Sir, with zeal most fervent,
Your much indebted, humble servant.

  But if, which Pow'rs above prevent,
That iron-hearted Carl, *Want*,
Attended, in his grim advances,
By *sad mistakes*, and *black mischances*,
While hopes, and joys, and pleasures fly him,
Make you as poor a dog as I am,
Your *humble servant* then no more;
For who would humbly serve the Poor?
But by a poor man's hopes in Heav'n!
While recollection's pow'r is giv'n,
If, in the vale of humble life,
The victim sad of Fortune's strife,
I, through the tender-gushing tear,
Should recognise my *Master dear*,
If friendless, low, we meet together,
Then, Sir, your hand – my FRIEND and BROTHER.

Address of Beelzebub

To the Rt Honble JOHN, EARL OF BREADALBANE, President of the Rt
Honble the HIGHLAND SOCIETY, which met, on the 23rd of May last, at the
Shakespeare, Covent garden, to concert ways and means to frustrate the
designs of FIVE HUNDRED HIGHLANDERS who, as the Society were informed
by Mr McKenzie of Applecross, were so audacious as to attempt an escape
from theire lawful lords and masters whose property they are by emigrating
from the lands of Mr McDonald of Glengary to the wilds of CANADA, in
search of that fantastic thing – LIBERTY –

> Long life, My lord, an’ health be yours,
> Unskaith’d by hunger’d HIGHLAN BOORS!
> Lord grant, nae duddie, desp’rate beggar,
> Wi’ durk, claymore, or rusty trigger
> May twin auld SCOTLAND O’ a LIFE,
> She likes – as BUTCHERS like a KNIFE!
>
> Faith, you and Applecross were right
> To keep the highlan hounds in sight!
> I doubt na! they wad bid nae better
> Than let them ance out owre the water;
> Then up amang thae lakes an’ seas
> They’ll mak what rules an’ laws they please.
>
> Some daring Hancocke, or a Frankline,
> May set their HIGHLAN bluid a ranklin;
> Some Washington again may head them,
> Or some MONTGOMERY, fearless, lead them;
> Till, God knows what may be effected,
> When by such HEADS an’ HEARTS directed:
> Poor, dunghill sons of dirt an’ mire,
> May to PATRICIAN RIGHTS ASPIRE;
> Nae sage North, now, nor sager Sackville,
> To watch an’ premier owre the pack vile!
> An’ whare will ye get Howes an’ Clintons
> To bring them to a right repentance,

To cowe the rebel generation,
An' save the honor o' the NATION?
THEY! an' be d—mn'd! what right hae they
To Meat, or Sleep, or light o' day,
Far less to riches, pow'r, or freedom,
But what your lordships PLEASE TO GIE THEM?

BUT, hear me, my lord! Glengary, hear!
Your HAND 'S OWRE LIGHT ON THEM, I fear:
Your FACTORS, GREIVES, TRUSTEES an' BAILIES,
I canna say but they do gailies;
They lay aside a' tender mercies
An' tirl the HALLIONS to the BIRSIES;
Yet, while they're only poin'd, and herriet,
They'll keep their stubborn Highlan spirit.
But smash them! crush them a' to spails!
An' rot the DYVORS i' the JAILS!
The young dogs, swinge them to the labour,
Let WARK an' HUNGER mak them sober!
The HIZZIES, if they're oughtlins fausont,
Let them in DRURY LANE be lesson'd!
An' if the wives, an' dirty brats,
Come thiggan at your doors an' yets,
Flaffan wi' duds, an' grey wi' beese,
Frightan awa your deucks an' geese;
Get out a HORSE-WHIP, or a JOWLER,
The langest thong, the fiercest growler,
An' gar the tatter'd gipseys pack
Wi' a' their bastarts on their back!

Go on, my lord! I lang to meet you
An' in my HOUSE AT HAME to greet you;
Wi' COMMON LORDS ye shanna mingle,
The benmost newk, beside the ingle
At my right hand, assign'd your seat
'Tween HEROD's hip, an' POLYCRATE;
Or, if ye on your station tarrow,
Between ALMAGRO and PIZARRO;

A seat, I'm sure ye're weel deservin 't;
An' till ye come – your humble servant
                                        BEELZEBUB.
HELL 1st June Anno Mundi 5790

Epitaph on a Wag in Mauchline

❧

Lament 'im Mauchline husbands a',
    He aften did assist ye;
For had ye staid whole weeks awa'
    Your wives they ne'er had miss'd ye.

Ye Mauchline bairns as on ye pass,
    To school in bands thegither,
O tread ye lightly on his grass,
    Perhaps he was your father.

A Dream

Thoughts, words and deeds, the Statute blames with reason;
But surely Dreams *were ne'er indicted Treason.*

On reading, in the public papers, the Laureate's Ode, with the other parade of June 4th, 1786, the Author was no sooner dropt asleep, than he imagined himself transported to the Birth-day Levee; and, in his dreaming fancy, made the following Address.

I

Guid-mornin to your MAJESTY!
    May heaven augment your blisses,
On ev'ry new *Birth-day* ye see,
    A humble Poet wishes!
My Bardship here, at your Levee,
    On sic a day as this is,
Is sure an uncouth sight to see,
    Amang thae Birth-day dresses
                Sae fine this day.

II

I see ye're complimented thrang,
    By many a *lord* an' *lady*;
'God save the King' 's a cukoo sang
    That 's unco easy said ay:
The *Poets* too, a venal gang,
    Wi' rhymes weel-turn'd an' ready,
Wad gar you trow ye ne'er do wrang,
    But ay unerring steady,
                On sic a day.

III

For me! before a Monarch's face,
    Ev'n *there* I winna flatter;

For neither Pension, Post, nor Place,
   Am I your humble debtor:
So, nae reflection on YOUR GRACE,
   Your Kingship to bespatter;
There 's monie *waur* been o' the Race,
   And aiblins *ane* been better
            Than You this day.

IV

'Tis very true, my sovereign King,
   My skill may weel be doubted;
But *Facts* are cheels that winna ding,
   An' downa be disputed:
Your *royal nest,* beneath *Your* wing,
   Is e'en right reft an' clouted,
And now the third part o' the string,
   An' less, will gang about it
            Than did ae day.

V

Far be 't frae me that I aspire
   To blame your Legislation,
Or say, ye wisdom want, or fire,
   To rule this mighty nation;
But faith! I muckle doubt, my SIRE,
   Ye've trusted 'Ministration,
To chaps, wha, in a *barn* or *byre,*
   Wad better fill'd their station
            Than *courts* yon day.

VI

And now Ye've gien auld *Britain* peace,
   Her broken shins to plaister;
Your sair taxation does her fleece,
   Till she has scarce a tester:
For me, thank God, my life 's a *lease,*
   Nae *bargain* wearing faster,

Or faith! I fear, that, wi' the geese,
    I shortly boost to pasture
            I' the craft some day.

VII

I'm no mistrusting *Willie Pit*,
    When taxes he enlarges,
(An' *Will* 's a true guid fallow's get,
    A Name not Envy spairges)
That he intends to pay your *debt*,
    An' lessen a' your *charges*;
But, G—d-sake! let nae *saving-fit*
    Abridge your bonie *Barges*
            An' *Boats* this day.

VIII

Adieu, my LIEGE! may Freedom geck
    Beneath your high protection;
An' may Ye rax Corruption's neck,
    And gie her for dissection!
But since I'm here, I'll no neglect,
    In loyal, true affection,
To pay your QUEEN, with due respect,
    My fealty an' subjection
            This great Birth-day.

IX

Hail, *Majesty most Excellent!*
    While Nobles strive to please Ye,
Will Ye accept a Compliment,
    A simple Poet gies Ye?
Thae bonie Bairntime, Heav'n has lent,
    Still higher may they heeze Ye
In bliss, till Fate some day is sent,
    For ever to release Ye
            Frae Care that day.

X

For you, young Potentate o' W—,
  I tell your *Highness* fairly,
Down Pleasure's stream, wi' swelling sails,
  I'm tauld ye're driving rarely;
But some day ye may gnaw your nails,
  An' curse your folly sairly,
That e'er ye brak *Diana*'s *pales*,
  Or rattl'd dice wi' *Charlie*
              By night or day.

XI

Yet aft a ragged *Cowte* 's been known,
  To mak a noble *Aiver*;
So, ye may dousely fill a Throne,
  For a' their clish-ma-claver:
There, Him at *Agincourt* wha shone,
  Few better were or braver;
And yet, wi' funny, queer *Sir* John*,
  He was an unco shaver
              For monie a day.

XII

For you, right rev'rend O—,
  Nane sets the *lawn-sleeve* sweeter,
Altho' a ribban at your lug
  Wad been a dress compleater:
As ye disown yon paughty dog,
  That *bears* the Keys of Peter,
Then swith! an' get a *wife* to hug,
  Or trouth! ye'll stain the *Mitre*
              Some luckless day.

* Sir John Falstaff, Vide Shakespeare.

XIII

Young, royal TARRY-BREEKS, I learn,
  Ye've lately come athwart her;
A glorious *Galley*, stem and stern,
  Weel rigg'd for *Venus barter*;
But first hang out that she'll discern
  Your *hymeneal Charter*,
Then heave aboard your *grapple airn*,
  An', large upon her *quarter*,
                    Come full that day.

XIV

Ye lastly, bonie blossoms a',
  Ye *royal Lasses* dainty,
Heav'n mak you guid as weel as braw,
  An' gie you *lads* a plenty:
But sneer na *British-boys* awa;
  For Kings are unco scant ay,
An' German-Gentles are but *sma'*,
  They're better just than *want ay*
                    On onie day.

XV

God bless you a'! consider now,
  Ye're unco muckle dautet;
But ere the *course* o' life be through,
  It may be bitter sautet:
An' I hae seen their *coggie* fou,
  That yet hae tarrow't at it,
But or the *day* was done, I trow,
  The laggen they hae clautet
                    Fu' clean that day.

* Alluding to the Newspaper account of a certain royal Sailor's Amour.

Tam Samson's* Elegy

◦◦◦◦

An honest man 's the noblest work of God –
POPE.

Has auld Kilmarnock seen the Deil?
Or great M'kinlay† thrawn his heel?
Or Robertson‡ again grown weel,
      To preach an' read?
'Na, waur than a'!' cries ilka chiel,
       '*Tam Samson* 's dead!'

Kilmarnock lang may grunt an' grane,
An' sigh an' sab, an' greet her lane,
An' cleed her bairns, man, wife, an' wean,
      In mourning weed;
To Death she 's dearly pay'd the kane,
      Tam Samson 's dead!

The Brethren o' the mystic *level*
May hing their head in wofu' bevel,
While by their nose the tears will revel,
      Like ony bead;
Death 's gien the Lodge an unco devel,
      Tam Samson 's dead!

When Winter muffles up his cloak,
And binds the mire like a rock;
When to the loughs the Curlers flock,
      Wi' gleesome speed,

* When this worthy old Sportsman went out last muir-fowl season, he supposed it was to be, in Ossian's phrase, 'the last of his fields;' and expressed an ardent wish to die and be buried in the muirs. On this hint the Author composed his Elegy and Epitaph.
  † A certain Preacher, a great favourite with the Million.
  ‡ Another Preacher, an equal favourite with the Few, who was at that time ailing.

Wha will they station at the *cock*,
        Tam Samson 's dead?

He was the king of a' the Core,
To guard, or draw, or wick a bore,
Or up the rink like *Jehu* roar
        In time o' need;
But now he lags on Death's *hog-score*,
        Tam Samson 's dead!

Now safe the stately Sawmont sail,
And Trouts bedropp'd wi' crimson hail,
And Eels weel kend for souple tail,
        And Geds for greed,
Since dark in Death's *fish-creel* we wail
        Tam Samson dead!

Rejoice, ye birring Paitricks a';
Ye cootie Moorcocks, crousely craw;
Ye Maukins, cock your fud fu' braw,
        Withoutten dread;
Your mortal Fae is now awa',
        Tam Samson 's dead!

That woefu' morn be ever mourn'd
Saw him in shootin graith adorn'd,
While pointers round impatient burn'd,
        Frae couples freed;
But, Och! he gaed and ne'er return'd!
        Tam Samson 's dead!

In vain Auld-age his body batters;
In vain the Gout his ancles fetters;
In vain the burns cam down like waters,
        An acre-braid!
Now ev'ry auld wife, greetin, clatters,
        'Tam Samson 's dead!'

Owre mony a weary hag he limpit,
An' ay the tither shot he thumpit,

Till coward Death behind him jumpit,
   Wi' deadly feide;
Now he proclaims, wi' tout o' trumpet,
   Tam Samson 's dead!

When at his heart he felt the dagger,
He reel'd his wonted bottle-swagger,
But yet he drew the mortal trigger
   Wi' weel-aim'd heed;
'L—d, five!' he cry'd, an' owre did stagger;
   Tam Samson 's dead!

Ilk hoary Hunter mourn'd a brither;
Ilk Sportsman-youth bemoan'd a father;
Yon auld gray stane, amang the heather,
   Marks out his head,
Whare *Burns* has wrote, in rhyming blether,
   Tam Samson 's dead!

There, low he lies, in lasting rest;
Perhaps upon his mould'ring breast
Some spitefu' muirfowl bigs her nest,
   To hatch an' breed:
Alas! nae mair he'll them molest!
   Tam Samson 's dead!

When August winds the heather wave,
And Sportsmen wander by yon grave,
Three vollies let his mem'ry crave
   O' pouther an' lead,
Till Echo answer frae her cave,
   Tam Samson 's dead!

Heav'n rest his saul, whare'er he be!
Is th' wish o' mony mae than me:
He had twa fauts, or may be three,
   Yet what remead?
Ae social, honest man want we:
   Tam Samson 's dead!

THE EPITAPH

Tam Samson's weel-worn clay here lies,
 Ye canting Zealots, spare him!
If Honest Worth in heaven rise,
 Ye'll mend or ye win near him.

PER CONTRA

Go, Fame, an' canter like a filly
Thro' a' the streets an' neuks o' *Killie,**
Tell ev'ry social, honest billie
     To cease his grievin,
For yet, unskaith'd by Death's gleg gullie,
    Tam Samson 's livin!

---

* Killie is a phrase the country-folks sometimes use for the name of a certain town in the West.

The Brigs of Ayr, a Poem. Inscribed to J. Ballantine, Esq; Ayr

The simple Bard, rough at the rustic plough,
Learning his tuneful trade from ev'ry bough;
The chanting linnet, or the mellow thrush,
Hailing the setting sun, sweet, in the green thorn bush,
The soaring lark, the perching red-breast shrill,
Or deep-ton'd plovers, grey, wild-whistling o'er the hill;
Shall he, nurst in the Peasant's lowly shed,
To hardy Independence bravely bred,
By early Poverty to hardship steel'd,
And train'd to arms in stern Misfortune's field,
Shall he be guilty of their hireling crimes,
The servile, mercenary Swiss of rhymes?
Or labour hard the panegyric close,
With all the venal soul of dedicating Prose?
No! though his artless strains he rudely sings,
And throws his hand uncouthly o'er the strings,
He glows with all the spirit of the Bard,
Fame, honest fame, his great, his dear reward.
Still, if some Patron's gen'rous care he trace,
Skill'd in the secret, to bestow with grace;
When Ballantine befriends his humble name,
And hands the rustic Stranger up to fame,
With heartfelt throes his grateful bosom swells,
The godlike bliss, to give, alone excels.

'Twas when the stacks get on their winter-hap,
And thack and rape secure the toil-won crap;
Potatoe-bings are snugged up frae skaith
Of coming Winter's biting, frosty breath;

The bees, rejoicing o'er their summer-toils,
Unnumber'd buds, an' flow'rs' delicious spoils,
Seal'd up with frugal care in massive, waxen piles,
Are doom'd by Man, that tyrant o'er the weak,
The death o' devils, smoor'd wi' brimstone reek:
The thund'ring guns are heard on ev'ry side,
The wounded coveys, reeling, scatter wide;
The feather'd field-mates, bound by Nature's tie,
Sires, mothers, children, in one carnage lie:
(What warm, poetic heart but inly bleeds,
And execrates man's savage, ruthless deeds!)
Nae mair the flow'r in field or meadow springs;
Nae mair the grove with airy concert rings,
Except perhaps the Robin's whistling glee,
Proud o' the height o' some bit half-lang tree:
The hoary morns precede the sunny days,
Mild, calm, serene, wide-spreads the noon-tide blaze,
While thick the gossamour waves wanton in the rays.
'Twas in that season when a simple Bard,
Unknown and poor, simplicity's reward,
Ae night, within the ancient brugh of *Ayr*,
By whim inspir'd, or haply prest wi' care,
He left his bed and took his wayward rout,
And down by *Simpson*'s* wheel'd the left about:
(Whether impell'd by all-directing Fate,
To witness what I after shall narrate;
Or whether, rapt in meditation high,
He wander'd out he knew not where nor why)
The drowsy *Dungeon-clock*† had number'd two,
And *Wallace Tow'r*† had sworn the fact was true:
The tide-swoln Firth, with sullen-sounding roar,
Through the still night dash'd hoarse along the shore,
All else was hush'd as Nature's closed e'e;
The silent moon shone high o'er tow'r and tree:
The chilly Frost, beneath the silver beam,
Crept, gently-crusting, o'er the glittering stream. —

---

* A noted tavern at the *Auld Brig* end.
† The two steeples.

When, lo! on either hand the list'ning Bard,
The clanging sugh of whistling wings is heard;
Two dusky forms dart thro' the midnight air,
Swift as the *Gos*** drives on the wheeling hare;
Ane on th' *Auld Brig* his airy shape uprears,
The ither flutters o'er the *rising piers*:
Our warlock Rhymer instantly descry'd
The Sprites that owre the *Brigs of Ayr* preside.
(That Bards are second-sighted is nae joke,
And ken the lingo of the sp'ritual folk;
Fays, Spunkies, Kelpies, a', they can explain them,
And ev'n the vera deils they brawly ken them.)
Auld Brig appear'd of ancient Pictish race,
The vera wrinkles Gothic in his face:
He seem'd as he wi' Time had warstl'd lang,
Yet, teughly doure, he bade an unco bang.
New Brig was buskit in a braw, new coat,
That he, at *Lon'on*, frae ane *Adams* got;
In 's hand five taper staves as smooth 's a bead,
Wi' virls an' whirlygigums at the head.
The Goth was stalking round with anxious search,
Spying the time-worn flaws in ev'ry arch;
It chanc'd his new-come neebor took his e'e,
And e'en a vex'd and angry heart had he!
Wi' thieveless sneer to see his modish mien,
He, down the water, gies him this guid-een —

AULD BRIG

I doubt na, frien', ye'll think ye're nae sheep-shank,
Ance ye were streekit owre frae bank to bank!
But gin ye be a Brig as auld as me,
Tho' faith, that date, I doubt, ye'll never see;
There'll be, if that day come, I'll wad a boddle,
Some fewer whigmeleeries in your noddle.

NEW BRIG

Auld Vandal, ye but show your little mense,
Just much about it wi' your scanty sense;

* The gos-hawk, or falcon.

Will your poor, narrow foot-path of a street,
Where twa wheel-barrows tremble when they meet,
Your ruin'd, formless bulk o' stane and lime,
Compare wi' bonie *Brigs* o' modern time?
There 's men of taste wou'd tak the *Ducat-stream*,*
Tho' they should cast the vera sark and swim,
Ere they would grate their feelings wi' the view
Of sic an ugly, Gothic hulk as you.

AULD BRIG

Conceited gowk! puff'd up wi' windy pride!
This mony a year I've stood the flood an' tide;
And tho' wi' crazy eild I'm sair forfairn,
I'll be a *Brig* when ye're a shapeless cairn!
As yet ye little ken about the matter,
But twa-three winters will inform ye better.
When heavy, dark, continued, a'-day rains
Wi' deepening deluges o'erflow the plains;
When from the hills where springs the brawling *Coil*,
Or stately *Lugar*'s mossy fountains boil,
Or where the *Greenock* winds his moorland course,
Or haunted *Garpal*† draws his feeble source,
Arous'd by blustering winds an' spotting thowes,
In mony a torrent down the snaw-broo rowes;
While crashing ice, borne on the roaring speat,
Sweeps dams, an' mills, an' brigs, a' to the gate;
And from *Glenbuck*,‡ down to the *Ratton-key*,§
Auld *Ayr* is just one lengthen'd, tumbling sea;
Then down ye'll hurl, deil nor ye never rise!
And dash the gumlie jaups up to the pouring skies.
A lesson sadly teaching, to your cost,
That Architecture's noble art is lost!

---

* A noted ford, just above the Auld Brig.

† The banks of *Garpal Water* is one of the few places in the West of Scotland where those fancy-scaring beings, known by the name of *Ghaists,* still continue pertinaciously to inhabit.

‡ The source of the river of Ayr.

§ A small landing-place above the large key.

NEW BRIG

Fine *architecture*, trowth, I needs must say 't o't!
The L—d be thankit that we've tint the gate o't!
Gaunt, ghastly, ghaist-alluring edifices,
Hanging with threat'ning jut like precipices;
O'er-arching, mouldy, gloom-inspiring coves,
Supporting roofs fantastic, stony groves:
Windows and doors in nameless sculptures drest,
With order, symmetry, or taste unblest;
Forms like some bedlam Statuary's dream,
The craz'd creations of misguided whim;
Forms might be worshipp'd on the bended knee,
And still the *second dread command* be free,
Their likeness is not found on earth, in air, or sea.
Mansions that would disgrace the building-taste
Of any mason reptile, bird, or beast;
Fit only for a doited Monkish race,
Or frosty maids forsworn the dear embrace,
Or Cuifs of latter times, wha held the notion,
That sullen gloom was sterling, true devotion:
Fancies that our guid Brugh denies protection,
And soon may they expire, unblest with resurrection!

AULD BRIG

O ye, my dear-remember'd, ancient yealings,
Were ye but here to share my wounded feelings!
Ye worthy *Proveses*, an' mony a *Bailie*,
Wha in the paths o' righteousness did toil ay;
Ye dainty *Deacons*, an' ye douce *Conveeners*,
To whom our moderns are but causey-cleaners;
Ye godly *Councils* wha hae blest this town;
Ye godly *Brethren* o' the sacred gown,
Wha meekly gae your *hurdies* to the *smiters*;
And (what would now be strange) ye *godly Writers*:
A' ye douce folk I've borne aboon the broo,
Were ye but here, what would ye say or do!
How would your spirits groan in deep vexation,
To see each melancholy alteration;

And, agonising, curse the time and place
When ye begat the base, degen'rate race!
Nae langer Rev'rend Men, their country's glory,
In plain, braid Scots hold forth a plain, braid story:
Nae langer thrifty Citizens, an' douce,
Meet owre a pint, or in the Council-house;
But staumrel, corky-headed, graceless Gentry,
The herryment and ruin of the country;
Men, three-parts made by Taylors and by Barbers,
Wha waste your weel-hain'd gear on d—d *new Brigs* and *Harbours*!

NEW BRIG

Now haud you there! for faith ye've said enough,
And muckle mair than ye can mak to through.
As for your Priesthood, I shall say but little,
Corbies and *Clergy* are a shot right kittle:
But, under favor o' your langer beard,
Abuse o' Magistrates might weel be spar'd;
To liken them to your auld-warld squad,
I must needs say, comparisons are odd.
In *Ayr*, Wag-wits nae mair can have a handle
To mouth 'A Citizen', a term o' scandal:
Nae mair the Council waddles down the street,
In all the pomp of ignorant conceit;
Men wha grew wise priggin owre hops an' raisins,
Or gather'd lib'ral views in Bonds and Seisins.
If haply Knowledge, on a random tramp,
Had shor'd them with a glimmer of his lamp,
And would to Common-sense for once betray'd them,
Plain, dull Stupidity stept kindly in to aid them.

———————

What farther clishmaclaver might been said,
What bloody wars, if Sprites had blood to shed,
No man can tell; but, all before their sight,
A fairy train appear'd in order bright:
Adown the glittering stream they featly danc'd;
Bright to the moon their various dresses glanc'd:
They footed o'er the wat'ry glass so neat,

The infant ice scarce bent beneath their feet:
While arts of Minstrelsy among them rung,
And soul-ennobling Bards heroic ditties sung.
O had *M'Lauchlan*,* thairm-inspiring Sage,
Been there to hear this heavenly band engage,
When thro' his dear *Strathspeys* they bore with Highland rage;
Or when they struck old Scotia's melting airs,
The lover's raptur'd joys or bleeding cares;
How would his Highland lug been nobler fir'd,
And ev'n his matchless hand with finer touch inspir'd!
No guess could tell what instrument appear'd,
But all the soul of Music's self was heard;
Harmonious concert rung in every part,
While simple melody pour'd moving on the heart.

The Genius of the Stream in front appears,
A venerable Chief advanc'd in years;
His hoary head with water-lilies crown'd,
His manly leg with garter tangle bound.
Next came the loveliest pair in all the ring,
Sweet Female Beauty hand in hand with Spring;
Then, crown'd with flow'ry hay, came Rural Joy,
And Summer, with his fervid-beaming eye:
All-chearing Plenty, with her flowing horn,
Led yellow Autumn wreath'd with nodding corn;
Then Winter's time-bleach'd locks did hoary show,
By Hospitality with cloudless brow.
Next follow'd Courage with his martial stride,
From where the *Feal* wild-woody coverts hide:
Benevolence, with mild, benignant air,
A female form, came from the tow'rs of *Stair*:
Learning and Worth in equal measures trode,
From simple *Catrine*, their long-lov'd abode:
Last, white-rob'd Peace, crown'd with a hazle wreath,
To rustic Agriculture did bequeath
The broken, iron instruments of Death,
At sight of whom our Sprites forgat their kindling wrath.

* A well known performer of Scottish music on the violin.

Epistle to Captn Willm Logan at Park

❦

Oct: 30th, 1786.

Hail, thairm-inspirin, rattlin Willie!
Though Fortune's road be rough an' hilly
To ev'ry fiddling, rhyming billie,
   We never heed;
But tak it like th' unbacked Fillie,
    Proud o' her speed.

When idly goavin whyles we saunter,
Yirr, Fancy barks, — awa we canter,
Up-hill, down-brae, till some mishanter,
   Some black Bog-hole,
Arreest us; then the scathe an' banter
    We're forc'd to thole.

Hale be your HEART! Hale be your FIDDLE!
Lang may your elbuck jink an' didle,
To chear you through the weary widdle
   O' this vile Warl:
Until ye on a cummock dridle,
    A gray-hair'd Carl!

Come WEALTH, come POORTITH, late or soon,
Heav'n send your HEART-STRINGS ay IN TUNE!
An' screw your TEMPER-PINS aboon,
   A FIFTH or mair,
The melancholious, sairie croon
    O' cankrie CARE!

May still your Life, from day to day,
Nae LENTE LARGO, in the play,
But ALLEGRETTO FORTE, gay,
   Harmonious flow:
A sweeping, kindling, bauld STRATHSPEY,
    Encore! Bravo!

A' blessins on the cheary *gang*
Wha dearly like a Jig or sang;
An' never balance RIGHT and WRANG
      By square and rule,
But as the CLEGS O' FEELING stang,
      Are wise or fool!

My hand-wal'd CURSE keep hard in chase
The harpy, hoodock, purse-proud RACE,
Wha count on POORTITH as disgrace!
      Their tuneless hearts,
May FIRE-SIDE DISCORDS jar a BASS
      To a' their PARTS!

But come – your hand – my careless brither –
I' th' tither WARLD, if there 's anither,
An' that there is, I've little swither
      About the matter;
We cheek-for-chow shall jog the gither,
      I 'se ne'er bid better.

We've fauts an' failins, – granted clearly:
We're frail, backsliding Mortals meerly:
Eve's bonie SQUAD, Priests wyte them sheerly,
      For our grand fa':
But still – but still – I like them dearly;
      GOD bless them a'!

Ochon! for poor CASTALIAN DRINKERS,
When they fa' foul o' earthly Jinkers!
The witching, curst, delicious blinkers
      Hae put me hyte;
An' gart me weet my waukrife winkers,
      Wi' girnan spite.

But by yon Moon! an' that 's high swearin;
An' every Star within my hearin!
An' by her een! wha was a dear ane,
      I'll ne'er forget;

I hope to gie the JADS a clearin
      In fair play yet!

My loss I mourn, but not repent it:
I'll seek my pursie whare I tint it:
Ance to the Indies I were wonted,
      Some cantraip hour,
By some sweet Elf I may be dinted,
      Then, VIVE L'AMOUR!

Faites mes BAISEMAINS respectueuse,
To sentimental Sister Susie,
An' honest LUCKY; no to roose ye,
      Ye may be proud,
That sic a couple Fate allows ye
      To grace your blood.

Nae mair, at present, can I measure;
An' trowth my rhymin ware 's nae treasure;
But when in Ayr, some half hour's leisure,
      Be 't light, be 't dark,
Sir Bard will do himsel the pleasure
      To call at PARK.

A Winter Night

❧❧❧

Poor naked wretches, wheresoe'er you are,
That bide the pelting of this pityless storm!
How shall your houseless heads, and unfed sides,
Your loop'd and window'd raggedness, defend you
From seasons such as these —

SHAKESPEARE.

When biting *Boreas*, fell and doure,
Sharp shivers thro' the leafless bow'r;
When *Phoebus* gies a short-liv'd glow'r,
   Far south the lift,
Dim-dark'ning thro' the flaky show'r,
   Or whirling drift.

Ae night the Storm the steeples rocked,
Poor Labour sweet in sleep was locked,
While burns, wi' snawy wreeths up-choked,
   Wild-eddying swirl,
On thro' the mining outlet bocked,
   Down headlong hurl.

List'ning, the doors an' winnocks rattle,
I thought me on the ourie cattle,
Or silly sheep, wha bide this brattle
   O' winter war,
And thro' the drift, deep-lairing, sprattle,
   Beneath a scar.

Ilk happing bird, wee, helpless thing!
That, in the merry months o' spring,
Delighted me to hear thee sing,
   What comes o' thee?
Whare wilt thou cow'r thy chittering wing,
   An' close thy e'e?

289

Ev'n you on murd'ring errands toil'd,
Lone from your savage homes exil'd,
The blood-stain'd roost, and sheep-cote spoil'd,
 My heart forgets,
While pityless the tempest wild
 Sore on you beats.

Now *Phoebe*, in her midnight reign,
Dark-muffl'd, view'd the dreary plain;
Still crouding thoughts, a pensive train,
 Rose in my soul,
When on my ear this plaintive strain,
 Slow-solemn, stole –

 'Blow, blow ye Winds, with heavier gust!
 'And freeze, thou bitter-biting Frost!
 'Descend, ye chilly, smothering Snows!
 'Not all your rage, as now, united shows
 'More hard unkindness, unrelenting,
 'Vengeful malice, unrepenting,
'Than heaven-illumin'd Man on brother Man bestows!

 'See stern Oppression's iron grip,
 'Or mad Ambition's gory hand,
 'Sending, like blood-hounds from the slip,
 'Woe, Want, and Murder o'er a land!
 'Ev'n in the peaceful rural vale,
 'Truth, weeping, tells the mournful tale,
'How pamper'd Luxury, Flatt'ry by her side,
 'The parasite empoisoning her ear,
 'With all the servile wretches in the rear,
'Looks o'er proud Property, extended wide;
 'And eyes the simple, rustic Hind,
 'Whose toil upholds the glitt'ring show,
 'A creature of another kind,
 'Some coarser substance, unrefin'd,
'Plac'd for her lordly use thus far, thus vile, below!

'Where, where is Love's fond, tender throe,
'With lordly Honor's lofty brow,
   'The pow'rs you proudly own?
'Is there, beneath Love's noble name,
'Can harbour, dark, the selfish aim,
   'To bless himself alone!
'Mark Maiden-innocence a prey
   'To love-pretending snares,
'This boasted Honor turns away,
'Shunning soft Pity's rising sway,
'Regardless of the tears, and unavailing pray'rs!
   'Perhaps, this hour, in Mis'ry's squalid nest,
   'She strains your infant to her joyless breast,
'And with a Mother's fears shrinks at the rocking blast!

   'Oh ye! who sunk in beds of down,
   'Feel not a want but what yourselves create,
   'Think, for a moment, on his wretched fate,
   'Whom friends and fortune quite disown!
'Ill-satisfy'd, keen Nature's clam'rous call,
   'Stretch'd on his straw he lays himself to sleep,
   'While thro' the ragged roof and chinky wall,
   'Chill, o'er his slumbers, piles the drifty heap!
   'Think on the dungeon's grim confine,
   'Where Guilt and poor Misfortune pine!
   'Guilt, erring Man, relenting view!
   'But shall thy legal rage pursue
   'The Wretch, already crushed low
   'By cruel Fortune's undeserved blow?
'Affliction's sons are brothers in distress;
'A Brother to relieve, how exquisite the bliss!'

   I heard nae mair, for *Chanticleer*
      Shook off the pouthery snaw,
   And hail'd the morning with a cheer,
      A cottage-rousing craw.

But deep this truth impress'd my mind –
   Thro' all his works abroad,
The heart benevolent and kind
   The most resembles GOD.

To a Haggis

Fair fa' your honest, sonsie face,
Great Chieftan o' the Puddin-race!
Aboon them a' ye tak your place,
      Painch, tripe, or thairm:
Weel are ye wordy of a *grace*
      As lang 's my arm.

The groaning trencher there ye fill,
Your hurdies like a distant hill,
Your *pin* wad help to mend a mill
      In time o' need,
While thro' your pores the dews distil
      Like amber bead.

His knife see Rustic-labour dight,
An' cut you up wi' ready slight,
Trenching your gushing entrails bright
      Like onie ditch;
And then, O what a glorious sight,
      Warm-reekin, rich!

Then, horn for horn they stretch an' strive,
Deil tak the hindmost, on they drive,
Till a' their weel-swall'd kytes belyve
      Are bent like drums;
Then auld Guidman, maist like to rive,
      Bethankit hums.

Is there that owre his French *ragout*,
Or *olio* that wad staw a sow,
Or *fricassee* wad mak her spew
      Wi' perfect sconner,
Looks down wi' sneering, scornfu' view
      On sic a dinner?

Poor devil! see him owre his trash,
As feckless as a wither'd rash,
His spindle shank a guid whip-lash,
        His nieve a nit;
Thro' bluidy flood or field to dash,
        O how unfit!

But mark the Rustic, *haggis-fed*,
The trembling earth resounds his tread,
Clap in his walie nieve a blade,
        He'll mak it whissle;
An' legs, an' arms, an' heads will sned,
        Like taps o' thrissle.

Ye Pow'rs wha mak mankind your care,
And dish them out their bill o' fare,
Auld Scotland wants nae skinking ware
        That jaups in luggies;
But, if ye wish her gratefu' pray'r,
        Gie her a *Haggis*!

1787

EDINBURGH; BORDER TOUR;
HIGHLAND TOURS

꘠꘠꘠

On Fergusson

꘠꘠꘠

Curse on ungrateful man, that can be pleas'd,
And yet can starve the author of the pleasure!

O thou, my elder brother in Misfortune,
By far my elder Brother in the muse,
With tears I pity thy unhappy fate!
Why is the Bard unfitted for the world,
Yet has so keen a relish of its Pleasures?

To a Painter

Dear —, I'll gie ye some advice,
   You'll tak it no uncivil:
You shouldna paint at angels, man,
   But try and paint the Devil.

To paint an angel 's kittle wark,
   Wi' Nick there 's little danger;
You'll easy draw a lang-kent face,
   But no sae weel a stranger.
                     R. B.

To William Creech

Selkirk 13th May 1787

AULD chuckie REEKIE 's sair distrest,
Down droops her ance weel-burnish'd crest,
Nae joy her bonie buskit nest
      Can yield ava;
Her darling bird that she loes best,
      Willie 's awa. —

O Willie was a witty wight,
And had o' things an unco slight;
Auld Reekie ay he keepit tight,
      And trig and braw:
But now they'll busk her like a fright,
      Willie 's awa. —

The stiffest o' them a' he bow'd,
The bauldest o' them a' he cow'd,
They durst nae mair than he allow'd,
      That was a law:
We've lost a birkie weel worth gowd,
      Willie 's awa. —

Now gawkies, tawpies, gowks and fools,
Frae colleges and boarding-schools,
May sprout like simmer puddock-stools
      In glen or shaw;
He wha could brush them down to mools
      Willie 's awa. —

The brethren o' the commerce-chaumer
May mourn their loss wi' doolfu' clamour;
He was a dictionar and grammar
      Amang them a':
I fear they'll now mak mony a stammer,
      Willie 's awa. —

Nae mair we see his levee door
Philosophers and Poets pour,
And toothy Critics by the score
          In bloody raw;
The Adjutant of a' the core
          Willie 's awa. –

Now worthy Greg'ry's latin face,
Tytler's and Greenfield's modest grace,
Mckenzie, Stuart, such a brace
          As Rome ne'er saw;
They a' maun meet some ither place,
          Willie 's awa. –

Poor BURNS – even Scotch Drink canna quicken,
He cheeps like some bewilder'd chicken,
Scar'd frae its minnie and the cleckin
          By hoodie-craw:
Grief 's gien his heart an unco kickin,
          Willie 's awa. –

Now ev'ry sour-mou'd, girnin blellum,
And Calvin's folk are fit to fell him;
Ilk self-conceited, critic skellum
          His quill may draw;
He wha could brawlie ward their bellum
          Willie 's awa. –

Up wimpling, stately Tweed I've sped,
And Eden scenes on chrystal Jed,
And Ettrick banks now roaring red
          While tempests blaw;
But ev'ry joy and pleasure 's fled,
          Willie 's awa. –

May I be Slander's common speech;
A text for Infamy to preach;
And lastly, streekit out to bleach
          In winter snaw

When I forget thee, WILLIE CREECH,
    Tho' far awa!

May never wicked Fortune touzle him,
May never wicked men bamboozle him,
Until a pow as auld 's Methusalem
    He canty claw:
Then to the blessed, new Jerusalem
    Fleet-wing awa. –

On a Schoolmaster in Cleish Parish, Fifeshire

Here lie Willie Michie's banes,
    O Satan, when ye tak him,
Gie him the schulin' o' your weans;
    For clever Deils he'll mak 'em!

1788–9

EDINBURGH AND ELLISLAND

❦❦

An Extemporaneous Effusion on being appointed to the Excise

❦❦

Searching auld wives' barrels,
  Ochon, the day!
That clarty barm should stain my laurels;
  But – what'll ye say!
These muvin' things ca'd wives and weans
Wad muve the very hearts o' stanes!

Epistle to Hugh Parker

In this strange land, this uncouth clime,
A land unknown to prose or rhyme;
Where words ne'er crost the muse's heckles,
Nor limpet in poetic shackles;
A land that prose did never view it,
Except when drunk he stacher't thro' it;
Here, ambush'd by the chimla cheek,
Hid in an atmosphere of reek,
I hear a wheel thrum i' the neuk,
I hear it – for in vain I leuk. –
The red peat gleams, a fiery kernel,
Enhusked by a fog infernal:
Here, for my wonted rhyming raptures,
I sit and count my sins by chapters;
For lief and spunk like ither Christians,
I'm dwindled down to mere existence,
Wi' nae converse but Gallowa' bodies,
Wi' nae kend face but Jenny Geddes.
Jenny, my Pegasean pride!
Dowie she saunters down Nithside,
And ay a westlin leuk she throws,
While tears hap o'er her auld brown nose!
Was it for this, wi' canny care,
Thou bure the Bard through many a shire?
At howes or hillocks never stumbled,
And late or early never grumbled? –
O, had I power like inclination,
I'd heeze thee up a constellation,
To canter with the Sagitarre,
Or loup the ecliptic like a bar;
Or turn the pole like any arrow;
Or, when auld Phebus bids good-morrow,

Down the zodiac urge the race,
And cast dirt on his godship's face;
For I could lay my bread and kail
He'd ne'er cast saut upo' thy tail. –
Wi' a' this care and a' this grief,
And sma', sma' prospect of relief,
And nought but peat reek i' my head,
How can I write what ye can read? –
Tarbolton, twenty-fourth o' June,
Ye'll find me in a better tune;
But till we meet and weet our whistle,
Tak this excuse for nae epistle.

       ROBERT BURNS.

Elegy on Capt. Matthew Henderson, A Gentleman *who held the Patent for his Honours immediately from Almighty God!*

❧❧❧

> *But now his radiant course is run,*
> *For Matthew's course was bright;*
> *His soul was like the glorious sun,*
> *A matchless Heavenly Light!*

O death! thou tyrant fell and bloody!
The meikle devil wi' a woodie
Haurl thee hame to his black smiddie,
   O'er hurcheon hides,
And like stock-fish come o'er his studdie
   Wi' thy auld sides!

He 's gane! he 's gane! he 's frae us torn,
The ae best fellow e'er was born!
Thee, Matthew, Nature's sel shall mourn
   By wood and wild,
Where, haply, Pity strays forlorn,
   Frae man exil'd.

Ye hills, near neebors o' the starns,
That proudly cock your cresting cairns;
Ye cliffs, the haunts of sailing yearns,
   Where Echo slumbers:
Come join, ye Nature's sturdiest bairns,
   My wailing numbers.

Mourn, ilka grove the cushat kens;
Ye hazly shaws and briery dens;
Ye burnies, wimplin down your glens,
   Wi' toddlin din,

Or foaming, strang, wi' hasty stens,
      Frae lin to lin.

Mourn, little harebells o'er the lee;
Ye stately foxgloves fair to see;
Ye woodbines hanging bonnilie,
      In scented bowers;
Ye roses on your thorny tree,
      The first o' flowers.

At dawn, when every grassy blade
Droops with a diamond at his head,
At even, when beans their fragrance shed,
      I' th' rustling gale,
Ye maukins whiddin thro' the glade,
      Come join my wail.

Mourn, ye wee songsters o' the wood;
Ye grouss that crap the heather bud;
Ye curlews calling thro' a clud;
      Ye whistling plover;
And mourn, ye whirring paitrick brood;
      He 's gane for ever!

Mourn, sooty coots, and speckled teals;
Ye fisher herons, watching eels;
Ye duck and drake, wi' airy wheels
      Circling the lake:
Ye bitterns, till the quagmire reels,
      Rair for his sake.

Mourn, clamouring craiks at close o' day,
'Mang fields o' flowering claver gay;
And when ye wing your annual way
      Frae our cauld shore,
Tell thae far warlds, wha lies in clay,
      Wham we deplore.

Ye houlets, frae your ivy bower,
In some auld tree, or eldritch tower,

What time the moon, wi' silent glowr,
        Sets up her horn,
Wail thro' the dreary midnight hour
        Till waukrife morn.

O, rivers, forests, hills, and plains!
Oft have ye heard my canty strains:
But now, what else for me remains
        But tales of woe;
And frae my een the drapping rains
        Maun ever flow.

Mourn, Spring, thou darling of the year;
Ilk cowslip cup shall kep a tear:
Thou, Simmer, while each corny spear
        Shoots up its head,
Thy gay, green, flowery tresses shear,
        For him that 's dead.

Thou, Autumn, wi' thy yellow hair,
In grief thy sallow mantle tear;
Thou, Winter, hurling thro' the air
        The roaring blast,
Wide o'er the naked world declare
        The worth we 've lost.

Mourn him thou Sun, great source of light;
Mourn, Empress of the silent night:
And you, ye twinkling starnies bright,
        My Matthew mourn;
For through your orbs he 's taen his flight,
        Ne'er to return.

O, Henderson! the man! the brother!
And art thou gone, and gone for ever!
And hast thou crost that unknown river,
        Life's dreary bound!
Like thee, where shall I find another,
        The world around!

Go to your sculptur'd tombs, ye Great,
In a' the tinsel trash o' state!
But by thy honest turf I'll wait,
            Thou man of worth!
And weep the ae best fellow's fate
            E'er lay in earth.

THE EPITAPH

Stop, passenger! my story 's brief,
    And truth I shall relate, man;
I tell nae common tale o' grief,
    For Matthew was a great man.

If thou uncommon merit hast,
    Yet spurn'd at Fortune's door, man;
A look of pity hither cast,
    For Matthew was a poor man.

If thou a noble sodger art,
    That passest by this grave, man;
There moulders here a gallant heart,
    For Matthew was a brave man.

If thou on men, their works and ways,
    Canst throw uncommon light, man;
Here lies wha weel had won thy praise,
    For Matthew was a bright man.

If thou at Friendship's sacred ca'
    Wad life itself resign, man;
Thy sympathetic tear maun fa',
    For Matthew was a kind man.

If thou art staunch without a stain,
    Like the unchanging blue, man;
This was a kinsman o' thy ain,
    For Matthew was a true man.

If thou hast wit, and fun, and fire,
    And ne'er gude wine did fear, man;
This was thy billie, dam, and sire,
    For Matthew was a queer man.

If ony whiggish whingin sot,
    To blame poor Matthew dare, man;
May dool and sorrow be his lot,
    For Matthew was a rare man.

Elegy on the Year 1788

For Lords or kings I dinna mourn,
E'en let them die – for that they're born!
But oh! prodigious to reflect,
A *Towmont*, Sirs, is gane to wreck!
O *Eighty-eight*, in thy sma' space
What dire events ha'e taken place!
Of what enjoyments thou hast reft us!
In what a pickle thou hast left us!

The Spanish empire 's tint a head,
An' my auld teethless Bawtie 's dead;
The toolzie 's teugh 'tween Pitt an' Fox,
An' our gudewife's wee birdy cocks;
The tane is game, a bluidy devil,
But to the *hen-birds* unco civil;
The tither 's dour, has nae sic breedin',
But better stuff ne'er claw'd a midden!

Ye ministers, come mount the pupit,
An' cry till ye be haerse an' rupit;
For *Eighty-eight* he wish'd you weel,
An' gied you a' baith gear an' meal;
E'en mony a plack, an' mony a peck,
Ye ken yoursels, for little feck!

Ye bonny lasses, dight your een,
For some o' you ha'e tint a frien';
In *Eighty-eight*, ye ken, was ta'en
What ye'll ne'er ha'e to gi'e again.

Observe the very nowt an' sheep,
How dowff an' dowie now they creep;
Nay, even the yirth itsel' does cry,
For Embro' wells are grutten dry.

O *Eighty-nine*, thou 's but a bairn,
An' no owre auld, I hope to learn!
Thou beardless boy, I pray tak' care,
Thou now has got thy Daddy's chair,
Nae hand-cuff'd, mizl'd, haff-shackl'd *Regent*,
But, like himsel', a full free agent.
Be sure ye follow out the plan
Nae war than he did, honest man!
As muckle better as you can.

January 1, 1789.

To Dr Blacklock

My Revd and dear Friend

Wow, but your letter made me vauntie!
And are ye hale, and weel, and cantie?
I kend it still your wee bit jauntie
      Wad bring ye to:
Lord send you ay as weel 's I want ye,
      And then ye'll do. –

The *Ill-thief* blaw the *Heron* south!
And never drink be near his drouth!
He tald mysel, by word o' mouth,
      He'd tak my letter;
I lippen'd to the chiel in trouth,
      And bade nae better. –

But aiblins honest Master Heron
Had at the time some dainty *Fair One*,
To ware his theologic care on,
      And holy study:
And tired o' *Sauls* to waste his lear on,
      E'en tried the *Body*. –

But what d'ye think, my trusty Fier,
I'm turn'd a Gauger – Peace be here!
Parnassian *Quines* I fear, I fear,
      Ye'll now disdain me,
And then my fifty pounds a year
      Will little gain me. –

Ye glaiket, gleesome, dainty Damies,
Wha by Castalia's wimplin streamies
Lowp, sing, and lave your pretty limbies,
      Ye ken, Ye ken,

That strang Necessity supreme is
       'Mang sons o' Men. –

I hae a wife and twa wee laddies,
They maun hae brose and brats o' duddies;
Ye ken yoursels my heart right proud is,
       I need na vaunt;
But I'll sned boosoms and thraw saugh-woodies
       Before they want. –

Lord help me thro' this warld o' care!
I'm weary sick o't late and air!
No but I hae a richer share
       Than mony ithers;
But why should ae man better fare,
       And a' Men brithers!

Come, *Firm Resolve* take thou the van,
Thou stalk o' carl-hemp in man!
And let us mind, faint heart ne'er wan
       A lady fair:
Wha does the utmost that he can,
       Will whyles do mair. –

But to conclude my silly rhyme,
(I'm scant o' verse and scant o' time,)
To make a happy fireside clime
       To weans and wife,
That 's the true *Pathos* and *Sublime*
       Of Human life. –

My Compliments to Sister Beckie;
And eke the same to honest Lucky,
I wat she is a dainty Chuckie
       As e'er tread clay!
And gratefully my gude auld Cockie
       I'm yours for ay. –
               ROBT BURNS

Ellisland
21st Oct. 1789

On the Late Captain Grose's Peregrinations thro' Scotland, collecting the Antiquities of that Kingdom

❦

Hear, Land o' Cakes, and brither Scots,
Frae Maidenkirk to Johny Groats! –
If there 's a hole in a' your coats,
        I rede you tent it:
A chield 's amang you, taking notes,
          And, faith, he'll prent it.

If in your bounds ye chance to light
Upon a fine, fat, fodgel wight,
O' stature short, but genius bright,
        That 's he, mark weel –
And wow! he has an unco slight
         O' cauk and keel.

By some auld, houlet-haunted, biggin*,
Or kirk deserted by its riggin,
It 's ten to ane ye'll find him snug in
        Some eldritch part,
Wi' deils, they say, L—d safe 's! colleaguin
        At some black art. –

Ilk ghaist that haunts auld ha' or chamer,
Ye gipsy-gang that deal in glamor,
And you, deep-read in hell's black grammar,
        Warlocks and witches;
Ye'll quake at his conjuring hammer,
        Ye midnight b—es.

It 's tauld he was a sodger bred,
And ane wad rather fa'n than fled;

* Vide his Antiquities of Scotland.

But now he 's quat the spurtle-blade,
      And dog-skin wallet,
And taen the – *Antiquarian trade*,
      I think they call it.

He has a fouth o' auld nick-nackets;
Rusty airn caps and jinglin jackets,*
Wad haud the Lothians three in tackets,
      A towmont gude;
And parritch-pats, and auld saut-backets,
      Before the Flood.

Of Eve's first fire he has a cinder;
Auld Tubalcain's fire-shool and fender;
That which distinguished the gender
      O' Balaam's ass;
A broom-stick o' the witch of Endor,
      Weel shod wi' brass.

Forbye, he'll shape you aff fu' gleg
The cut of Adam's philibeg;
The knife that nicket Abel's craig
      He'll prove you fully,
It was a faulding jocteleg,
      Or lang-kail gullie. –

But wad ye see him in his glee,
For meikle glee and fun has he,
Then set him down, and twa or three
      Gude fellows wi' him;
And *port, O port!* shine thou a wee,
      And THEN ye'll see him!

Now, by the Powers o' Verse and Prose!
Thou art a dainty chield, O Grose! –
Whae'er o' thee shall ill suppose,
      They sair misca' thee;
I'd take the rascal by the nose,
      Wad say, Shame fa' thee.

---

* Vide his treatise on ancient armour and weapons.

ELLISLAND AND DUMFRIES

✧◦✧◦✧

To a Gentleman who had sent him a News-paper, and offered to continue it free of expense

✧◦✧◦✧

Kind Sir, I've read your paper through,
And faith, to me, 'twas really new!
How guessed ye, Sir, what maist I wanted?
This mony a day I've grain'd and gaunted,
To ken what French mischief was brewin;
Or what the drumlie Dutch were doin;
That vile doup-skelper, Emperor Joseph,
If Venus yet had got his nose off;
Or how the collieshangie works
Atween the Russians and the Turks;
Or if the Swede, before he halt,
Would play anither Charles the twalt:
If Denmark, any body spak o't;
Or Poland, wha had now the tack o't;
How cut-throat Prussian blades were hingin;
How libbet Italy was singin;
If Spaniard, Portuguese, or Swiss,
Were sayin or takin aught amiss:
Or how our merry lads at hame,
In Britain's court kept up the game:
How royal George, the Lord leuk o'er him!
Was managing St Stephen's quorum;

If sleekit Chatham Will was livin,
Or glaikit Charlie got his nieve in;
How daddie Burke the plea was cookin,
If Warren Hastings' neck was yeukin;
How cesses, stents, and fees were rax'd,
Or if bare a—s yet were tax'd;
The news o' princes, dukes, and earls,
Pimps, sharpers, bawds, and opera-girls;
If that daft buckie, Geordie W***s,
Was threshin still at hizzies' tails,
Or if he was grown oughtlins douser,
And no a perfect kintra cooser,
A' this and mair I never heard of;
And but for you I might despair'd of.
So gratefu', back your news I send you,
And pray, a' gude things may attend you!

Ellisland, Monday morning

Tam o' Shanter. A Tale

❧•❀•❧

Of Brownyis and of Bogillis full is this buke.

GAWIN DOUGLAS.

When chapman billies leave the street,
And drouthy neebors, neebors meet,
As market-days are wearing late,
An' folk begin to tak the gate;
While we sit bousing at the nappy,
And getting fou and unco happy,
We think na on the lang Scots miles,
The mosses, waters, slaps, and styles,
That lie between us and our hame,
Whare sits our sulky sullen dame,
Gathering her brows like gathering storm,
Nursing her wrath to keep it warm.

This truth fand honest *Tam o' Shanter*,
As he frae Ayr ae night did canter,
(Auld Ayr, wham ne'er a town surpasses,
For honest men and bonny lasses.)

O *Tam*! hadst thou but been sae wise,
As ta'en thy ain wife *Kate*'s advice!
She tauld thee weel thou was a skellum,
A blethering, blustering, drunken blellum;
That frae November till October,
Ae market-day thou was nae sober;
That ilka melder, wi' the miller,
Thou sat as lang as thou had siller;
That every naig was ca'd a shoe on,
The smith and thee gat roaring fou on;
That at the L—d 's house, even on Sunday,
Thou drank wi' Kirkton Jean till Monday.

316

She prophesied that late or soon,
Thou would be found deep drown'd in Doon;
Or catch'd wi' warlocks in the mirk,
By *Alloway*'s auld haunted kirk.

Ah, gentle dames! it gars me greet,
To think how mony counsels sweet,
How mony lengthen'd sage advices,
The husband frae the wife despises!

But to our tale: Ae market-night,
Tam had got planted unco right;
Fast by an ingle, bleezing finely,
Wi' reaming swats, that drank divinely;
And at his elbow, Souter *Johnny*,
His ancient, trusty, drouthy crony;
Tam lo'ed him like a vera brither;
They had been fou for weeks thegither.
The night drave on wi' sangs and clatter;
And ay the ale was growing better:
The landlady and *Tam* grew gracious,
Wi' favours, secret, sweet, and precious:
The Souter tauld his queerest stories;
The landlord's laugh was ready chorus:
The storm without might rair and rustle,
Tam did na mind the storm a whistle.

Care, mad to see a man sae happy,
E'en drown'd himsel amang the nappy:
As bees flee hame wi' lades o' treasure,
The minutes wing'd their way wi' pleasure:
Kings may be blest, but *Tam* was glorious,
O'er a' the ills o' life victorious!

But pleasures are like poppies spread,
You seize the flower, its bloom is shed;
Or like the snow falls in the river,
A moment white – then melts for ever;
Or like the borealis race,
That flit ere you can point their place;

Or like the rainbow's lovely form
Evanishing amid the storm. –
Nae man can tether time or tide;
The hour approaches *Tam* maun ride;
That hour, o' night's black arch the key-stane,
That dreary hour he mounts his beast in;
And sic a night he taks the road in,
As ne'er poor sinner was abroad in.

The wind blew as 'twad blawn its last;
The rattling showers rose on the blast;
The speedy gleams the darkness swallow'd;
Loud, deep, and lang, the thunder bellow'd:
That night, a child might understand,
The Deil had business on his hand.

Weel mounted on his gray mare, *Meg*,
A better never lifted leg,
Tam skelpit on thro' dub and mire,
Despising wind, and rain, and fire;
Whiles holding fast his gude blue bonnet;
Whiles crooning o'er some auld Scots sonnet;
Whiles glowring round wi' prudent cares,
Lest bogles catch him unawares:
Kirk-Alloway was drawing nigh,
Whare ghaists and houlets nightly cry. –

By this time he was cross the ford,
Whare, in the snaw, the chapman smoor'd;
And past the birks and meikle stane,
Whare drunken *Charlie* brak 's neck-bane;
And thro' the whins, and by the cairn,
Whare hunters fand the murder'd bairn;
And near the thorn, aboon the well,
Whare *Mungo*'s mither hang'd hersel. –
Before him *Doon* pours all his floods;
The doubling storm roars thro' the woods;
The lightnings flash from pole to pole;
Near and more near the thunders roll:

When, glimmering thro' the groaning trees,
Kirk-Alloway seem'd in a bleeze;
Thro' ilka bore the beams were glancing;
And loud resounded mirth and dancing. –

Inspiring bold *John Barleycorn*!
What dangers thou canst make us scorn!
Wi' tippeny, we fear nae evil;
Wi' usquabae, we'll face the devil! –
The swats sae ream'd in *Tammie*'s noddle,
Fair play, he car'd na deils a boddle.
But *Maggie* stood right sair astonish'd,
Till, by the heel and hand admonish'd,
She ventured forward on the light;
And, vow! *Tam* saw an unco sight!
Warlocks and witches in a dance;
Nae cotillion brent new frae *France*,
But hornpipes, jigs, strathspeys, and reels,
Put life and mettle in their heels.
A winnock-bunker in the east,
There sat auld Nick, in shape o' beast;
A towzie tyke, black, grim, and large,
To gie them music was his charge:
He screw'd the pipes and gart them skirl,
Till roof and rafters a' did dirl. –
Coffins stood round, like open presses,
That shaw'd the dead in their last dresses;
And by some devilish cantraip slight
Each in its cauld hand held a light. –
By which heroic *Tam* was able
To note upon the haly table,
A murderer's banes in gibbet airns;
Twa span-lang, wee, unchristen'd bairns;
A thief, new-cutted frae a rape,
Wi' his last gasp his gab did gape;
Five tomahawks, wi' blude red-rusted;
Five scymitars, wi' murder crusted;

A garter, which a babe had strangled;
A knife, a father's throat had mangled,
Whom his ain son o' life bereft,
The grey hairs yet stack to the heft;
Wi' mair o' horrible and awefu',
Which even to name wad be unlawfu'.

Three Lawyers' tongues, turn'd inside out,
Wi' lies seam'd like a beggar's clout;
And Priests' hearts, rotten, black as muck,
Lay stinking, vile, in every neuk. –

As *Tammie* glow'rd, amaz'd, and curious,
The mirth and fun grew fast and furious:
The piper loud and louder blew;
The dancers quick and quicker flew;
They reel'd, they set, they cross'd, they cleekit,
Till ilka carlin swat and reekit,
And coost her duddies to the wark,
And linket at it in her sark!

Now, *Tam*, O *Tam*! had thae been queans,
A' plump and strapping in their teens,
Their sarks, instead o' creeshie flannen,
Been snaw-white seventeen hunder linnen!
Thir breeks o' mine, my only pair,
That ance were plush, o' gude blue hair,
I wad hae gi'en them off my hurdies,
For ae blink o' the bonie burdies!

But wither'd beldams, auld and droll,
Rigwoodie hags wad spean a foal,
Lowping and flinging on a crummock,
I wonder didna turn thy stomach.

But *Tam* kend what was what fu' brawlie,
There was ae winsome wench and wawlie,
That night enlisted in the core,
(Lang after kend on *Carrick* shore;

For mony a beast to dead she shot,
And perish'd mony a bony boat,
And shook baith meikle corn and bear,
And kept the country-side in fear:)
Her cutty sark, o' Paisley harn,
That while a lassie she had worn,
In longitude tho' sorely scanty,
It was her best, and she was vauntie. –
Ah! little kend thy reverend grannie,
That sark she coft for her wee Nannie,
Wi' twa pund Scots, ('twas a' her riches),
Wad ever grac'd a dance of witches!

But here my Muse her wing maun cour;
Sic flights are far beyond her pow'r;
To sing how Nannie lap and flang,
(A souple jade she was, and strang),
And how *Tam* stood, like ane bewitch'd,
And thought his very een enrich'd;
Even Satan glowr'd, and fidg'd fu' fain,
And hotch'd and blew wi' might and main:
Till first ae caper, syne anither,
Tam tint his reason a' thegither,
And roars out, 'Weel done, Cutty-sark!'
And in an instant all was dark:
And scarcely had he Maggie rallied,
When out the hellish legion sallied.

As bees bizz out wi' angry fyke,
When plundering herds assail their byke;
As open pussie's mortal foes,
When, pop! she starts before their nose;
As eager runs the market-crowd,
When 'Catch the thief!' resounds aloud;
So Maggie runs, the witches follow,
Wi' mony an eldritch skreech and hollow.

Ah, *Tam*! Ah, *Tam*! thou'll get thy fairin!
In hell they'll roast thee like a herrin!

In vain thy *Kate* awaits thy comin!
Kate soon will be a woefu' woman!
Now, do thy speedy utmost, Meg,
And win the key-stane* of the brig;
There at them thou thy tail may toss,
A running stream they dare na cross.
But ere the key-stane she could make,
The fient a tail she had to shake!
For Nannie, far before the rest,
Hard upon noble Maggie prest,
And flew at *Tam* wi' furious ettle;
But little wist she Maggie's mettle –
Ae spring brought off her master hale,
But left behind her ain gray tail:
The carlin claught her by the rump,
And left poor Maggie scarce a stump.

Now, wha this tale o' truth shall read,
Ilk man and mother's son, take heed:
Whene'er to drink you are inclin'd,
Or cutty-sarks run in your mind,
Think, ye may buy the joys o'er dear,
Remember Tam o' Shanter's mare.

---

* It is a well known fact that witches, or any evil spirits, have no power to follow a poor wight any farther than the middle of the next running stream. – It may be proper likewise to mention to the benighted traveller, that when he falls in with *bogles*, whatever danger may be in his going forward, there is much more hazard in turning back.

Epigram on Capt. Francis Grose, The Celebrated Antiquary

❦❧❦

The following epigram, written in a moment of festivity by Burns, was so much relished by Grose, that he made it serve as an excuse for prolonging the convivial occasion that gave it birth to a very late hour.

The Devil got notice that GROSE was a-dying,
So whip! at the summons, old Satan came flying;
But when he approach'd where poor FRANCIS lay moaning,
And saw each bed-post with its burden a-groaning,
Astonished! confounded! cry'd Satan, by G—d,
I'll want 'im, ere I take such a d—ble load.

Extempore – on some Commemorations of Thomson

Dost thou not rise, indignant Shade,
  And smile wi' spurning scorn,
When they wha wad hae starv'd thy life,
  Thy senseless turf adorn. –

They wha about thee mak sic fuss
  Now thou art but a name,
Wad seen thee d–mn'd ere they had spar'd
  Ae plack to fill thy wame. –

Helpless, alane, thou clamb the brae,
  Wi' meikle, meikle toil,
And claught th' unfading garland there,
  Thy sair-won, rightful spoil. –

And wear it there! and call aloud,
  This axiom undoubted –
'Wouldst thou hae Nobles' patronage,
  First learn to live without it!'

To whom hae much, shall yet be given,
  Is every Great man's faith;
But he, the helpless, needful wretch,
  Shall lose the mite he hath. –

DUMFRIES

❧❧❧

Here 's a Health to them that 's awa

❧❧❧

Here 's a health to them that 's awa,
Here 's a health to them that 's awa;
And wha winna wish gude luck to our cause,
May never gude luck be their fa'!
It 's gude to be merry and wise,
It 's gude to be honest and true,
It 's gude to support Caledonia's cause,
And bide by the Buff and the Blue.

Here 's a health to them that 's awa,
Here 's a health to them that 's awa;
Here 's a health to Charlie, the chief o' the clan,
Altho' that his band be sma'.
May Liberty meet wi' success!
May Prudence protect her frae evil!
May Tyrants and Tyranny tine i' the mist,
And wander their way to the devil!

Here 's a health to them that 's awa,
Here 's a health to them that 's awa;
Here 's a health to Tammie, the Norland laddie,
That lives at the lug o' the law!
Here 's freedom to him that wad read,
Here 's freedom to him that wad write!
There 's nane ever fear'd that the Truth should be heard,
But they whom the Truth wad indite.

Here 's a health to them that 's awa,
An' here 's to them that 's awa!
Here 's to Maitland and Wycombe! Let wha does na like 'em
Be built in a hole in the wa'!
Here 's timmer that 's red at the heart,
Here 's fruit that is sound at the core;
And may he that wad turn the buff and blue coat
Be turn'd to the back o' the door!

Here 's a health to them that 's awa,
Here 's a health to them that 's awa;
Here 's Chieftan Mcleod, a chieftan worth gowd
Tho' bred amang mountains o' snaw!
Here 's friends on baith sides o' the Forth,
And friends on baith sides o' the Tweed;
And wha wad betray old Albion's right,
May they never eat of her bread!

Ode for General Washington's Birthday

No Spartan tube, no Attic shell,
   No lyre Eolian I awake;
'Tis Liberty's bold note I swell,
   Thy harp, Columbia, let me take.
See gathering thousands, while I sing,
A broken chain, exulting, bring,
   And dash it in a tyrant's face!
And dare him to his very beard,
And tell him, he no more is feared,
No more the Despot of Columbia's race.
A tyrant's proudest insults braved,
They shout, a People freed! They hail an Empire saved.

   Where is Man's godlike form?
Where is that brow erect and bold,
That eye that can, unmoved, behold
The wildest rage, the loudest storm,
That e'er created fury dared to raise!
   Avaunt! thou caitiff, servile, base,
   That tremblest at a Despot's nod,
   Yet, crouching under th' iron rod,
Canst laud the arm that struck th' insulting blow!
   Art thou of man's imperial line?
   Dost boast that countenance divine?
   Each sculking feature answers, No!
   But come, ye sons of Liberty,
   Columbia's offspring, brave as free,
In danger's hour still flaming in the van:
Ye know, and dare maintain, The Royalty of Man.

   Alfred, on thy starry throne,
   Surrounded by the tuneful choir,
The Bards that erst have struck the patriot lyre,
And roused the freeborn Briton's soul of fire,

No more thy England own. –
Dare injured nations form the great design,
   To make detested tyrants bleed?
Thy England execrates the glorious deed!
    Beneath her hostile banners waving,
    Every pang of honor braving,
England in thunders calls – 'The Tyrant's cause is mine!'
That hour accurst, how did the fiends rejoice,
And hell thro' all her confines raise th' exulting voice,
  That hour which saw the generous English name
Linkt with such damned deeds of everlasting shame!

Thee, Caledonia, thy wild heaths among,
Famed for the martial deed, the heaven-taught song,
    To thee, I turn with swimming eyes. –
    Where is that soul of Freedom fled?
    Immingled with the mighty Dead!
Beneath that hallowed turf where WALLACE lies!
Hear it not, Wallace, in thy bed of death!
    Ye babbling winds in silence sweep;
    Disturb not ye the hero's sleep,
    Nor give the coward secret breath. –
Is this the ancient Caledonian form,
Firm as her rock, resistless as her storm?
Shew me that eye which shot immortal hate,
    Blasting the Despot's proudest bearing:
Shew me that arm which, nerved with thundering fate,
    Braved Usurpation's boldest daring!
    Dark-quenched as yonder sinking star,
    No more that glance lightens afar;
That palsied arm no more whirls on the waste of war.

Address to the Tooth-Ache

(*Written by the Author at a time when he was grievously tormented by that Disorder.*)

My curse on your envenom'd stang,
That shoots my tortur'd gums alang,
An' thro' my lugs gies mony a bang
                    Wi' gnawin vengeance;
Tearing my nerves wi' bitter twang,
                    Like racking engines.

A' down my beard the slavers trickle,
I cast the wee stools owre the meikle,
While round the fire the hav'rels keckle,
                    To see me loup;
I curse an' ban, an' wish a heckle
                    Were i' their doup.

Whan fevers burn, or agues freeze us,
Rheumatics gnaw, or colics squeeze us,
Our neebors sympathize, to ease us,
                    Wi' pitying moan;
But thou – the hell o' a' diseases,
                    They mock our groan.

O' a' the num'rous human dools,
Ill har'sts, daft bargains, *cutty-stools*,
Or worthy friends laid i' the mools,
                    Sad sight to see!
The tricks o' knaves, or fash o' fools,
                    Thou bear'st the gree.

Whare'er that place be, priests ca' hell,
Whare a' the tones o' mis'ry yell,
An' plagues in ranked number tell
                    In deadly raw,

Thou, *Tooth-ache*, surely bear'st the bell
          Aboon them a'!

O! thou grim mischief-making chiel,
That gars the notes o' discord squeel,
Till human-kind aft dance a reel
          In gore a shoe thick,
Gie a' the faes o' Scotland's weal
          A TOWMOND'S TOOTH-ACHE!

Poem

Addressed to Mr Mitchell, Collector of Excise, Dumfries.

Friend o' the Poet, tried and leal,
Wha, wanting thee, might beg, or steal:
Alake! Alake! the meikle Deil
   Wi' a' his witches
Are at it, skelpin! jig and reel,
    In my poor pouches.

Fu' fain I, modestly, would hint it,
That ONE POUND, ONE, I sairly want it;
If wi' the hizzie down ye sent it,
   It would be kind;
And while my heart wi' life-blood dunted,
    I'd bear 't in mind.

So may the AULD YEAR gang out moaning,
To see the NEW come, laden, groaning,
With double plenty, o'er the loaning,
   To THEE and THINE;
DOMESTIC PEACE and COMFORT crowning
    The hail DESIGN.

      Hogmanai eve: 1795.
      R. Burns.

POSTSCRIPT

Ye've heard this while how I've been licket,
And by fell Death 'maist nearly nicket;
Grim loon! he gat me by the fecket,
   And sair he sheuk;
But by good luck, I lap a wicket,
    And turn'd a neuk.

But by that HEALTH, I've got a share o't!
And by that LIFE, I'm promis'd mair o't!

My hale and weel I'll take a care o't
    A tentier way:
So fareweel, FOLLY, hilt and hair o't,
    For ance and ay!
                       R. B.

Poem on Life

Addressed to Colonel De Peyster, Dumfries, 1796.

My honored colonel, deep I feel
Your interest in the Poet's weal;
Ah! now sma' heart hae I to speel
   The steep Parnassus,
Surrounded thus by bolus pill,
   And potion glasses.

O what a canty warld were it,
Would pain and care, and sickness spare it;
And fortune favor worth and merit,
   As they deserve:
(And aye a rowth, roast beef and claret;
   Syne wha would starve?)

Dame life, tho' fiction out may trick her,
And in paste gems and frippery deck her;
Oh! flickering, feeble, and unsicker
   I've found her still,
Ay wavering like the willow wicker,
   'Tween good and ill.

Then that curst carmagnole, auld Satan,
Watches, like bawd'rons by a rattan,
Our sinfu' saul to get a claute on
   Wi' felon ire;
Syne, whip! his tail ye'll ne'er cast saut on,
   He 's off like fire.

Ah! Nick, ah Nick it is na fair,
First shewing us the tempting ware,
Bright wines and bonnie lasses rare,
   To put us daft;
Syne weave, unseen, thy spider snare
   O' hell's damned waft.

Poor man the flie, aft bizzes bye,
And aft as chance he comes thee nigh,
Thy auld damned elbow yeuks wi' joy,
          And hellish pleasure;
Already in thy fancy's eye,
          Thy sicker treasure.

Soon heels o'er gowdie! in he gangs,
And like a sheep-head on a tangs,
Thy girning laugh enjoys his pangs
          And murdering wrestle,
As dangling in the wind he hangs
          A gibbet's tassel.

But lest you think I am uncivil,
To plague you with this draunting drivel,
Abjuring a' intentions evil,
          I quat my pen:
The Lord preserve us frae the devil!
          Amen! Amen!

UNDATED

A CODA

ᵔᵕᐯᵕᐯ

The Tree of Liberty

ᵔᵕᐯᵕᐯ

Heard ye o' the tree o' France,
   I watna what 's the name o't;
Around it a' the patriots dance,
   Weel Europe kens the fame o't.
It stands where ance the Bastile stood,
   A prison built by kings, man,
When Superstition's hellish brood
   Kept France in leading strings, man.

Upo' this tree there grows sic fruit,
   Its virtues a' can tell, man;
It raises man aboon the brute,
   It maks him ken himsel, man.
Gif ance the peasant taste a bit,
   He 's greater than a lord, man,
An' wi' the beggar shares a mite
   O' a' he can afford, man.

This fruit is worth a' Afric's wealth,
   To comfort us 'twas sent, man:
To gie the sweetest blush o' health,
   An' mak us a' content, man.
It clears the een, it cheers the heart,
   Maks high and low gude friends, man;
And he wha acts the traitor's part
   It to perdition sends, man.

My blessings aye attend the chiel
   Wha pitied Gallia's slaves, man,
And staw a branch, spite o' the deil,
   Frae yont the western waves, man.
Fair Virtue water'd it wi' care,
   And now she sees wi' pride, man,
How weel it buds and blossoms there,
   Its branches spreading wide, man.

But vicious folks aye hate to see
   The works o' Virtue thrive, man;
The courtly vermin 's banned the tree,
   And grat to see it thrive, man;
King Loui' thought to cut it down,
   When it was unco sma', man;
For this the watchman cracked his crown,
   Cut aff his head and a', man.

A wicked crew syne, on a time,
   Did tak a solemn aith, man,
It ne'er should flourish to its prime,
   I wat they pledged their faith, man.
Awa' they gaed wi' mock parade,
   Like beagles hunting game, man,
But soon grew weary o' the trade
   And wished they'd been at hame, man.

For Freedom, standing by the tree,
   Her sons did loudly ca', man;
She sang a sang o' liberty,
   Which pleased them ane and a', man.
By her inspired, the new-born race
   Soon drew the avenging steel, man;
The hirelings ran – her foes gied chase,
   And banged the despot weel, man.

Let Britain boast her hardy oak,
   Her poplar and her pine, man,
Auld Britain ance could crack her joke,
   And o'er her neighbours shine, man.

But seek the forest round and round,
    And soon 'twill be agreed, man,
That sic a tree can not be found,
    'Twixt London and the Tweed, man.

Without this tree, alake this life
    Is but a vale o' woe, man;
A scene o' sorrow mixed wi' strife,
    Nae real joys we know, man.
We labour soon, we labour late,
    To feed the titled knave, man;
And a' the comfort we're to get
    Is that ayont the grave, man.

Wi' plenty o' sic trees, I trow,
    The warld would live in peace, man;
The sword would help to mak a plough,
    The din o' war wad cease, man.
Like brethren in a common cause,
    We'd on each other smile, man;
And equal rights and equal laws
    Wad gladden every isle, man.

Wae worth the loon wha wadna eat
    Sic halesome dainty cheer, man;
I'd gie my shoon frae aff my feet,
    To taste sic fruit, I swear, man.
Syne let us pray, auld England may
    Sure plant this far-famed tree, man;
And blythe we'll sing, and hail the day
    That gave us liberty, man.

NOTES

Notes begin with reference to the earliest printing of each poem. This does not indicate the text followed, but does make it possible to distinguish between poems seen through the press by Burns himself and those published after his death. A key is supplied below. The number in brackets after each title is that given by Kinsley in his edition and is offered to facilitate the use of Kinsley's voluminous notes, where further information is required. Similarly, Burns's letters are referred to by their numbers in G. Ross Roy's revision (Oxford, 1985) of J. De Lancey Ferguson's edition.

Books containing first printings are as follows:

Chambers   *Life and Works*, ed. Robert Chambers, 1851 and subsequent revisions, including that by William Wallace, 1896.

Cromek   *Reliques of Robert Burns*, ed. R. H. Cromek, 1808.

Cunningham   *Works*, ed. Allan Cunningham, 1834.

Currie   *Works*, ed. James Currie, 1800; 2nd edn 1801.

Edinburgh   *Poems, chiefly in the Scottish Dialect*, by Robert Burns, Edinburgh, 1787, new edn 1793, reprinted 1794.

Kilmarnock   *Poems, chiefly in the Scottish Dialect*, by Robert Burns, Kilmarnock, 1786.

Kinsley   *The Poems and Songs of Robert Burns*, ed. James Kinsley, Oxford, 1968.

SC   *A Select Collection of Original Scotish Airs for the Voice*, ed. George Thomson, in eight parts (1793, 1798, 1799, ?1799, 1802, 1803, 1805, 1818).

SMM   *The Scots Musical Museum*, ed. James Johnson (1787, 1788, 1790, 1792, 1796, 1803).

Stewart   *Poems Ascribed to Robert Burns*, ed. Thomas Stewart, 1801, 2nd edn 1802.

References to OED are to the Oxford English Dictionary, and SND, to the Scottish National Dictionary.

PART ONE: SONGS

BEFORE 1788

O Tibbie I hae seen the day (6)
SMM, 1788, but written much earlier. Burns noted in his own copy of SMM, 'This song I composed about the age of seventeen.'

Corn rigs are bonie (8)
Kilmarnock, 1786, but written before 1782.

John Barleycorn. A Ballad (23)
Edinburgh, 1787. Burns's published note: 'This is partly composed on the plan of an old song known by the same name.' It is clear that he built into his own song verses and scraps that he remembered from the older one. The mythology evoked is ancient: the corn spirit, driven out at the threshing, returns at sowing time. The earliest-known Scottish precedent for Burns's verses is 'Quhy sowld not Allane honorit be' in the Bannatyne MS of 1568. It had several successors.

Mary Morison (30)
Currie, 1800. Hugh MacDiarmid commented (1959) on 'the supreme power of Burns's finest line, "Ye are na Mary Morison"' (quoted in Donald A. Low, *Burns*, Edinburgh, 1986, 1).

In Mauchline there dwells (42)
Kinsley, from Glenriddell MS. Probably written late 1784 or early 1785. Jean Armour, seventeen when she met Burns at the end of 1784, was acknowledged as his wife in April 1788, after bearing him two sets of twins.

O leave novels (43)
Currie, 1800. 'Rob Mossgiel' is the poet, so named from his farm. The novels mentioned are Fielding's *Tom Jones* and *Sir Charles Grandison* by Samuel Richardson.

Green grow the rashes (45)
Edinburgh, 1787.

The rantin dog the daddie o't (80)
SMM, 1790. The woman could be either Elizabeth Paton, who bore Burns a daughter in May 1785, or Jean Armour, whose first offspring by him arrived in September 1786.

faut: 'faulter' was the official term for an offender against Kirk discipline, especially in sexual matters.

groanin maut: drink provided for those attending a childbirth.

Creepie-chair: the famous 'stool of repentance', raised on a pedestal directly facing the pulpit, on which fornicators were punished. Man and woman alike, with uncovered faces, were placed on this for three successive Sundays.

There was a lad (140)
Cromek, 1808.

Ca' the ewes (*A*) (185)
SMM, 1790. Burns by his own account took this from the singing of a clergyman (John Clunie) but 'added some stanzas and mended others'. He produced a second version for SC, also in this selection.

AFTER 1788

I'm o'er young to Marry Yet (195)
SMM, 1788. Burns stated that the chorus was traditional, the rest his own.

McPherson's Farewell (196)
SMM, 1788. Burns averred that this was all his 'excepting the chorus and one stanza' (Letter 644). James Macpherson, a cattle rustler hanged at Banff in 1700, was said himself to have composed the tune to which these words are sung, in lament for being sentenced.

What will I do gin my Hoggie die (198)
SMM, 1788.

Up in the Morning Early (200)
SMM, 1788. Burns noted, 'the chorus is old, the two stanzas are mine'.

To daunton me (209)
SMM, 1788. The theme is medieval. Cf. Dunbar's 'Tretis of the Tua Marriit Wemen and the Wedo'.

O'er the water to Charlie (211)
SMM, 1788. 'Charlie' is, of course, Prince Charles Edward Stewart, 'The Young Pretender'.

Up and warn a' Willie (212)

SMM, 1788. Here Burns 'mends' a common song theme. At Sherriffmuir, near Dunblane, on 13 November 1715, the climax of the Jacobite rebellion saw the Earl of Mar's men line up against Hanoverian forces led by the Duke of Argyll. The left of each army was routed by the other's right, but Argyll was able to hold the field.

whigs: this wonderfully confusing term originally derived from the cries of Galloway drovers ('whiggam! whiggam!') herding cattle to market in Edinburgh. Since the south-west heavily supported the Presbyterian, Covenanting cause in the seventeenth-century religious struggles, 'whig' came to mean 'anti-Royalist'. But after the Revolution of 1688-9, its application in British politics broadened at last to include generally all those who supported the Hanoverian settlement and the Whig oligarchy, which before long came to dominate politics. Burns uses it here to mean 'Hanoverian', but in his Ayrshire satires employs it in a narrower sense, identifying it with strict, old-fashioned Presbyterianism. However, the Foxite faction he supported in verse were now, politically, the Whigs, following the fragmentation of the old Whig oligarchy after the accession of George III in 1760.

And I'll kiss thee yet, yet (215)

SMM, 1788.

Rattlin, roarin Willie (216)

SMM, 1788.

I love my Jean (227)

SMM, 1790. Written for Jean Armour after she became Mrs Burns.

O, were I on Parnassus Hill (228)

SMM, 1790. Nith is a river in Dumfriesshire, Corsincon a hill in Ayrshire visible from Ellisland.

Whistle o'er the lave o't (235)

SMM, 1790. In the medieval *chanson de malmarie* tradition.

Tam Glen (236)

SMM, 1790.
gude hunder marks ten: about £700 Scots, then equivalent to £55 sterling.

But, if it 's ordain'd: Burnsian fun with the Calvinist idea of predestination.
Valentines' dealing: sweethearts chosen by lot on St Valentine's Day.

Auld lang syne (240)
SMM, 1796. Burns said he had taken one of his drafts of this down from 'an old man's singing' (Letter 586). There were many existing variants on the theme, and there is no hard evidence that Burns's versions contain anything wholly original. The tune for which Burns wrote it, cited in SMM, differs from that in SC, 1799, which is universally associated with the words today. Burns's most famous single song exposes with especial acuteness the difficulty of separating his individual contribution from the tradition in which he lived and wrote.

My bony Mary (242)
SMM, 1790. Burns claimed all but the first half-stanza as his own.
Lieth: as in Kinsley. Leith is the port of Edinburgh.

Louis what reck I by thee (248)
SMM, 1796. Probably written on Jean Armour's joining Burns at Ellisland in December 1788. 'Geordie' is George III, nominal ruler of the world's greatest naval power; 'Louis' (XVI) of France was at this date in considerable trouble.

Robin shure in hairst (251)
SMM, 1803. Robin Ainslie was a womanizing law student whom Burns met in Edinburgh in 1787; the quills and pen-knife in the last stanza are tools of the legal profession.

Afton Water (257)
SMM, 1792. Afton is a stream that joins the Nith near New Cumnock in Ayrshire.

Willie brew'd a peck o' maut (268)
SMM, 1790. An original contribution to the Bacchanalian tradition, prompted by a meeting with two friends who were schoolteachers – William Nicol (1744–97) and Allan Masterton, who wrote the tune.

Ay waukin O (287)
SMM, 1790.

Lassie lie near me (290)
SMM, 1790.

My love she 's but a lassie yet (293)
SMM, 1790.

There's a youth in this City (300)
SMM, 1790. Burns claimed that only the first four lines were traditional.

John Anderson my Jo (302)
SMM, 1790. The impotence of ageing husbands is a traditional theme, and versions of this song existed that exploited it for bawdy humour. Burns turned it round to tender sentiment.

Awa whigs awa (303)
SMM, 1790. Whigs here are anti-Jacobites.

Merry hae I been teethin a heckle (305)
SMM, 1790. In the popular tradition of tinker songs with sexual resonance.

The Battle of Sherra-moor (308)
SMM, 1790. For Sherriffmuir (1715), see notes to 'Up and warn a' Willie' above. Here, Burns built on an earlier broadside, a dialogue between two shepherds, by one Barclay.

Ken ye ought o' Captain Grose? (322)
Currie, 1801. For Grose, see notes below to 'On the Late Captain Grose's Peregrinations' and 'Tam o' Shanter'. Burns's model is an oyster-dredging ('dreg') song from the river Forth, and the tune is said to be good for rowing to. The chorus is dog Latin.

There'll never be peace till Jamie comes hame (326)
SMM, 1792. James VII, or his son James, 'The Old Pretender'.

The Banks o' Doon (*A*) and (*B*) (328)
The first version, printed by Cromek, 1808, was sent by Burns in a letter (441) of March 1791. The second, in SMM, 1792, had been revised for publication and set to a different air.

Ae fond kiss (337)
SMM, 1792. Sent in a letter (486) of 27 December 1791 to 'Clarinda' – Mrs Agnes McLehose, a genteel Edinburgh lady with whom Burns had been conducting a sentimental affair since meeting her in December 1787.

O saw ye bonie Lesley (339)
SC, 1798. The subject was a Miss Lesley Baillie, of Mayville, Ayrshire.

My Tochers the Jewel (345)
SMM, 1792. Burns wrote this from traditional fragments.

I do confess thou art sae fair (349)
SMM, 1792. Burns worked on a poem 'To His Forsaken Mistress' by the talented Sir Robert Aytoun (1570–1638), which he found in James Watson's *Collection of Scots Poems* (1711). He wrote in his interleaved copy of SMM, 'I think I have improved the simplicity of the sentiments by giving them a Scots dress.'

It is na, Jean, thy bonie face (354)
SMM, 1792. Written for Jean Armour, Mrs Burns.

The bonny wee thing (357)
SMM, 1792.

The weary pund o' tow (360)
SMM, 1792.
At last her feet . . . o'er the knowe: she was taken to be buried.

I hae a wife o' my ain (361)
SMM, 1792. Burns refurbishes traditional verses.

When she cam ben she bobbed (362)
SMM, 1792. Burns again reworks an old song. A 'Collier-lassie' is a coal-miner's daughter.

O, for ane and twenty Tam (363)
SMM, 1792.

Bessy and her spinning wheel (365)
SMM, 1792.

Ye Jacobites by name (371)
SMM, 1792. The words may be wholly or largely traditional. As Thomas Crawford points out (*Burns: A Study of the Poems and Songs*, Edinburgh,

1960, reprinted 1978, 240), the song, at face value anti-Jacobite, is bitterly ironical. The brutal advice from the winning side to 'leave a Man undone/To his fate' is offensive to moral instinct.

Song – Sic a wife as Willie's wife (373)
SMM, 1792.

Such a parcel of rogues in a nation (375)
SMM, 1792. Subject and refrain appear in many variants subsequent to the Union of 1707, but Burns makes of his sources an exceptionally powerful assessment of the event.

Hey Ca' thro' (381)
SMM, 1792. The place names are in Fife, which Burns had visited in 1787. He may have learnt the song there and simply transmitted it to SMM.

The De'il's awa wi' th' Exciseman (386)
SMM, 1792. Burns jokes against his own job.

The lea-rig (392)
Currie, 1800. An earlier version in SMM, 1787, was attributed by Burns there to Fergusson. This in turn was probably built upon an earlier fragment.

Duncan Gray (394)
SC, 1798.

Here awa', there awa' (396)
SC, 1793. Modelled on an earlier song. He offered both to Thomson for SC: the editor chose Burns's version.

O poortith cauld, and restless love (398)
SC, 1798.

O, Logan, sweetly didst thou glide (409)
SC, 1803. Earlier lyrics to this tune were bawdy, but Burns found the melody appropriate, as he explained to Thomson in June 1793 (Letter 566), to 'the plaintive indignation of some swelling, suffering heart, fired at the tyrannic strides of some Public Destroyer'. At this time six European powers were allied against Revolutionary France, which may have impressed Burns more than the movement towards Terror in Paris.

O whistle, and I'll come to ye, my lad (420)
SC, 1799. Based on a traditional fragment.

Robert Bruce's March to Bannockburn (425)
Morning Chronicle, 8 May 1794; SC, 1799; SMM, 1803. Burns was always enthusiastic about Scotland's fight for freedom under Wallace and Bruce. But he wrote to Thomson (Letter 582, end of August 1793) that his inspiration in this case sprang from the 'accidental recollection of that glorious struggle . . . associated with the glowing ideas of some other struggles of the same nature, *not quite so ancient*'. The air 'Hey tutti taiti', which Burns had in mind, was by tradition Bruce's march at Bannockburn.

A red red Rose (453)
SMM, 1796, but see below. There are chapbook models for almost every line of this song. For instance, compare the last stanza with 'The True Lover's Farewell', published in 1792:

> Fare you well, my own true love,
> And fare you well for a while,
> And I will be sure to return back again,
> If I go ten thousand mile.

This itself echoes an English broadside ballad of *c.* 1690. Burns told Alexander Cunningham in November 1794 that the song was *in its entirety* 'a simple old Scots song which I had pickt up in this country', and which he had passed on to the musician Urbani for setting (Letter 642). Urbani duly published it, as collected by a 'celebrated Scot's poet' in a *Selection of Scots Songs* (April 1794). If we trust Burns's word, this wonderful set of verses is the 'simple' and 'wild' production of popular tradition, though perhaps feeding on printed sources.

Ca' the yowes to the knowes (B) (456)
Kinsley, from Dalhousie MS, as offered to Thomson (Letter 636) in September 1794 – a revised version of the song published in SMM, 1790.
Clouden: a tributary of the river Nith.
silent towers: Lincluden Abbey.

Contented wi' little (471)
SC, 1799.

For a' that and a' that (482)
Glasgow Magazine, August 1795; SC, 1805. The air had been turned to both bawdy and Jacobite uses.

The Dumfries Volunteers (484)
Edinburgh Courant, 4 May 1795; SMM, 1803. Written while Burns was helping to organize Volunteer forces to resist French invasion.

Scotish Ballad (503)
SC, 1799.

Hey for a lass wi' a tocher (516)
SC, 1799.

The lovely lass o' Inverness (554)
SMM, 1796. Laments the rout of the Jacobite clans at Drumossie (Culloden) Moor. Burns seems to have refined old words and set them to another air.

As I stood by yon roofless tower (555)
SMM, 1796. The 'roofless tower' is Lincluden Abbey at Maxwelltown, near Dumfries. The chorus and the last two stanzas may relate to Burns's reaction to Britain's attempts to destroy the French Republic.

Comin thro' the rye (560)
SMM, 1796. Burns reworks a traditional theme.

Charlie he 's my darling (562)
SMM, 1796. Burns's distillation and improvement of a long broadside ballad. 'Charlie' is Prince Charles Edward Stewart.

For the sake o' Somebody (566)
SMM, 1796. 'Somebody' in such a context was often a Jacobite reference to Charles Edward Stewart.

The cardin o't (567)
SMM, 1796.

Tibbie Fowler (569)
SMM, 1796. A refinement of traditional material found in fragments.
Tintock: a hill in Lanarkshire.

I'll ay ca' in by yon town (574)
SMM, 1796. Again, written from traditional fragments.

Bannocks o' bear-meal (581)
SMM, 1796. Burns's version of a theme associated with several Jacobite songs.

It was a' for our rightfu' king (589)
SMM, 1796. Burns's reworking of a chapbook ballad, 'Molly Stewart'. Though
this source is *c.* 1746, the song may be construed as referring to the supporters of
James VII's campaign in Ireland in 1690 after he had lost the throne of England.

My Lady's gown there's gairs upon't (597)
SMM, 1803.
Cassillis: an ancient noble family in Ayrshire.

Oh wert thou in the cauld blast (524)
Currie, 1801. We print this out of Kinsley's order because, although not quite
Burns's last song, it is one of the very latest, and one of the finest. It is said to
have been written (as other poems certainly were) for Jessy Lewars (1778–
1855), sister of a friend in the Excise and the woman who nursed Burns in
his last sickness.

PART TWO: POEMS, EPISTLES, EPIGRAMS

BEFORE 1784: LOCHLIE AND MOUNT OLIPHANT

Winter, A Dirge (10)
Kilmarnock, 1786. Melancholy contemplation of nature often occurs in Burns's
early work. This may be related to his Calvinistic background and the
anxieties it involved, but also to literary sources such as *The Seasons* by the

Scottish poet James Thomson (1700–1748) and the work of Edward Young (1683–1765), whose *Ocean: An Ode* is echoed in l. 9.

Extempore (18)
Currie, 1800. Dated April 1782.

The Death and Dying Words of Poor Mailie (24)
Kilmarnock, 1786. The mock-testament has a long history in Scottish letters. See, for example, David Lindsay's sixteenth-century 'Testament of our Soverane Lordis Papyngo' (parrot).

Poor Mailie's Elegy (25)
Kilmarnock, 1786. The six-line stanza used here, the commonest in Burns's poetry, was so popular in eighteenth-century Scotland that Allan Ramsay dubbed it 'Standart Habbie', from its use in a seventeenth-century comic elegy 'The Life and Death of Habbie Simson, the piper of Kilbarchan' by Robert Sempill of Beltrees (?1590–?1660). It is well discussed by Low (*Burns*, 48–52). Doon and Aire are rivers in Ayrshire.

1784–5: MOSSGIEL

Mock Epitaphs: On Wee Johnie, For G. H. Esq; (34, 37)
Kilmarnock, 1786. 'Wee Johnie' was probably John Wilson, schoolmaster and session clerk of Tarbolton. 'G. H.' was Burns's friend Gavin Hamilton, fellow freemason, lawyer in Mauchline and a major influence on the poet's life.

Address to the Unco Guid, or the Rigidly Righteous (39)
Edinburgh, 1787. Date of composition is uncertain, but this may well be the first of Burns's satirical assaults on the foibles he sees as attendant upon traditional, Auld Licht Calvinism. The doctrine of predestination leads the 'Unco Guid' to the assumption that they are saved while lesser mortals are damned. Burns counters this by appeal to ideas of natural and supernatural benevolence, compatible with the tone of David Hume and other 'Enlightened' Scottish philosophers and with the literary convention of 'sentimentality'. This aligned him with the views of the more generous New Licht wing within the Church.

Epistle to J. Ranken (47)

Kilmarnock, 1786. John Rankine (d. 1810) was a tenant farmer at Adamhill, Tarbolton. The epistle uses hunting as a source of sexual symbolism – this was traditional – and was occasioned by the pregnancy of Elizabeth Paton, a servant girl at Lochlie, who bore Burns a daughter on 22 May 1785.

Korah-like: see Numbers 16:32 – 'And the earth opened her mouth and swallowed . . . all the men that appertained unto Korah.'

Blue-gown badge: from the Middle Ages, the Blue-gown was the costume of a class of paupers with a special licence to beg denied to the ordinary poor. Burns compares this to the spiritual privilege assumed by the 'lads in *black*'.

Bunker's hill: a battle in the American War of Independence, 17 June 1775.

Poacher-Court: an allusion to the kirk session and its strictures against fornication. Culprits, male and female, were set for three consecutive Sundays on a raised seat, known as the 'stool of repentance', wearing black sackcloth and facing the preacher. Financial pledges against future behaviour were also exacted.

gat the whissle o' my groat: to play a losing game.

buckskin: a term for 'American'. Kinsley suggests that the 'kye' could be black slaves.

yellow George: the guinea fine.

pennyworths again is fair: you shall have a fair return, good value for money.

Verses (49)

Stewart, 1801.

The breaking of ae point: cf. James 2:10 – 'For whosoever shall keep the whole law, and yet offend in one point, he is guilty of all.'

whaup: the curlew is known by its wailing note.

Epistle to Davie, a Brother Poet (51)

Kilmarnock, 1786. David Sillar (1760–1830) was a native of Tarbolton and a member, with Burns, of its Batchelor's Club (a debating society). He was at various times teacher, grocer, bankrupt and, eventually, a successful magistrate at Irvine. A noted fiddler, he published his *Poems* at Kilmarnock in 1789. Addressing him, Burns uses a stanza form he would have found in *The Cherrie and the Slae* by Alexander Montgomerie, published in 1597 and reprinted many times.

The sentiment in the fifth stanza is central to Burns's philosophy. Pride, material and spiritual, is contrasted unfavourably to the essential honesty of those who obey the heart.

'*Mair spier na, nor fear na*': cf. Allan Ramsay, 'The Poet's Wish'. Echoes of Ramsay are so frequent in Burns's verse that they will not normally be noted here.

tenebrific: 'tending to darkness' – this is the earliest use of the word cited in OED.

But least: but lest.

The Holy Tulzie (52)

'The first of my poetic offspring that saw the light', according to Burns (Letter 125), who circulated it in ms in late 1784 or early 1785. But it was not printed in his lifetime. It appeared in different versions in 1796 and 1799 and Stewart, 1801. Kinsley's text, used here, follows the Egerton MS.

Alexander Moodie (1728–99), minister at Riccarton, and John Russel (*c.* 1740–1817), incumbent at Kilmarnock, fell into furious public dispute over parish boundaries, though both were of the Auld Licht faction (see note to 'Address to the Unco Guid' above). This refused to accept the Patronage Act of 1712, which had restored to lay patrons ('Lairds', st. iv) the right to present ministers to vacant parishes. Duncan, Peebles and Auld were Auld Licht clergymen; the last, minister at Mauchline, was an especially close enemy of Burns. Dalrymple, McGill, McQuhey, the Shaws, Wodrow, M'Math and Smith were all 'Moderate' (cf. New Licht) ministers.

Epigraph: Pope, *The Dunciad* (1742), iii.173–4.

Ariminian: Arminius of Leyden (d. 1609) was an opponent of Calvinism. The New Lichts were 'smeared' as 'Arminians'.

Common Sense: a less innocent-seeming term in Burns's day than now. The 'Common Sense' school of 'Enlightened' Scottish philosophers countered David Hume's scepticism without supporting religious bigotry. In the words of John Wilson (one of two Scots who signed the US Declaration of Independence in 1776, and also one of the chief authors of the US Constitution of 1787): 'This philosophy will teach us that first principles are in themselves apparent; that to make nothing self-evident is to take away all possibility of knowing anything; that without first principles there can be neither reason nor reasoning ... Consequently, all sound reasoning must rest ultimately on the principles of common sense' (quoted in David Daiches *et al.*, eds., *A Hotbed of Genius*, Edinburgh, 1986, 149). But 'Common Sense' here is not the inert, lowest common denominator of ideology it has since become. G. E. Davie describes thus the conception of Common Sense held by Thomas Reid (1710–96), the leader of the school: 'Common sense knowledge is ... knowledge of bodies which we could not get from the senses when they are in isolation from one another but which can be got from the senses when they are employed in co-operation so as to enable us to compare them together ... [This] gives us a

knowledge of aspects of things which in a genuine way transcends the senses
and which thus is rightly called intellectual knowledge' (*The Crisis of the
Democratic Intellect*, Edinburgh, 1986, 187).

Holy Willie's Prayer (53)

Stewart, 1801. William Fisher (1739–1809) was a farmer and elder of the
parish of Mauchline. Burns's satire was probably written early in 1785.
Epigraph: Pope, *The Rape of the Lock*, iv.64.
Argument: Gavin Hamilton, Burns's lawyer friend, had been cited in August
1784, before the annual communion at Mauchline, for neglecting public
worship. In January 1785, the 'Moderate' Presbytery of Ayr ordered the
erasure of the Mauchline session minutes against Hamilton. For ample annota-
tion of the biblical and theological references with which this text is loaded,
see Kinsley. Willie is an orthodox Auld Licht Calvinist, accepting that God
has predestinated his 'elect' to eternal life, the rest to damnation, immovably
from all eternity.

Epitaph on Holy Willie (54)

Stewart, 1801.
left-hand road: sinister, leading to Hell.

Death and Doctor Hornbook. A True Story (55)

Edinburgh, 1787. John Wilson (*c.* 1751–1839), schoolmaster in Tarbolton
from 1781, sought to set up as a physician with the aid of a few medical books.
The standard tool of education at primary level was a sheet of paper with the
basics on it, mounted on wood and protected by transparent horn. Hence
'hornbook' is a nickname for a schoolmaster.
Buchan: Hornbook's handbook was really 'state of the art'. *Domestic Medicine*,
by the Edinburgh-trained William Buchan (1729–1805), provided sensible
medical advice for the general public. First published in 1769, it ran to some
twenty-two editions by 1822 and was translated into all the major European
languages.

On Tam the Chapman (56)

Aldine edition, 1839.

Epistle to J. Lapraik, An Old Scotch Bard (57)

Kilmarnock, 1786. John Lapraik (1727–1807), a farmer, turned to writing
verse when imprisoned for debt in Ayr in 1785.

Fasteneen: Shrove Tuesday evening. The 'rocking' was a convivial evening visit to which the 'rock', or distaff, was taken so that spinning could continue.

ae sang: Lapraik's 'When I upon thy bosom lean'.

Pope ... Steele ... Beattie: Alexander Pope (1688–1744) was the dominant English poet of Burns's century. Richard Steele (1672–1729) was better known for elegant prose. James Beattie (1735–1803) was professor of moral philosophy at Aberdeen University, venerated by moderate Christians for his attacks on Hume: he was an important poet in *English* who wrote a book against *Scotticisms*, but nevertheless influenced Burns.

ALLAN: Allan Ramsay (1685–1758) was immensely influential, both as editor and poet, in the revival of Scots as a literary medium.

FERGUSON: Robert Fergusson (1750–74). See note to 'On Fergusson' below. His vigorous poetry in Scots broke much new ground and provided Burns with inspiration and direction in his own career. As with Ramsay, echoes of his poetry in Burns's are so frequent that we rarely note them.

kirs'n him: christen, i.e. dilute with water.

To the Same (58)

Kilmarnock, 1786.

Baillie: 'a town magistrate next in rank to the Provost' (SND).

cits: derogatory abbreviation of 'citizens' in Augustan poetry, now cordially applied to the Citizens Theatre, Glasgow.

the ragged Nine: the Muses.

Their worthless ... shun the light: Burns here flirts with the notion of metempsychosis, a classical one he might have found in well-known verse by Dryden and Pope.

To W. Simpson, Ochiltree (59)

Kilmarnock, 1786. William Simson (1758–1815) was schoolmaster at Ochiltree and then Cumnock.

in a creel: 'creeling' was a Scottish custom by which, after a wedding-night, a creel (basket) full of stones was tied to the groom's back. The haste, or otherwise, with which his wife helped relieve him was considered a sign of his success – or otherwise – in consummating the marriage. Burns parallels this test with that of his poetic prowess relative to Ramsay *et al*.

Allan ... Ferguson: Allan Ramsay and Robert Fergusson. See notes to 'Epistle to J. Lapraik' above. Fergusson worked in the commissionary office at one penny per page transcribed, and Burns clearly associates this poor pay with his early death.

COILA: Kyle, the area of Ayrshire in which Burns was born. See his note to 'The Vision'.

New Holland: Australia.

Magellan: the straits between the Atlantic and Pacific, discovered by Ferdinand Magellan in 1520.

WALLACE: Sir William Wallace (?1272–1305), Scottish patriot of the Wars of Independence, was a countryman who took up the Scottish cause while the nobility stoof aloof; he appealed to both Burns's patriotism and his democratic impulses.

guid, fat braxies: braxy is a fatal disease in sheep, but its victims, remaining edible, were a welcome supplement to the shepherd's diet.

Postscript: this is where Burns most explicitly places the confrontation between the Auld and New Lichts (see note above to 'Address to the Unco Guid') in the context of the great cleavage in human thought between religion and science, dogma and reason, which began during the Renaissance.

new-light and Burns's note: in 1740 Dr Taylor published *The Scripture Doctrine of Original Sin Proposed to free and candid examination*, asserting the need to interpret the Bible in the light of reason.

plain, braid lallans: Burns associates Lowland Scots ('lallans') with a pre-rational cast of mind.

Frae less to mair ...: there had been religious dispute and persecution 'in monie lands' in the seventeenth century.

bure sic hands: fought so strongly.

took the sands: took to the wilderness, fled.

A Poet's Welcome to his love-begotten Daughter (60)

Stewart, 1801. Addressed to Burns's daughter Elizabeth, born to Elizabeth Paton on 22 May 1785. Burns provided for her financially, and was prepared to make her part of his family after he married Jean Armour.

The Vision (62)

Kilmarnock, 1786. For this poem's complex textual history, see Kinsley. Crawford has a long and convincing discussion of this work (*Burns*, 182–92). Burns told his friend Mrs Dunlop (Letter 219) that he took the idea of 'Coila' from Alexander Ross's muse 'Scota' in the latter's poem *Helenore* (1768).

Curlers: curling is a sport, originally Scottish, played with heavy stones on ice – outdoors in Burns's time. It is traditionally known as the 'roaring game'.

flingin-tree: the part of the flail that strikes the grain.

her robe: tartan, symbolic of ancient Scottish traditions, was proscribed from 1746, after the Battle of Culloden, until 1782.

ancient BOROUGH: Ayr.

Suthron: traditional term for the English.

COUNTRY's SAVIOUR: Sir William Wallace. See notes above to 'To W.

Simpson'. Wallace was an Ayrshire man. One of the earliest influences on Burns had been the medieval poet Blind Hary's *Wallace* in an edition of 1722.

And He whom ruthless Fates: Kinsley believes this to be a reference to Sir Thomas Wallace Dunlop, eldest son of Burns's friend Mrs Dunlop, who was forced by debts in 1783 to sell his estate at Craigie and died in England in 1786.

wild, romantic grove: the Lord Justice Clerk whose seat was at Barskimming was Sir Thomas Miller, Bt (1717–89), dedicated in his spare time to landscape gardening.

BRYDON's brave Ward: William Fullarton (1754–1808) travelled to Europe in the care of Patrick Brydone. He became soldier, politician and notable agricultural 'improver'.

the great Genius: here, the guiding spirit of the nation.

FULLARTON ... DEMPSTER ... BEATTIE: for Fullarton, see above. George Dempster (1732–1818) was another agricultural 'improver' and an MP much admired for his 'independent mind'. James Beattie's long poem *The Minstrel* was written in 1771–4. He was also praised for his attack on Hume's scepticism in his *Essay on the Nature and Immutability of Truth* (1770).

Thomson ... Shenstone ... Gray: noted poets in English (though James Thomson was a Border Scot). There is no need to doubt Burns's genuine admiration. But the close of this poem is an assertion of Burns's own genius cloaked in modesty. This is in a longstanding tradition – cf. the 'Remonstrance to the King' by James IV's great court poet, William Dunbar.

Potosi's mine: in Bolivia, a great source of silver.

Epistle to John Goldie in Kilmarnock (63)

Stewart, 1802, and Cromek, 1808, printed parts only. Kinsley's full text is from the Glenriddell MS. Goldie (1717–1809) was a cabinet-maker and wine merchant as well as amateur theologian. Burns's epistle was prompted by Goldie's publications, notably *Essays on Various Important Subjects Moral and Divine* (1780), which put forward a liberal position and offended the Auld Lichts.

whigs: see notes above to 'Up and warn a' Willie'. Here, the word denotes Auld Lichts.

Taylor: see notes above to 'To W. Simpson'.

A toom tar-barrel: presumably Burns is referring to a variant of the old punishment of standing barelegged in a tub of water at the church door.

'mang hands: at intervals.

see a styme: see the least, tiny thing.

Man was Made to Mourn, A Dirge (64)
Kilmarnock, 1786. Echoes of notable recent poems in English by Shenstone, Young, Blair and Thomson make this, on the one hand, an exercise in conventional eighteenth-century discourse. On the other, the note of disgust over class pride is characteristically Burnsian.

Third Epistle to J. Lapraik (67)
Cromek, 1808.
jads frae heathen hills: the Muses.
Till kye be gaun: till after harvest, when the herdsman no longer needs to keep livestock from the crops.
RAB THE RANTER: the name of the singer in Francis Sempill's song 'Maggie Lauder', where his piper's chanter has clear phallic connotations.

To the Rev. John M'Math (68)
Cromek, 1808. M'Math (d. 1825) was a New Licht minister at Tarbolton.
gown, an' ban': the dress of the clergy.
douse black bonnet: as worn by elders.
Gaun: Gavin Hamilton. See 'Holy Willie's Prayer', 'Extempore – to Mr Gavin Hamilton' and 'A Dedication to Gavin Hamilton' and notes.

To a Mouse (69)
Kilmarnock, 1786.
A daimen-icker in a thrave: David Murison of SND (in Donald A. Low, ed., *Critical Essays on Robert Burns*, London and Boston, 1974, 63) notes that Burns here uses no fewer than three words peculiar to Kyle, a 'debatable land' between the dialect regions of Strathclyde and Galloway. It means 'occasional ear of corn in a measure equivalent to two stooks of corn, or twenty-four sheaves'.
I'll get a blessin: Low (*Burns*, 44) points out that the recollection of Deuteronomy 24:19 here associates the mouse with 'the stranger . . . the fatherless and . . . the widow': charity towards these is blessed by the Lord.
Still, thou art blest: Burns echoes Samuel Johnson's tale, *Rasselas* (1759), ch. 2.

The Holy Fair (70)
Kilmarnock, 1786. The occasion (at Mauchline) is the annual parish communion day, which in country districts was combined with the merrymaking of the fair, as in pre-Reformation holy-days. The celebration of the excesses of such gatherings is also of medieval provenance. Ramsay, in 1721, had printed the two most famous Scottish precedents, 'Chrystis Kirk on the Grene' and

'Peblis to the Play', both found in sixteenth-century mss. Fergusson had adopted the 'Chrystis Kirk' stanza for 'Hallow-Fair' and 'Leith Races', providing Burns with recent and first-rate precedents in form and content. But the development of the central tension between religious and secular aspects of the occasion is all Burns's own.

Epigraph: Tom Brown's play of 1704, *The Stage Beaux Toss'd in a Blanket; or, Hypocrisie Alamode*.

FUN: Fergusson has Mirth as companion in 'Leith Races': Burns adds Hypocrisy and Superstition.

Black-bonnet: once worn by the Covenanters, now a sign of Auld Licht opinion.

Racer-Jess: Janet Gibson, the simpleton daughter of 'Poosie Nansie', the inn-keeper.

Sawnie: so named in ms, but not in the Kilmarnock edition, 'Sawnie' was Alexander Moodie, a fire-and-brimstone Auld Licht preacher. See 'The Holy Tulzie' and notes.

Hornie: the devil.

cantharidian plaisters: Cantharides ('Spanish Fly') was used medicinally or as an aphrodisiac.

Smith: George Smith (d. 1823), minister of Galston and New Licht 'Moderate', is not named in ms or printed text, but is a convincing suggestion by Kinsley. For Auld and New Lichts, see note to 'Address to the Unco Guid' above. Despite Burns's sympathy with the New, he reports the crowd's lack of interest in Smith's moral instructions, by contrast to the spellbinding effect of Moodie's 'tidings', and the jibe at 'English style' may hint that Burns felt such sensible stuff to be out of place at the fair.

Peebles: an Auld Licht preacher, William Peebles. He never forgave Burns.

Miller: Alexander Miller, obviously seen as a closet 'Moderate'.

Russel: John Russel, minister of Kilmarnock. See 'The Holy Tulzie' and notes.

Clinkumbell: Burns owed this word for 'town crier' to the chapbook-writer Dougal Graham (Murison, in Low, ed., *Critical Essays*).

The Twa Dogs. A Tale (71)

Kilmarnock, 1786. Burns's favourite dog, Luath, died in 1784 and the poet, according to his brother Gilbert, resolved to produce a poetic memento. Henryson's *Moral Fables* provide a fifteenth-century Scottish instance of dialogue between animals. Fergusson's 'Mutual Complaint of Plainstanes and Causey', in octosyllabic couplets, was a more immediate influence.

auld king COIL: imaginary eponymous king of Kyle.

Ceasar: the classically named canine gentleman is a Newfoundland, of a breed recently introduced to Scotland.

Luath: in giving his collie this name Burns shows, as he does elsewhere, that James Macpherson's 'translations' of 'Ossian's' ancient Gaelic poetry, published in the 1760s, had made an impression on him.

lord knows how lang: this, however, hints that he was sceptical about their authenticity.

tight in thack an' raep: safe in comfort and security.

a factor's snash: Burns claimed that this passage refers to the experience of his own family in his youth (Letter 125).

patronage: see notes above to 'The Holy Tulzie'.

Some rascal: the factor again – landowner's agent and immediate persecutor of the cotter.

Fient haet o' them: none of them.

devil's pictur'd beuks: playing-cards.

The Cotter's Saturday Night (72)

Kilmarnock, 1786. Burns uses the Spenserian stanza, as rediscovered in the eighteenth century and used by Thomson and Beattie (see notes above to 'The Vision'), Scottish poets who wrote in English. At the same time flourished the literary cult of the worthy rustic, typically celebrated in such meditative language as we find in Burns's epigraph here, from Thomas Gray's *Elegy Written in a Country Churchyard*. Besides these three writers, Burns echoes Milton, Pope, Shenstone and the Bible. But, as so often, Fergusson provided the most important precedent. In 'The Farmer's Ingle' (1773) he had used Scots in the Spenserian stanza while praising rustic worth.

   This was long the most popular (or, which is not quite the same thing, most praised) of Burns's poems. For a defence of its morality against present-day taste, which finds the poem mawkish, see Crawford, *Burns*, 174–82.

My lov'd . . . friend: for Robert Aitken, see 'Holy Willie's Prayer'.

Dundee . . . Martyrs . . . Elgin: psalm-tunes.

'*An honest man . . . work of GOD*': the line is from Pope's *Essay on Man*, iv. 248, slightly misquoted (should be 'noblest').

Halloween (73)

Kilmarnock, 1786. This poem uses the 'Chrystis Kirk' stanza, like 'The Holy Fair'. As his own notes to it show, Burns's antiquarian impulse was well developed before he met Captain Grose (see notes below to 'On the Late Captain Grose's Peregrinations' and 'Tam o' Shanter') or the Edinburgh literati. The detailed recording of complex and vanishing social traditions foreshadows Burns's later commitment to preserving Scottish song.

Epigraph: Oliver Goldsmith, *The Deserted Village* (1770), ii.251–4.

Colean: Culzean Castle at Kirkoswald in Ayrshire.

Sherra-moor: battle of 1715. See notes to 'Up and warn a' Willie' above.

hoy't: to cry 'hoy' – to summon or encourage.

timmer-propt for thrawin: propped with lengths of timber to prevent warping.

Leezie's heart maist lap the hool: Leezie's heart was in her mouth.

Mar's-year: the Earl of Mar led the Jacobite Rising of 1715.

So'ns: left-over oats, mixed with water and left to sour somewhat, produced a paste used in puddings.

The Auld Farmer's New-year-morning Salutation to his Auld Mare, Maggie (75)

Kilmarnock, 1786.

KYLE-STEWART: the area between the rivers Ayr and Doon to which Burns had moved in 1777.

Brooses: races, including that from the church door to the house of a new bride-groom.

pay't them hollow: beat them hollow, beat them utterly.

Fittie-lan': 'The left-hand horse of the hinder pair in the plough, treading the unploughed land while its neighbour walks in the furrow' (Kinsley).

fow . . . Stimpart: measures – fractions of a bushel.

hain'd rig: an area enclosed to preserve and promote the growth of fodder.

Address to the Deil (76)

Kilmarnock, 1786. The epigraph is from *Paradise Lost*, i.128–9. In a letter (114) to his rather disreputable friend William Nicol, Burns wrote that he carried a pocket Milton 'perpetually about with me, in order to study the sentiments – the dauntless magnanimity; the intrepid, unyielding independence; the desperate daring and noble defiance of hardship, in that great Personage, Satan'. A letter to Dr John Moore (125) exposes another influence on this poem. Burns writes of an old maid of his mother's who 'had, I suppose, the largest collection in the country of tales and songs concerning devils, ghosts, fairies, brownies, witches, warlocks, spunkies, kelpies, elf-candles, dead-lights, wraiths, apparitions, cantraips, giants, inchanted towers, dragons, and other trumpery'. The 'Address' jibes, once again, at the belief of the Auld Lichts, by inverting the Calvinist idea that all are damned save the elect: even the Devil, Burns suggests, might change his ways and be saved.

like a roaring lion: 1 Peter 5:8.

boortries: elder trees, planted close to houses as a guard against the super-natural.

ragweed nags: steeds made from the ragwort plant – cf. witches' broomsticks.

yellow treasure . . . warklum: witches were thought to spirit away dairy produce and undo the work of the weaver. Loom (tool) has sexual overtones. Burns cancelled an earlier version of this stanza which referred to a bewitched bridegroom, rather than weaver, but even so that noted literary man Hugh Blair advised him to leave out the present stanza as indecent.

Water-kelpies: in Celtic lore, water-spirits, usually in the shape of a horse.

Spunkies: marsh-lights that lured the traveller to his death.

the man of Uz: Job in the Old Testament.

MICHAEL: the archangel who drove Satan from Heaven, often depicted as piercing the serpent-devil with a lance.

Scotch Drink (77)

Kilmarnock, 1786.

wimplin worms: spiral tubes employed in distilling.

Ev'n goodly meetings . . .: cf. 'The Holy Fair'.

burn: water used in distilling.

fumbling: sexually impotent or clumsy.

Ferintosh: A whisky distilled at Ferintosh on the Cromarty Firth, exempted from duty from 1695. When Forbes of Culloden's 'charter' was taken away in 1785, the price of whisky in general rose.

To J. Smith (79)

Kilmarnock, 1786. James Smith (1765–1823) was a close friend of Burns in Mauchline, for a time a draper in the village.

Epigraph: from *The Grave* (1743) by Robert Blair (1699–1746), another important Scottish poet writing in English.

the russet coat: the apparel – and the role – of country farmer.

DEMPSTER: see notes above to 'The Vision'.

WILLIE PIT: William Pitt the Younger, Prime Minister.

The Author's Earnest Cry and Prayer, to . . . the Scotch Representatives (81)

Kilmarnock, 1786. The question of whisky at this time was not trivial. Spirits were a bone of contention between Scotland and England, where the Westminster Parliament hearkened to pleas from English distillers that Scottish competition was unfair. The increase of illicit distilling in Scotland had prompted licit enterprises to export to England. The Scotch Distillery Act of 1786, to which Burns refers in his note, followed the unsatisfactory 'Wash Act' of 1784, which had resulted in Scotch distillers being squeezed out of business, between newly zealous excisemen on the one hand and their illicit rivals on the other. The new legislation taxed Scottish spirits at 6d. a gallon, and added import duty on whisky brought into England at 2s. a gallon, to match overall the 2s. 6d. per gallon tax on English-distilled spirits.

Epigraph: cf. *Paradise Lost*, ix.896 and ix.900.

IRISH LORDS: those who held Scottish seats in Parliament.

AQUAVITAE: alcoholic spirit. Cf. the Gaelic *uisge beatha*, 'water of life', from which 'whisky' derives.

yon PREMIER YOUTH: William Pitt the Younger, Prime Minister.

MONTGOMERIES: the family of the Earls of Eglinton, famous in military history. Archibald, the eleventh Earl, was one of the sixteen representative Scottish peers in the House of Lords.

BOSWEL: another local name. James Boswell (1740–95) was an advocate, as well as being Dr Johnson's biographer.

Saint Stephen's wa's: the chapel of St Stephen's in the Palace of Westminster.

Dempster ... Kilkerran, et al.: Scots MPs. Henry Dundas (1742–1811), 'auldfarran' in his use of 'auld Scotch', was a very powerful colleague of Pitt, and the political controller of Scotland; he was known as 'King Harry the Ninth'.

lost Militia: the Militia Bill for Scotland of 1782 was rejected after Dempster and others objected to its provision for enlistment from the militia into the army.

straik her cannie: stroke her hair nicely.

Charlie Fox: Charles James Fox, a leader of opposition to Pitt, was famous for his non-parliamentary pleasures.

Boconnock's: Pitt's grandfather was Robert Pitt of Boconnoc in Cornwall.

tea an' winnocks: in 1784 Pitt reduced the excise duty on tea (to check smuggling) and introduced a tax on windows to make up the lost revenue.

FIVE AND FORTY: Scotland's forty-five representatives in the House of Commons.

royal GEORGE's will: Burns in his postscript echoes the *British* patriotism of the eighteenth century, which (cf. Hogarth) despised Europeans as cowardly starvelings. Here, he is loyally Hanoverian.

Till whare ye sit ... Tak aff your dram!: Kinsley substituted for these famous lines a late emendation in Burns's own hand, but we follow the printed editions.

Sketch (82)

Currie, 1800.

Barbauld: Anna Laetitia Barbauld (1743–1825), whose *Poems* appeared in 1773.

Herd's ballats, Maro's catches: David Herd (?1731–1810) published his *Ancient and Modern Scottish Songs* in 1769. Maro is a puzzle. It is a name for Virgil, who hardly wrote 'catches' – this might be Burns's joke. But he may have been thinking of Clément Marot (1496–1544), a French writer of songs.

honest Allan: Allan Ramsay.

Tamtallan: a castle in East Lothian (Tantallon). Burns is echoing Hamilton of Gilbertfield's verse epistle to Ramsay of 26 June 1719.

To a Louse (83)
Kilmarnock, 1786.

toy: a tight-fitting cap with flaps going down to the shoulders.

wylecoat: under-waistcoat or undercoat – or maybe a kind of frock worn by a child (SND).

Lunardi: a bonnet in the shape of a balloon. Vincenzo Lunardi's pioneering flights took place in the 1780s, several of them in Scotland.

winks and finger-ends: the congregation was winking and pointing.

Love and Liberty – A Cantata (84)
Stewart and Meikle, 1799. Thomas Stewart, the first publisher of this 'Cantata', said that he had the 'Merry Andrew' section from an uncle, John Richmond, who was with Burns in Poosie Nansie's howff in Mauchline on the night when the poet saw this 'merry core' of beggars. Be that as it may, the Jolly Beggar had been a ballad motif for centuries, and John Gay's *Beggar's Opera* was one of the best-known works of the eighteenth century. The Cantata might be taken to be descriptive, or an exercise within established conventions. Crawford regards it as a critique of society (*Society and the Lyric: A Study of the Song Culture of Eighteenth-Century Scotland*, Edinburgh, 1979, 185–210).

the heights of ABRAM: General Wolfe died as the British force under him routed the French at the Heights of Abraham near Quebec in 1759.

the MORO: the fortress defending Santiago in Cuba when British forces captured the island in 1762.

Curtis ... Elliot: Admiral Curtis destroyed floating batteries sent by the French and Spanish attackers against Gibraltar in 1782, while General George Elliot defended the Rock.

the PEACE: Treaty of Versailles, 1783.

CUNNINGHAM: district in northern Ayrshire.

ty'd up like a stirk: publicly punished in the 'jougs', an iron collar chained to a post.

abus'd i' the kirk: see notes to 'Epistle to J. Ranken' above.

in mony a well been douked: punishment for pilfering.

waefu' woodie: hangman's rope.

Philibeg: kilt – the *feileadh beag*, or 'little kilt'.

Claymore: originally the great two-handed sword, but later used of swords of every sort.

kittle hair on thairms: tickle hair on fiddle strings – a *double entendre*.

shor'd them DAINTY DAVIE/O' boot that night: he offered them Dainty Davie into the bargain. The reference is to David Williamson (cf. Speedy Gonzales), a seventeenth-century minister famed for his sexual accomplishments. The bard has three women in tow; when one, the Dame, defects to the fiddler, the bard gives the couple his blessing; get on with it.

FLIE: desire.

VARIORUM: shifting scene.

1786: MOSSGIEL AND EDINBURGH

The Inventory (86)

Stewart, 1801. In the years 1784–6 Pitt introduced taxes on the items mentioned in Burns's headnote. A bachelor paid a higher rate than a married man. Robert Aitken (see 'Holy Willie's Prayer') was the Surveyor of Taxes in Ayr.

carriage cattle: 'carriage' applies to any wheeled vehicle, and 'cattle' could still refer to horses at this time. But Burns is humorously stretching the terms of Aitken's mandate.

Kilburnie: in north-west Ayrshire.

Wee Davock: David Hutcheson, an orphan adopted into the Burns family.

the questions: the Shorter Catechism of the Church of Scotland, which householders were expected to instil into children and servants.

Effectual Calling: a key concept in Scottish Presbyterian theology – 'the work of God's spirit, whereby . . . he doth persuade and enable us to embrace Jesus Christ'.

misses: mistresses.

dear-bought Bess: see 'A Poet's Welcome to his love-begotten Daughter'.

Letter to James Tennant of Glenconner (90)

Oliver and Duncan, 1801. 'Auld Glen' was John Tennant, factor on the Countess of Glencairn's Ochiltree estates. His son James (1755–1835), miller in Ochiltree, had several brothers and sisters who are mentioned in Burns's epistle to him.

Johnie Simson: said to have been a dancing master in Ochiltree.

Smith . . . Reid: so far from being the ruthless advocate of profitable free enterprise at all costs that misreading of his *Wealth of Nations* has made him seem, Adam Smith, famous for his *Theory of Moral Sentiments* (1759), was a proponent of 'sympathetic feeling'. For Reid, and 'common sense', see notes above to 'The Holy Tulzie'.

Bunyan, Brown and Boston: John Bunyan's *Pilgrim's Progress* was popular in Scotland, as were the works of such Calvinist divines as John Brown (1722–87) and Thomas Boston (1676–1732). Burns is joking that, left to such influences, he might turn Auld Licht.

RAB THE RANTER: see notes to 'Third Epistle to J. Lapraik' above.

To a Mountain-Daisy (92)

Kilmarnock, 1786. As Daiches points out (*Robert Burns*, London, 1952, revised 1966, reprinted 1981, 155), 'It is significant that Burns changed the title of this poem from "The Gowan" ("gowan" being the regular Scots word for daisy).' Burns was seeking to appeal to the 'sentimental' taste of genteel readers – and struck home: Henry Mackenzie himself, author of *The Man of Feeling*, that classic of Sentiment, acclaimed it in his *Lounger* review of December 1786.

Extempore – to Mr Gavin Hamilton (99)

Kinsley, like previous editors, takes the text from ms, Burns's Second Commonplace Book. For Gavin Hamilton (1751–1805), writer (solicitor) in Mauchline, see 'Holy Willie's Prayer' and notes.

whig: here, strict Presbyterian.

On a Scotch Bard Gone to the West Indies (100)

Kilmarnock, 1786. It should not be supposed that Burns had a peculiar, cynical wish to profit from the slave system in the Caribbean, against which protest was beginning on a large scale in Britain. There was a well-beaten path from Ayrshire to the New World, which beckoned him: the minister of Irvine wrote in 1791 that the young men of the port, where Burns had once worked, were in general sailors, or went 'abroad to the West Indies and America as storekeepers and planters' (quoted in Daiches, *Robert Burns*, 64). Burns's first reference to his intention to emigrate is in a letter of April 1786. He was supposed to sail in July or early August, but departure was postponed and, after Jean Armour bore him twins (September), the 'feelings of a father' persuaded him to stay in Scotland.

Auld, cantie KYLE: Burns's home district is here his muse.

weepers: a widow's broad white cuffs.

drummock: raw oatmeal mixed with cold water (Gaelic, *dramaig*).

Second Epistle to Davie (101)

In David Sillar, *Poems*, 1789. See 'Epistle to Davie' and notes.

A Dedication to Gavin Hamilton Esq; (103)

Kilmarnock, 1786. Since Burns's friend Hamilton (see 'Holy Willie's Prayer' and 'Extempore – to Gavin Hamilton' and notes) had encouraged him to print his poems, the Kilmarnock volume is aptly dedicated to him.

His Grace: the Duke of Hamilton.

godly symptom: Calvinists believed that the good deeds and virtues of those not predestined to election could have no redemptive effect; they were damned.

Gentoos: Hindus.

Ponotaxi: Burns may be thinking of Cotopaxi, a volcano in the Andes.

the CLERK: Hamilton himself, Clerk of Court.

Kennedy: Hamilton's wife was Helen Kennedy.

Address of Beelzebub (108)

Scots Magazine, February 1818. The meeting referred to took place in May 1786. It was not until 1802 that fears of overpopulation in the Highlands arose, and even then most opinion there 'remained strongly opposed to emigration for another decade or so. It was only after 1818 that landlords shifted from opposition to ambivalence, and then to promotion of emigration' (Eric Richards, *A History of the Highland Clearances*, London, 1982, 103–4).

Hancocke . . . Frankline . . . MONTGOMERY: heroes of the American Revolution. Burns characteristically sets in capitals the Ayrshire name of the American commander who captured Montreal from the British but died attacking Quebec.

North . . . Sackville: Lord North was Prime Minister, Sackville his Secretary of State for the Colonies, when the American colonists triumphed. Howe and Clinton were among the unsuccessful British commanders.

DRURY LANE: a centre of prostitution in London.

HEROD . . . POLYCRATE: ancient tyrants.

ALMAGRO . . . PIZARRO: Pizarro, conqueror of Inca Peru, later had his lieutenant Almagro executed.

Anno Mundi 5790: by generally accepted computation, the world had been created in 4004 BC. Hence, for the Devil, 1786 equals 5790.

Epitaph on a Wag in Mauchline (111)

Stewart, 1801.

A Dream (113)

Kilmarnock, 1786. After Thomas Warton supplied an ode in celebration of George III's birthday on 4 June 1786, Burns quickly produced this poem for inclusion among the work that went to the Kilmarnock printer in the same month.

aiblins ane: Prince Charles Edward Stewart.

And now the third part: refers to the lost American colonies.

Willie Pit . . . get: the Prime Minister was the offspring ('get') of Lord Chatham, who had spoken up for the American colonists.

rax . . . dissection: since 1694 surgeons in Edinburgh had been granted the remains of executed persons for dissection.

W—: George, Prince of Wales (1762–1830), later George IV.

Diana . . . Charlie: Diana was patroness of chastity in classical mythology. The

Prince, besides his womanizing, affected Opposition views and consorted with the dissolute Charles James Fox.

O—: Osnabrück. Prince Frederick Augustus, Duke of York, was elected by George III to the bishopric of this town in Westphalia in 1764.

TARRY-BREEKS: Prince William (1765–1837) – William IV from 1830 – had entered the navy in 1779. The 'amour' referred to in Burns's note may have been the one rumoured between William and the daughter of a Portsmouth official.

royal Lasses: George III had five daughters.

Tam Samson's Elegy (117)

Edinburgh, 1787. The burial place of Thomas Samson (1722–95) in Kilmarnock churchyard is marked by Burns's (premature) epitaph.

M'kinlay . . . Robertson: ministers respectively of Auld Licht and New Licht persuasions.

The Brethren: freemasons of the Kilmarnock Lodge, of which Burns became an honorary member in October 1786.

cock, etc.: references to the sport of curling – see notes above to 'The Vision'. *Cock* – the circle on the ice at which the stones are aimed. *Guard* – a defensive stone played to lie in front of a scoring stone. *Draw* – to 'curl' the revolving stone to the required spot. *Wick a bore* – send a stone between two opposing guard stones. *Hog-score* (nowadays 'hog-line') – a line on the ice beyond which a stone has to pass in order to count.

The Brigs of Ayr, A Poem (120)

Edinburgh, 1787. The old bridge dated from the fifteenth century, and was inadequate for modern traffic. The new bridge was begun in 1786 and completed in 1788. John Ballantine (1743–1812) was a merchant of Ayr who was soon, in the course of 1787, to become the town's provost. He was a generous supporter of Burns's poetry.

Adams: Robert Adam, the major Scottish architect (1728–92), planned the New Brig. His name epitomized up-to-date Neo-classical fashion. The origins of the Picts were mysterious (they are now believed to have been Celts), but Burns was happy to use the then current theory that they were 'Goths'. Hence the debate is polarized between a 'Gothic' architectural tradition, with very ancient local roots, and polite new London style.

second dread command: the second of the Ten Commandments forbids the making of likenesses of 'anything there is in heaven above, or . . . in the earth beneath, or . . . in the water under the earth'.

godly Writers: Writers to the Signet (solicitors) like Burns's friends Aitken (see 'The Inventory') and Hamilton (see 'Holy Willie's Prayer', 'Extempore – to Mr Gavin Hamilton' and 'A Dedication to Gavin Hamilton' and notes).

Courage . . . *the Feal*: the Fail is a tributary of the Ayr. These lines compliment
Hugh Montgomerie (1740–1819), MP for Ayrshire at the time, later twelfth
Earl of Eglinton.

Epistle to Captn Willm Logan at Park (129)

Cunningham, 1834. William Logan, an infantry officer, lived in Ayr with his
sister Susan. 'Honest Lucky' was his mother.
CASTALIAN DRINKERS: at a fountain on Mount Parnassus sacred to the
Muses.

A Winter Night (130)

Edinburgh, 1787. To John Ballantine (see notes to 'The Brigs of Ayr' above).
Burns described this as his 'first attempt' at an ode in an 'irregular kind of
measure' – that is, 'Pindaric' (Letter 59).
Epigraph: *King Lear*, III, iv.
'*Blow, blow . . . the bliss!*': cf. the song in *As You Like It*, II, vii; and *King
Lear*, III, ii.

To a Haggis (136)

Caledonian Mercury, 19 December 1786; Edinburgh, 1786. This poem, written
soon after Burns's arrival in Edinburgh, was quickly included in two of the
city's periodicals. Appropriately, it is reminiscent of Edinburgh's own poet
Fergusson – see his 'Caller Oysters'.

1787: EDINBURGH; BORDER TOUR; HIGHLAND TOURS

On Fergusson (143)

Cromek, 1808. Robert Fergusson (1750–74) was Burns's most important
recent precursor in Scots verse. Burns inscribed these lines in a copy of
Fergusson's poems presented to an Edinburgh friend in March 1787, when he
was arranging the erection of the stone which now stands above Fergusson's
grave in the Canongate Churchyard.

To a Painter (145)

Wallace's revision of Chambers, 1896. Burns is said to have written this in the
studio of a well-known Edinburgh painter.

To William Creech (154)

Cromek, 1808. Creech (1745–1815) was Burns's publisher, later Lord Provost
of Edinburgh. In the seventh stanza Burns names five of Edinburgh's most
distinguished literati: James Gregory, professor of medicine; Alexander Tytler,

judge and professor of universal history; William Greenfield, minister of the High Church of St Giles; Henry Mackenzie, novelist and man of letters; and Dugald Stewart, professor of moral philosophy.

AULD . . . REEKIE: Edinburgh, so called because of the smoke of its many chimneys.

On a Schoolmaster in Cleish Parish, Fifeshire (167)

Cromek, 1808. A Mr Michie, whom Burns met in Edinburgh.

1788–9: EDINBURGH AND ELLISLAND

An Extemporaneous Effusion on being appointed to the Excise (193)

Cromek, 1808. Burns began to train as an excise officer in April 1788, having left Edinburgh the month before.

Epistle to Hugh Parker (222)

Cunningham, 1834. Dated June 1788. Parker was an old Ayrshire friend. Burns moved into Ellisland farm in Dumfriesshire in June 1788. Jean Armour, acknowledged as his wife in April, did not join him there till December.

Elegy on Capt. Matthew Henderson (239)

Edinburgh, 1793. Henderson (1737–88) served as a soldier and later held a civil service post. He was forced by convivial extravagance to sell his property and, when Burns met him the year before he died, he was subsisting on a pension. The elegy's rhetoric has innumerable precedents – classical, English and Scots – but the detail is Burnsian and fresh.

Elegy on the Year 1788 (250)

Edinburgh Evening Courant, 1 January 1789; Stewart, 1801.

Spanish empire: Charles III of Spain died on 13 December 1788.

Pitt an' Fox: when George III became temporarily insane in November 1788, Pitt proposed that the Prince of Wales should be Regent under parliamentary restrictions, Fox that the Prince should have full power. The last stanza of this poem hints at Burns's sympathy with Fox's Opposition Whigs.

For Embro' wells: there was a water shortage in Edinburgh during 1788.

To Dr Blacklock (273)

Currie, 1800. Thomas Blacklock (1721–91) was a blind poet and one-time minister. His enthusiastic reception of the Kilmarnock edition of Burns's poems helped turn the poet's mind from emigration. In replying to an epistle from Blacklock, Burns refers to a mutual friend, Robert Heron (1764–1807), literary hack and drunk, who died in Newgate Debtors Prison.

carl-hemp: proverbially associated with courage.

On the Late Captain Grose's Peregrinations thro' Scotland (275)

Edinburgh Evening Courant, 27 August 1789; Edinburgh, 1793 (hence 'Late'). Francis Grose (1731–91) was soldier, artist and author of *The Antiquities of England and Wales* (6 vols., 1773–87). Burns met him in 1789 when he was collecting material for *The Antiquities of Scotand* (2 vols., 1789 and 1791).

Land o' Cakes: a popular term for Scotland, where oatcakes were so prevalent.

Frae Maidenkirk to Johny Groats: from Maidenkirk in Wigtownshire, the most southerly Scottish parish, to John o' Groats in Caithness, at the northern extreme of the mainland.

slight/O' cauk and keel: skill in drawing.

Tubalcain: in the Bible, the first blacksmith (Genesis 4:22).

Balaam's ass . . . witch of Endor: see Numbers 22:21ff and 1 Samuel 28:7ff.

1790–91: ELLISLAND AND DUMFRIES

To a Gentleman who had sent him a News-paper (282)

Currie, 1801. The gentleman has not been identified. Among the many topical references:

Charles the twalt: Charles XII, King of Sweden (1697–1718), was a legendary conqueror. Gustavus III of Sweden, like his famous predecessor, had attacked Russia in 1787.

libbet Italy: a reference to operatic castrati.

Chatham Will . . . glaikit Charlie: William Pitt and Charles James Fox.

*Geordie W***s*: George, Prince of Wales.

Tam o' Shanter. A Tale (321)

First published in 1791 in Grose's *Antiquities of Scotland*, vol. 2, the *Edinburgh Magazine*, March, and the *Edinburgh Herald*, March; Edinburgh, 1793. When Francis Grose (see notes above to 'On the Late Captain Grose's Peregrinations') was collecting materials for his *Antiquities* in Dumfriesshire in the summer of 1790, he asked Burns to write him an account of the witches' meetings in Alloway Kirk in the poet's native Ayrshire. This poem was Burns's response. Tam is traditionally supposed to be based on Douglas Graham (1739–1811), tenant of the farm of Shanter, who liked a convivial evening in Ayr and had a shrewish wife.

Epigraph: Gavin Douglas, *Eneados* (1513), vi, Proloug, l. 18. Burns could have found this in Douglas's *Select Works*, published in Perth in 1787.

Kirkton Jean: Jean Kennedy kept a public house at Kirkoswald with her sister, known as 'the Leddies' House' – hence, probably, Burns's *L—d's house*.

Souter Johnny: may be either John Davidson (1728–1806), a cobbler at Kirkoswald, or John Lachlan (d. 1819), a shoemaker in Ayr.

John Barleycorn: see 'John Barleycorn' and notes.

Three Lawyers' tongues . . . in every neuk: these four lines occurred in the early printings but were omitted in the Edinburgh edition of 1793. Burns was persuaded by the arguments of Alexander Fraser Tytler, who was a judge himself, and not disinterested. The cut has been praised on aesthetic grounds, however (see, for example, Crawford, *Burns*, 231).

seventeen hunder linnen: woven with 1,700 threads to the warp.

spean a foal: wean through sheer fright.

As open pussie's . . .: 'pussie' here is the hare; dogs 'open', or give voice, when they see her.

Epigram on Capt. Francis Grose, The Celebrated Antiquary (323)

Stewart, 1801. See 'On the Late Captain Grose's Peregrinations' and notes.

Extempore – on some Commemorations of Thomson (332)

Chambers, 1856. Burns's reaction to the eccentric Earl of Buchan's intention to erect a bust commemorating the Scottish poet James Thomson, author of *The Seasons* (1730), at his birthplace, Ednam.

1792–6: DUMFRIES

Here's a Health to them that's awa (391)

Edinburgh Gazeteer, 1792. This is modelled on a Jacobite motif, of which there are versions in SMM, 1796, and Hogg's *Jacobite Relics* (1819). But it would be absurd to include this with Burns's 'songs' – he has twisted his model into topical support for the Whig faction, who were currently suffering odium for their favourable attitude towards the French Revolution. The third stanza refers to recent government action against 'seditious' writing.

the Buff and the Blue: the colours of the Whigs.

Charlie: not 'Bonny Prince', but Charles James Fox, leader of the Whigs.

Tammie: Thomas Erskine, the distinguished Scottish lawyer who defended Tom Paine and other democrats.

Maitland and Wycombe: James Maitland, Earl of Lauderdale, and John Henry Petty, Earl of Wycombe, had spoken in the House of Lords in May 1792, objecting to the Royal Proclamation against seditious writing.

Chieftan Mcleod: Colonel Norman McLeod of McLeod (1754–1801), MP for Inverness, was at this time a political reformer. In October 1792 he went so far as to join the Glasgow branch of the Society of the Friends of the People, which pressed for more equal representation and shorter parliaments. But after a few months, he got cold feet. (See I. F. Grant, *The Macleods . . . 1200–1956*, London, 1981 edition, 519ff.)

Ode for General Washington's Birthday (451)
Part in Cromek, 1808. After 'A Winter Night', Burns's second attempt at a Pindaric ode. Written in 1794. Formal praise of Washington and American liberty gives way in the last two strophes to condemnation of Britain's part in the coalition against the French Republic.
WALLACE: see notes to 'To W. Simpson' above.

Address to the Tooth-Ache (500)
Scots Magazine, October 1797; Stewart, 1801.

Poem (*Addressed to Mr Mitchell*) (514)
Currie, 1801. This poem is a reminder of Burns's fragile financial position. Moreover, the hopes expressed in the third stanza would be dashed by a famine in Dumfriesshire in the months to come. The Postscript refers to the rheumatic fever that had kept Burns in bed for some time – in this case, his hopes have an even more pathetic ring in retrospect.

Poem on Life (517)
Currie, 1801. Colonel De Peyster (1736–1822) was at this time major-commandant of the Dumfries Volunteers.

Undated: A Coda

The Tree of Liberty (625)
In 1838 the Edinburgh firm of W. and R. Chambers added Burns to their 'People's Edition of Standard Works'. They took the much reprinted Currie edition of the poems and augmented it. 'The Tree of Liberty' appears on p. 87 with a note: 'Here printed for the first time, from a MS in the possession of Mr James Duncan, Mosesfield, near Glasgow.' That manuscript was lost, and hence Burns's authorship may still be disputed.

Crawford (*Burns*, 246–51) argues that if it is a later forgery, 'The Tree of Liberty' is an amazing feat of imaginative projection back into the 1790s, and if it is by some other hand of the French Revolutionary period, we must wonder who this 'anonymous democrat' was who 'wrote nothing else of value which has been preserved'. If it *is* by Burns, as Crawford says, it is 'the most extreme development of his political thoughts and emotions that we possess' – and also a plea to the English to follow the example of the Scots, who in the 1790s, despite repression, set up 'Trees of Liberty' as revolutionary symbols in many places. Robert Chambers was a Burnsian scholar of repute, but it has to be noted that he published this poem at the height of the Chartist phase in British popular politics, in an edition intended for wide readership. Sixty years later, at the zenith of imperialism, W. E. Henley and T. F. Henderson in their expensive edition of *The Poetry of Robert Burns* (vol. 4, Edinburgh, 1897, 107) confidently dismissed the 'trash' as spurious. The general belief in Scotland around 1990 that this remarkable poem *is* by Burns no doubt relates to the new national truculence.

Frae yont the western waves: from the USA.

GLOSSARY

A

a, *v. inf.* have (reduced form of **hae**)

a', *adj., adv., n.* all

aback, *adv.* in the rear; 'away, aloof' (B)

abiegh, *adv.* aside, 'at a shy distance' (B)

ablins, see **a(i)blins**

(a)boon, *adv.* up; *prep.* above, over; **get aboon,** rejoice

about, *adv.* here and there; alternately; *prep.* in the neighbourhood of

abread, abreed, *adv.* wide, 'in breadth' (B); 'abroad, in sight' (B)

abus't, *v. pa. t.* abused

acquaint, acquent, *ppl. adj.* familiar; acquainted with each other

acre-braid, *n.* an acre in breadth (22 yards)

advices, *n.* counsels

ae, *adj.* one, a certain; one of two; only; emphatic before a superlative

aff, *adv., prep.* off, away

aff-loof, *adv.* 'unpremeditated' (B)

aff 's, off his

a-fiel, *adv.* in the field, outside

afore, *prep.* before; in front of

aft(en), aft(en)-times, *adv.* often

agley, *adv.* awry, wrong

ahin(t), *prep.* behind. See **furr ahin, lan' ahin**

a(i)blins, *adv.* perhaps

aik, *n.* oak; **aiken,** *adj.*

ain, *adj.* own

air, *adv.* early

airles, *n.* payment made in token of employment; **airle-penny,** earnest money

airn, *n.* iron; *pl.* fetters

airt, *n.* quarter, direction; *v.* guide

aith, *n.* oath

aits, *n. pl.* oats

aiver, *n.* 'an old horse' (B); cart-horse

aizle, n. 'a hot cinder' (B); ember of tobacco

a-jee, *adv.* ajar

alake, *interj.* alas

alane, *adj., adv.* alone

alarms, *n. pl.* provocations

amaist, *adv.* almost

amang, *prep.* among

an('), *conj.* (1) and; (2) if; **an 't,** if it

anathem, *v.* curse

ance, *adv.* once

ane, *adj., pron.* one, a(n)

aneuch, *adj., n.* enough

anger, *v.* make angry; become angry

anither, *adj., pron.* another

an's, and am; and is; and his

aqua-fontis, *n.* spring water

aqua-vitae, *n.* alcohol, whisky

arch, *v.* rise in a curve

ase, auss, *n.* ashes

asklent, *adv.* askew, on the side; askance

aspar, *adv.* aspread, with legs apart

asteer, *adj.* 'abroad, stirring' (B)

athort, *prep.* across

atween, *prep.* between

aught, *adj.* eight

aught, *n.* anything

auld, *adj.* old

auldfarran, auld-farrent, *adj.* old-fashioned, hence 'sagacious, cunning, prudent' (B); wise, witty

auld-warld, *adj.* old-fashioned, antiquated

aumous (dish), *n.* alms-dish

auss, see ase

ava, *adv. phr.* of all; at all

awa, *adv., interj.* away

awauk, *v.* awake

awee, *adv.* for a moment
awkart, *adj.* obstinate, cantankerous
awnie, *adj.* having awns, bearded
ayont, *prep., adv.* beyond, past

B

ba', *n.* ball; game of handball
babie-clouts, *n. pl.* baby-linen
backlins, *adv.* backwards; **backlins-comin**, *ppl. phr.* returning
back-style, back-yett, *nn.* the stile, gate in the rear fence of the house. See yett
bade, see **bid, bide**
baggie, *n.* belly
baiginets, *n. pl.* bayonets
bail(l)ie, *n.* landlord's deputy; borough officer corresponding to alderman
bair, *v.* uncover, clear
bairn, *n.* child
bairn-time, *n.* all the offspring of one mother, 'a family of children, a brood' (B)
baith, *pron., adj., conj.* both
bakes, *n. pl.* biscuits
ballat, *n.* ballad, traditional verse tale
ban, *v. tr.* curse; *intr.* swear; *n.* curse
ban(d), *n.* white linen strip attached to clerical collar
banditti, *n. attrib.* treacherous, vicious
bane, *n.* bone; bone-comb
bang, *v.* thrash, thump, hammer
bang, *n.* blow, pain, 'effort' (B)
banie, *adj.* bony, big-boned, 'stout' (B)
bannock, bonnock, *n.* round, flat girdle-baked cake of oatmeal, barley, pease or flour
bardie, *n.* minor poet
barefit, *adj.* barefooted
barley-bree, *n.* whisky
barm, *n.* yeast; **barmie**, *adj.* passionate, fermenting with ideas
bastart, *n.* bastard
batch, *n.* 'crew, gang' (B), set

batts, *n*. colic, 'botts' (B)

bauckie-bird, *n*. bat

baudrans, baudrons, bawd'rons, *n*. cat

bauk, *n*. cross-beam, tying the rafters in a roof; **bauk-en'**, *n*. end of a cross-beam

bauld, *adj*. bold, audacious

bawbee, *n*. coin of 6 pennies Scots originally struck in base silver by James V, a halfpenny

bawd'rons, see **baudrans**

baws'nt, *adj*. 'having a white stripe down the face' (B), brindled

bawtie, *n*. name given to a dog

be, see **let be**

bead, *n*. drop of liquor

bear, *v*. allow, suffer, admit

bear, beir, *n*. barley

bearers, *n. pl*. legs

beat, see **beet**

bedeen, *adv*. early, quickly, anon

bedlam, *adj*. fit for Bedlam, mad

beese, *n*. vermin

beet, beat, *v*. mend, kindle, 'add fuel to fire' (B)

befa', *v*. befall

behin(t), *prep*., *adv*. behind

beild, see **biel(d)**

beir, see **bear**

belang, *v*. belong to

beld, *adj*. bald

bellum, *n*. rumpus, force, onslaught

bellys, *n*. bellows

belted, *adj*. descr. the distinctive belt of an earl or a knight

belyve, *adv*. quickly, at once, soon

ben, *adv*., *prep*. indoors, within, 'into the *spence* or parlour' (B); *n*. parlour, inner room. See **but(t) and ben**

benmost, *adj*. furthest in, innermost

bent, *n*. hillside, ridge of a hill

beside our han', see **han(d)**

besouth, *prep*. to the south of

bestead, *pa. pple*. placed, circumstanced

bethankit, *pa. pple.* (God) be thanked, 'the grace after meat' (B)

beuk, *n.* book

bevel, *n.* mason's rule; **in . . . bevel**, on the line set by the bevel, obliquely

bewaure, *v.* beware

beyont, *prep.* beyond, on the far side of

bicker, *v.* rush, scurry; *n.* short rush, stagger

bicker, *n.* wooden drinking vessel with one or two staves extended to form lugs

bid, *v.* ask, desire; **bade**, *pa. t.*

bide, *v.* remain, await, stay for; stand, endure; **bade**, *pa. t.*

biel(d), **beild**, *n.* protection, shelter, cover

bien, *adj.* cosy, comfortable, well-stocked; *adv.* **bien(ly)**, comfortably, warmly

big, *adj.* elated, passionate

big, *v.* build; **biggin**, *n.* building, cottage

bill, *n.* bull

billie, **billy**, *n.* craft-brother; friend, comrade; fellow, lad

bird(ie), see **burd(ie)**

birdy, *adj.* chicken, poultry

birk, *n.* birch tree

birkie, *n.* lively, spry fellow

birrin(g), *ppl. adj.* whirring, 'the noise of partridges, etc., when they spring' (B)

birsie, *n.* bristle, hair

birth, *n.* berth, place on board ship

bit, (1) *n.* 'crisis, nick of time' (B); (2) *quasi-adj.* by omission of *of*, indicating littleness, affection, contempt

bitch, *n.* term of contempt

bizz, *v.* buzz; *n.* stir, flurry

black, *adj.* dark, swarthy; foul, ugly; wicked, malignant, sinister; disastrous

blackguarding, *pres. pple.* roistering

blae, *adj.* blue, livid, bitter

blast, *v.* blow, curse, wither; **blast(i)et**, *ppl. adj.* accursed, dwarfish; **blastie**, *n.* ill-tempered beast, ill-disposed creature

blate, *adj.* bashful, diffident

blather, *n.* bladder

blaud, *n.* piece, specimen, selection

blaud, *v.* slap, beat; *ppl. adj.* pelting

blaw, *v.* (1) blow; (2) get breath back; (3) boast; **blawn,** *pa. pple.* (have) blown

blaze, *n.* brilliance, display

blear, bleer(i)t, *adj.* watery-eyed, bleary

bleeze, *n.,* *v.* blaze

blellum, *n.* idle babbler; blusterer, railer

blether, *v.* talk foolishly, babble, boast; **blethers,** *n. pl.*

blin', *v., adj.* blind; **blin't,** *pa. t.*

blink, *v.* glance fondly; leer flirtatiously; gleam, 'shine by fits' (B)

blink, *n.* instant; short time, moment

blinkers, *n. pl.* ogling, alluring girls; spies, cheats ('a term of contempt' (B))

blin't, see **blin'**

blitter, *n.* 'bleater', snipe

blue-clue, *n.* ball of blue yarn used for divining

blue-gown, *n. attrib.* 'one of those beggars who get annually, on the King's birthday, a blue cloke or gown with a badge' (B)

bluid, *n.* blood; offspring; **bluidy,** *adj.*

bluntie, *n.* fool

blype, *n.* 'a layer of skin as it peels or is rubbed off' (SND)

bob, *v.* move up and down; curtsey

bock, *v.* 'to vomit, to gush intermittently' (B)

bod(d)le, *n.* copper coin first struck by Charles I, equivalent to a sixth of an English penny

bodie, body, *n.* person, fellow; *pl.* folk; **a body's sel,** oneself

boggie, *n.* bog, marsh

bogle, *n.* ghost, spectre, goblin

bole, *n.* recess in wall, serving as shelf or cupboard

bolus, *n.* large medicinal pill

bon ton, good breeding

bon(n)ie, bony, *adj.* fair, pretty, sweet; fine, splendid, handsome

bonnock, see **bannock**

boon, see **(a)boon**

boord, *n.* surface, layer (of ice)

boord-en', *n.* end of a table

boortree, *n.* 'the shrub elder planted much of old in hedges of barn-yards, etc.' (B)

boosom, *n.* besom, twig-broom

boost, *v.* must, ought

boot, o', into the bargain, as well

bore, *n.* crevice, crack; curling term, passage between two guarding stones

botch, *n.* 'an angry tumour' (B)

bother, *v.* fuss, give trouble

bouk, *n.* body, carcase

bow, *v.* bend; subdue; **bow't,** *ppl. adj.* crooked, bent

bow-hough'd, *adj.* bandy-legged

bow-kail, *n.* cabbage. See **kail**

bowse, *v.* drink heavily; **bowse about,** drink in turn

bow't, see **bow**

bra', see **braw**

brachen, *n.* bracken, coarse fern

brae, *n.* hill, hillside, high ground by a river

brag, *v.* challenge; **bragged,** have challenged

braid, *adj.* broad, plain; **braid sword,** broad-bladed cutting sword

braid-claith, *n.* broad-cloth

braik, *n.* heavy harrow

brainge, *v.* plunge, 'draw unsteadily' (B)

brak, *pa. t.* of *brek*, break; **brak 's,** broke his

branks, *n.* halter, bridle

bran'y, *n.* brandy

brash, *n.* 'a sudden illness' (B)

brats, *n. pl.* rags

brattle, *n.* clutter; hurry; short race; noisy onset

braw, bra', *adj.* fine, splendid; handsome; finely dressed; **braulies, brawlie, brawly,** *adv.* admirably, very much; *intensive* very

braxies, *n. pl.* sheep that have died of braxy

breastet, *v. pa. t.* pulled forward

breastie, *n.* a little breast

brechan, *n.* horse-collar made of, or lined with, straw

bree, *n.* whisky

breeks, *n.* breeches, trousers

breer, brier, *n., adj.* briar

brent, *adj.* smooth, unwrinkled

brent, *ppl. adj.* branded, brand (new)

brewn, *ppl. adj.* brewed

brief, *n.* writing; literary skill. Cf. **warlock-breef**

brier(-bush), see **breer**

brig, *n.* bridge

brisket, *n.* breast

brither, *n.* brother

brock, *n.* badger

brogue, *n.* trick, hoax

broo, *n.* water, soup; **snaw-broo**, half-melted snow, slush

broose, *n.* wedding race

brose, *n.* oatmeal mixed with boiling water or milk, and salt and butter added

browster, *n.* brewer; **browster wives**, ale-wives, landladies

brugh, *n.* borough

brulzie, *n.* uproar, affray, quarrel

brunstane, *n., adj.* brimstone

brunt, *v.* burnt

brust, *v.* burst

buckie, *n.* buck, 'gay debauchee'

buckle, *n.* curliness

buckskin, *n., adj.* American

budget, *n.* leather bag

buff, *v.* thrash, beat

bught, *v.* fold sheep; **bughtin-time**, time in the evening when ewes are milked

buirdly, *adj.* stalwart, stately

bum, *v.* hum; **bum-clock**, *n.* 'a humming beetle that flies in the evening' (B), cockchafer

bummle, *n.* idle, impotent bungler

burd(ie), **bird(ie)**, *n.* lady, girl

bure, *v. pa. t.* bore, carried, won; **bure sic hands**, fought so vigorously

burnewin, *n.* burn-the-wind, blacksmith

burn(ie), *n.* water, stream; water used in brewing

busk, *v.* prepare, dress; dress up; *ppl. adj.* well-furnished, splendid

bussle, *n.* commotion, fuss

but, *prep.* without; but that, other than that; lacking, less

butching, *vbl. n.* butchering

but(t), *prep., adv.* out, to the outer room; **butt the house**, in the kitchen; **but(t) and ben**, in the kitchen or outer room, and in the parlour or inner room of a cottage

by, *prep.*, *adv.* concerning, about (it); over, past; **by himself**, beside himself, 'lunatic distracted' (B)

byke, *n.* hive; swarm, crowd

byre, *n.* cowshed

C

ca', *v.* (1) call; **ca't**, *pa. t.*; name; **ca't**, name it; **ca'd**, *pa. pple.*; (2) urge forward, drive; (3) *phr.* **ca' the crack**, gossip, talk; **ca' thro'**, work away, get work done

cad(d)ie, *n.* fellow, ragamuffin, rascal

cadger, *n.* travelling hawker

caff, *n.* chaff

caird, *n.* tinker, gypsy

calces, *pl.* of *calx*, powder

calf-ward, *n.* 'a small enclosure for calves' (B), the churchyard

callan(t), *n.* stripling, lad

caller, callor, *adj.* fresh, cool

callet, *n.* wench, trull

cam, *pa. t.* of *come*

canie, see **can(n)ie**

canker, *v.* become peevish; **cankert, cankrie**, *adj.* ill-natured

canna, *v.* cannot

can(n)ie, can(n)y, *adj.*, *adv.* (1) knowing, shrewd; careful, cautious, frugal; (2) favourable, lucky; (3) gentle, steady, kindly, pleasant

cant, *n.* song, merry tale

cantan, *ppl. adj.* whining, hypocritical

cantie, canty, *adj.*, *adv.* lively, cheerful(ly), pleasant(ly)

cantraip, *n.* magic, witching

cany, see **can(n)ie**

cape-stane, *n.* coping-stone

cap'rin, *n.* capering

car, *n.* crude cart without wheels; carriage

card, *n.* chart

care, *n.* sweetheart

careerin, *pres. pple.* running this way and that

careless, *adj.* free from anxiety, untroubled

caretna by, cared nothing, not at all

carl(e), carlie, *n.* fellow, old man

carl-hemp, *n.* seed-bearing hemp

carlin, *n.* old woman, witch; old fellow

carmagnole, *n.* rascal

carte(s), *n.* card(s)

cast out, *v.* fall out, quarrel

catch'd, *v. pa. t., pa. pple.* caught

catch-the-plack, *n.* money-grubbing. See **plack**

cattle, *n.* horses, beasts

caudron, *n.* cauldron

cauf, *n.* calf; **cauf-leather,** *adj.* calfskin

cauk and keel, *n. phr.* drawing, sketching

cauld, *n., adj.* cold

caup, *n.* wooden bowl

causey-cleaner, *n.* street-cleaner

cavie, *n.* (hen-)coop

cess, *n.* land-tax

chamer, *n.* bed-chamber

change-house, *n.* ale-house

chantan, *pres. pple.* singing

chanter, *n.* the part of a bagpipe on which the melody is played;
  pastoral pipe

chap, *n.* fellow

chap, *n.* blow, stroke; *v.* knock, thrash, beat

chap, chappin, *n.* liquid measure, half a Scots pint; drink of liquor

chapman, *n.* pedlar

chearfu', *adj.* cheerful

cheek, *n.* side-piece

cheek-for-chow (jow), *adv. phr.* cheek by jowl, side by side

cheel, chiel(d), *n.* lad, young fellow, chap

chimla, chimlie, *n.* fireplace, hearth

chittering, *ppl. adj.* trembling, shivering

chow, *v.* chew

chuck(ie), *n.* mother hen; sweetheart, dear

chuffie, *adj.* portly, 'fat-faced' (B)

cit, *n.* citizen, townsman

clachan, *n.* village; *attrib.* ale-house

claes, claise, claething, claith(ing), *n.* clothes, dress

clamb, *v. pa. t.* climbed

clarket, *pa. pple.* written up

clarty, *adj.* sticky, dirty

clash, *n.* chatter, 'an idle tale, the story of the day' (B); *v.* gossip, talk scandal

clatter, *n.* uproar, chatter, gossip

claught, see **cleek**

claut(e), *n.* clutch, grip; handful, lump

claver, *n.* clover

clavers, *n.* idle talk, chatter

claw, *n.* scratching; *v.* scratch, beat, thrash

claymore, *n.* two-handed Highland sword

clean, *adj.* comely, shapely; empty; *adv.* quite, utterly

clear, *adj.* quite free

clearin, *n.* beating

cleckin, *n.* brood

cleed, *v.* clothe

cleek, *v.* clutch, lay hold of, pilfer; link arms in the dance; **claught,** *pa. t.*

cleg, *n.* gadfly

clink, *n.* (1) cash; (2) jingle (of verse); *v.* (1) ring, rhyme; (2) sit down smartly

clips, *n.* shears, clippers

clishmaclaver(s), *n.* wordy discourse, tittle-tattle, blethers

clockin-time, *n.* hatching-time, child-bearing

cloot, *n.* division of the hoof, the hoof; **Clooty, Cloots,** the (cloven-footed) Devil

close, *adj.* constant, unrelieved

clour, *n.* 'a bump or swelling after a blow' (B)

clout, *n., v.* patch

clud, *n.* cloud

clunk, *v.* gurgle

coat(ie), *n.* petticoat, skirt

coaxin, *ppl. adj.* making a 'cokes' of, wheedling, flattering

coble, see **saumont**

cock, *n.* (1) good fellow, chap; **cockie,** crony; (2) circle at which the stones are aimed in curling

coff, *v.* buy; **coft,** *pa. t.*

cog(gie), *n.* wooden vessel made of staves and girded with metal bands, for drinking liquor; as a corn measure

colleaguin, *v. pres. pple.* associating, conspiring

collieshangie, *n.* dispute, uproar

command, *n.* commandment

commen', *v.* commend

commerce-chaumer, *n.* chamber of commerce

conveener, *n.* president of a trades court

cood, *n.* cud

coof, cuif, *n.* fool, clown, lout

cooket, *v. pa. t.* 'appeared and disappeared by fits' (B)

coor, *v.* cover, protect

cooser, *n.* stallion; lecher

coost, *v. pa. t.* cast, threw off, discarded (for battle); tossed; looped

cootie, *n.* (milk-)basin, (wash-)tub

cootie, *adj.* with feathered legs

corbie, *n.* raven

core, *n.* band of dancers; party, merry company; team of curlers

corn't, *v. pa. pple.* fed with corn

cot(-house), *n.* cottage; **cot-folk**, cottagers

cotillion, *n.* eighteenth-century French dance

cotter(-man), *n.* farm tenant, cottager

couldna, *v.* could not

countra, *adj.* country, rustic. See **kintra**

coup, see **cowp**

couper, *n.* cooper; *v.* repair

cour, cow'r, *v.* lower, fold; **cowran**, *ppl. adj.* cringing, timid

court-day, *n.* rent-day

couthie, couthy, *adj.* loving, kind

cow(e), *v.* berate, scold, beat thoroughly, humiliate; *n.* trouncing

cowe, *v.* terrify; *n.* terror, hobgoblin

cowp, coup, *v.* upset, capsize; *pa. pple.* blown over, laid low

cow'r, cowran, see **cour**

cowt(e), *n.* colt; *transf.* awkward fellow

cozie, *adj.* snug, comfortable

crabbet, *adj.* crabbed, ill-natured

crack, *n.* gossip, chat; *pl.* jokes, talk; story, scandalous tale; *v.* talk, chat, make (a jest)

craft, *n*. croft, infield, land adjoining farm-house

craig(ie), *n*. neck, throat, gullet

craik, *n*. land-rail, corn-crake

crambo-clink, crambo-jingle, *n*. doggerel verse

crank, *n*. harsh sound, 'the noise of an ungreased wheel' (B); *pl.* grating lines

crankous, *adj*. fretful, captious, awkward

cranreuch, *n*. hoar-frost

crap, *n*. (1) top, head; (2) crop; *v*. crop

craw, *n*. (1) crow; (2) cock's crow

crazy, *adj*. crazed, infirm

creel, *n*. wicker basket carried on the back; '*to have one's wits in a creel*, to be craz'd, to be fascinated' (B)

creepie-chair, *n*. three-legged stool, used as stool of repentance in church

creeshie, *adj*. greasy, filthy

critic, *adj*. critical, practising criticism

crock, *n*. old ewe past bearing

crood, croud, *v*. coo, wail

croon, *n*. (1) moan, whine; (2) low, bellow; *v*. boom (of a bell), hum

croose, see **crouse**

cross, *prep*. across

crouch, *v*. bend, cringe submissively

crouchie, *adj*. hump-backed

croud, see **crood**

crouse, croose, *adj*. merry, cocksure

crowdie, *n*. oatmeal mixed with water and eaten raw; porridge; **crowdie-time**, *n*. breakfast-time

crowlan, *ppl. adj.* creeping

crummock, *n*. stick with crooked head, crook

crump, *adj*. 'hard and brittle, *spoken of bread*' (B), baked dry

crunt, *n*. 'a blow on the head with a cudgel' (B)

cry, *v*. call, summon; protest, claim

cuif, see **coof**

cummock, *n*. 'a short staff with a crooked head' (B)

curchie, *n*. curtsey

curler, *n*. player in curling

curmurring, *n*. 'slight, rumbling noise' (B), flatulence

curpan, *n.* rump

curry, *n.* dressing, beating

cushat, *n.* wood-pigeon

custoc(k), *n.* kale-stalk, cabbage stem

cutty, *adj.* short, brief; **cutty-stool,** *n.* stool of repentance in church, cf. **creepie-chair**

D

dadie, *n.* father

daez't, *ppl. adj.* stupefied, besotted

daffin, *n.* fooling, frolic, flirtation, dallying

daft, *adj.* silly, foolish; libertine; wild with excitement

dail, *n.* dale

dail, *n,* deal, fir- or pine-wood plank

daimen-icker, *n.* occasional ear of corn

dainty, *n.* treat; *adj.* (1) worthy, open-hearted; (2) 'pleasant, good-humoured, agreeable' (B); (3) stately

daud, *v.* 'to thrash, abuse' (B), pelt. See **dawd**

daunton, *v.* subdue, discourage, cast down

daur, *v.* dare; **daur't, durst,** *pa. t.* dared (do)

daurk, *n.* day's labour. Cf. **han'-daurk**

daut, dawt(e), *v.* fondle, caress, pet; *ppl. adj.* treasured, spoiled

daw, *v.* dawn; **dawin,** *n.*

dawd, daud, *n.* hunk, large piece

dawt(e), see **daut**

deacon, *n.* president of a trade, and *ex officio* town councillor

dead, *n.* death

dead-sweer, *adj.* quite disinclined

deal about, *v.* divide, distribute

dearthfu', *adj.* costly

deave, *v.* deafen

deep-lairing, *ppl. adj.* sinking deep into the drifts

deevil, de'il, diel, *n.* devil, the Devil

de'il a (ane), not a (one), no (one) at all; **deil na, deil nor** (expressing strong negation); **deil-mak-matter,** no matter. See **hair, deil a; hae't**

deleeret, deliret, *ppl. adj.* delirious, crazed

delver, *n.* gardener, labourer; **delvin,** *n.* digging

den, *n.* dingle

deu(c)k, *n.* duck

devel, *n.* violent blow

devil-haet, see **hae't**

dictionar, *n.* dictionary

did(d)le, *n.* jig, move jerkily, fiddle

diel, see **deevil**

dight, *v.* make ready; wipe, rub down; wipe ready, dry, clean; winnow

din, *adj.* dark, dingy

dine, *n.* dinner-time

ding, *v.* overcome, weary; *neut. pass.* be shifted, be worn out; **dung in,** *pa. pple.* beaten into

dink, *adj.* trim, finely dressed

dinna, *v.* do not

dinsome, *adj.* noisy

dint, *n.* occasion, chance; *v.* pierce with an arrow

dirl, *v.* shake, rattle; play vigorously, reel off; as *adv.* with a clatter, 'slight tremulous stroke or pain' (B)

diz(ze)n, *n., adj.* dozen; hank, dozen 'cuts' (each 310 yards) of yarn, the standard of a day's spinning

do, *v.* put up with, stand

docht, see **dow**

doit, *v.* to be crazed, enfeebled by age or drink; **doited,** *pa. t.* acted stupid, blundered, *trans.* enfeebled, dulled; **doytan,** *ppl. adj.* stumbling, blundering; **doited,** *ppl. adj.* muddled, 'stupified, hebetated' (B)

donsie, *adj.* hapless, unlucky; ill-tempered, unmanageable

dool, *n.* sorrow, misery

dorty, *adj.* supercilious, haughty

doubt, *v.* fear, think, suspect, with the implication of probability

douce, douse, *adj.* sedate, sober, prudent, kindly; **douse(ly),** circumspectly, decorously

dought, see **dow**

douk, *v.* duck, dip

douna, see **downa**

doup, *n.* backside, buttocks; **doup-skelper,** *n.* lecher

dour(e), dowr(e), *adj.* harsh, severe; pertinacious, unyielding; sullen

douse, see **douce**

dow, *n.* pigeon

dow, *v.* be able, have courage (to do), dare; **docht, dought**, *pa. t.*

dowf(f), *adj.* listless, 'pithless, wanting force' (B), melancholy, dull

dowie, *adj.* sad, dismal, melancholy; sickly, dejected

downa, douna, *v.* cannot

down-brae, *adv.* downhill

dowr(e), see **dour(e)**

doxy, *n.* beggar's wench

doylt, *ppl. adj.* dazed, muddled, stupid

doytan, see **doit**

dozen, dozin, *ppl. adj.* impotent; **dozen'd**, *pa. pple.* made impotent

draigle, *v.* bedraggle, bespatter

drank, *v. pa. t. intr.* tasted

drant, drunt, *n.* sulks

drap, *n.* drop; amount of; **drappie**, *n.* (a little) liquor

draunt, *v.* whine, drone out

drave on, *v. pa. t.* passed

dreeping, *ppl. adj.* dripping (with gravy)

dreigh, driegh, *adj.* slow, tedious, dreary

dress, see **droddum**

drid(d)le, *v.* dawdle, saunter; totter

driegh, see **dreigh**

drift, *n.* (1) flock, herd; (2) falling snow driven by the wind; hence **drifty**, *adj.*

droddum, *n.* backside; **dress your droddum**, thrash you

droop-rumpl't, *adj. comb.* with drooping haunches

drouk, *v.* soak, drench; **droukit**, *ppl. adj.*

drouth, *n.* thirst; **drouthy**, *adj.*

dru(c)ken, *ppl. adj.* drunken, tipsy

drumlie, *adj.* sedimented, cloudy; gloomy, thick-skulled

drummock, *n.* oatmeal and cold water

drunt, see **drant**

dry, *adj.* thirsty

duan, *n.* canto

dub, *n.* stagnant pool, puddle, pond; mud, mire

duddie, *adj.* ragged, tattered

dud(d)ies, duds, *n. pl.* (1) clothes; (2) rags, tatters

dung, see **ding**

dunt, *n*. dull knock, blow; *v*. strike, thump, throb

durk, *n*. short Highland dagger, worn in the belt

durst, see daur

dusht, *n. pa. pple.* 'pushed by a ram, ox, etc.' (B)

dwall, *v*. dwell; dwalling, *n*. dwelling, cottage

dyke, *n*. low dry-stone wall

dyvor, *n*. bankrupt

E

eastlin, *adj*. easterly

easy, *adv*. easily

e'e, *n*. eye; een, ein, *pl*.

e'en, *n*. evening

e'en, *adv*. even; just, simply

eerie, irie, *adj*. (1) apprehensive, 'frighted, *dreading spirits*' (B); (2) weird, ghostly, uncanny; (3) gloomy, melancholy

efter, *adv*. afterwards

eild, *n*. old age

ein, see e'e

elbuck, *n*. elbow

eldritch, *adj*. uncanny, unearthly; 'ghastly, frightful' (B), hideous; haunted

eleckit, *pa. pple*. elected, chosen

elf, *n*. dwarf; hideous creature, bewitching girl

ell, *n*. unit of measurement (*c*. 37 inches)

eller, *n*. (Presbyterian) elder

Embro', Enbrugh, *n*. familiar forms of *Edinburgh*

eneuch, eneugh, *adj., adv*. enough

enow, *adj*. enough, sufficient

Erse, *adj*. Highland, Gaelic

ettle, *n*. purpose, aim

ev'n down, *adj. phr*. downright, sheer

expeckit, *pa. pple*. (have) expected

eydent, *adj*. assiduous, diligent

F

fa', *v*. (1) fall; (2) befall; lay claim to; fa'n, faun, *pa. pple*.

fa', *n*. (1) fortune; (2) turn of events; (3) the Fall

facket, fecket, *n.* woollen waistcoat, vest

factor, *n.* steward, agent of an estate

faddom, *v.* measure by the fathom

fae, *n.* foe

faem, *n.* foam, froth

faikit, *ppl. adj.* excused, given a respite

fain, *adj.* glad, content; **fain o' ither,** fond of each other. See **fidge**

fair, *adj.* easy; *adv.* fairly, openly; **fairly,** *adv.* clearly, indeed; **fair fa',** good luck to

fairin, *n.* present from a fair; in *phr.* **give, get, take a fairin,** reward, deserts, punishment

fairy, *adj.* dwarfish

faith ye, *interj.* confound you

fallow, *n.* fellow, chap

famous, *adj.* grand, fine

fa'n, see fa'

fand, see fin'

farina, *n.* flour, meal

farl, *n.* quarter of the circular oaten bannock

fash, *v.* bother, trouble; *pa. pple.* afflicted; **fash ... thumb,** pay heed; *n.* trouble, annoyance

fashious, *adj.* tricky, awkward, irksome

Fasteneen, *n.* Shrove Tuesday (evening)

fatherly, *adv.* with a father's affection

fatt'rels, *n. pl.* 'ribbon ends' (B)

faught, see fecht

fauld, *v.* enfold, enclose, gather; **fauld,** *pa. pple.;' ppl. adj.* **faulding-(jocteleg),** clasp-(knife)

fauld, *n.* (sheep) fold; *v.* to gather in, pen; **a faulding,** *vbl. n.*

faun, see fa'

fause, *adj.* false

fausont, fawsont, *ppl. adj.* respectable, 'decent, seemly' (B)

faut(e), fau't, *n.* fault, (sexual) failing

fear, *v.* frighten, scare; **fear'd, fear't,** *pa. pple.* and *ppl. adj.* frightened

feat, *adj.* spruce, trim

fecht, *v.* fight; **faught,** *pa. t.;* **fechtan,** *ppl. adj.* fighting, disputatious

feck, *n.* value, return, advantage; **the feck,** the majority, most; **feckly,** *adv.* for the most part, almost

fecket, see **facket**

fee, *v.* hire (as a servant); **fee(s),** *n.* servant's (half-yearly) wages

feg, *n.* fig

feide, *n.* enmity

fell, *adj.* potent, pungent; harsh, cruel, keen

fen', fend, *v.* support, fend (for themselves); *n.* shift, effort

Ferintosh, *n.* a whisky

ferlie, *v.* marvel, wonder; *n.* 'a term of contempt' (B)

fetch, *v.* draw breath painfully, gasp; 'to stop suddenly in the draught, and then come on too hastily' (B)

fey, *adj.* doomed

fidge, *v.* shrug, twitch, frisk; **fidge fu' fain,** twitch with excitement; **fidgean-fain, fidgin fain,** *adj. phr.* excited, eager

fiel, *adv.* cosily, softly

fi(e)nt a, *strong neg.* the devil a; **fien' a hair,** see **hair; fien(t) haet (o't),** see **hae't**

fier, *adj.* hearty, sound

fier(e), *n.* companion, comrade

fin', *v.* find; **fand,** *pa. t.*

fint, see **fi(e)nt a**

fire-shool, see **shool**

fiscal, *n.* procurator fiscal, attorney (practising in the lower courts)

fish-creel, see **creel**

fissle, *v.* make a rustling noise; bustle, get excited

fit, *n.* poem, strain of music

fit(t), *n.* foot; foothold

fittie-lan', *n.* rear left-hand horse in the plough

flaff, *v.* flap, flutter; **flaffan,** *pres. pple.*

flainen, flannen, *n.* flannel

flairing, *ppl. adj.* gaudy, extravagant

flang, see **fling**

flannen, see **flainen**

flee, *v.* fly

fleech, *v.* wheedle, coax, flatter; **fleechan,** *ppl. adj.*

fleesh, *n.* fleece

fleet-wing, *v.* fly swiftly; *adv.* in swift flight

fleg, *n.* blow, kick; fling

fleth'ran, *ppl. adj.* wheedling, cajoling

fley, *v.* terrify, frighten

flichter, *v.* 'to flutter *as young nestlings when their dam approaches*' (B)

flie, *n.* fly; hence, something of no value (following a *neg.*)

flinders, *n. pl.* fragments, smithereens

fling, *v.* throw, kick; **flang,** *pa. t.*; *pres. pple.* capering; **fling,** *n.* jump; *comb.* **flingin-tree,** swingle of a flail, 'a flail' (B)

flisk, *v.* 'to fret at the yoke' (B)

flit, *v. tr.* shift, move; *intr.* go, depart; change abode

fodgel, *adj.* plump and good-humoured

foggage, *n.* rank grass

fool, play the, indulge in sexual dalliance

for, *prep.* of

forbear, *n.* ancestor, forefather

for(e)by(e), *prep.* besides, as well as; *adv.* what is more

forehammer, *n.* hammer with which the smith strikes first, sledge-hammer

forfairn, *ppl. adj.* undone, exhausted, worn out

forgather, *v.* assemble, congregate; encounter; **forgather up,** take up with, keep company with

forgie, *v.* forgive

forjesket, *ppl. adj.* 'jaded with fatigue' (B), worn out

forrit, *adv.* forward

fother, *n.* fodder, hay

fou, fow, fu', *adj.* full; drunk; *adv.* very, quite

foughten, *pa. pple.* of fecht; *ppl. adj.* harassed, worn out

foumart, fulmart, *n.* pole-cat

fouth, *n.* plenty, abundance

fow, *n.* firlot ('fill', full measure). See **fou**

frae, *prep.* from

fraeth, *v.* foam, froth

frank, *adj.* generous, lavish

freak, *n.* odd notion, fancy

free, *v.* clear, leap over

frien', *n.* friend; **freens,** *pl.*

fright, *n.* ridiculous creature; *v.* frighten, scare

fu', see **fou**

fud, *n.* backside; tail, scut

fuff, *v.* puff, smoke

fulmart, see foumart

fumble, *v.* act awkwardly, impotently

fun, *n.* boisterous sport

funny, *adj.* sportive, whimsical, facetious

furder, *n.* progress, good luck

furm, *n.* form, bench

furr, *n.* furrow, ditch

furr ahin, *n.* right-hand horse immediately in front of the plough

fusionless, *adj.* pithless, dry, weak

fyke, *v.* fidget, 'to piddle, to be in a fuss about trifles' (B), fiddle, twitch; *n.* fuss, commotion

fyle, *v.* defile, foul

G

gab, *n.* (1) bold, entertaining chatter; *v.* talk readily, eloquently; (2) mouth

gae, *v.* go, walk; gaen, gane, *pa. pple.*; gaun, *pres. pple.*

gae, see gie

gaets, see gate

gager, see gauge

gailies, *adv.* tolerably, well enough

gair, *n.* strip of cloth, gusset

gane, see gae

gang, *v.* go, depart, walk

gangrel, *n.* vagrant, tramp

gar, *v.* make, cause, compel; gart, gar't, *pa. t., pa. pple.*

garten, *n.* garter; *v., pa. pple.* gartered

gash, (1) *v.* chat volubly, prattle; (2) *adj.* shrewd, witty; smart, respectable, neat

gat, *v. pa. t.* of *get*; gat the whissle, see groat

gate, *n.* road, way, fashion; gaets, *pl.* habits

gaud, *n.* goad for driving cattle in the plough; gaudsman, *n.* boy who 'goads' the team

gauge, *v.* measure the contents of a cask; ga(u)ger, *n.* exciseman

gaun, see gae

Gaun, *n.* Gavin

gaunt, *v.* gape, gasp

gausie, gawsy, *adj.* ample, jovial-looking; fine, full, showy; plump

gawkie, *n.* booby, fool

gear, *n.* possessions, money, property; livestock

geck, *v.* toss the head in scorn, scoff (at)

ged, *n.* pike

gent, *n.* gentleman, fellow. See genty

gentles, *n. pl.* 'great folks' (B), gentry

gent(y), *adj.* dainty, graceful, slender

Geordie, George (yellow), *n.* guinea

get, *n.* offspring, brat

ghaist, *n.* ghost

gie, *v.* give; **giein**, *pres. pple.*; **gae**, *pa. t.*; **gien**, *pa. pple.* (have given); **gies**, give us, give me; **gied**, *pa. t.*; **gie up**, offer for intercession

gif, *conj.* if

giftie, *n.* dim. of *gift*; power, talent

giga, *n.* gigue, lively air

gill, *n.* Scots measure, quarter-mutchkin (*c.* three-quarters of the imperial gill); **gillie**, vessel holding a gill

gilpey, *n.* young girl

gimmer(-pet), *n.* yearling ewe kept as pet

gimp, see jimp

gin, *prep.*, *conj.* before, by (of time)

gin, *conj.* if, whether

girdle, *n.* griddle for baking scones

girn, *v.* grin, snarl, 'twist the features in rage, agony, etc.' (B)

giz(z), *n.* wig

glaiket, glaikit, *adj.* careless, foolish, carefree, inattentive, irresponsible, giddy

glaizie, *adj.* 'glittering, smooth like glass' (B), glossy

glamor, *n.* enchantment, magic

glaum, *v.* snatch, grab, lay hold of

gleesome, *adj.* cheerful, merry

gleg, *adj.* quick, lively; quick-witted, smart; keen-edged

gleib, *n.* portion of land

glib-gabbet, *adj.* smooth-tongued

glimpse, *v.* take a look (at)

gloamin, *n.* twilight, dusk

glowr, (1) *v.* stare wide-eyed, gaze intently; (2) gleam, shine out (of the sun, moon); (3) *n.* scowl

glunch, *v.*, *n.* look sullen, scowl, frown

goave, *v.* stare stupidly, vacantly

goom, *n.* gum

gor-cock, *n.* male of the red grouse

gos, *n.* goshawk

gossip, *n.* neighbour-woman

gowan, *n.* 'the flower of the daisy, dandelion, hawkweed, etc.' (B)

gowd, *n.* gold; **gowden,** *adj.*; **gowdie,** *n.* (golden) head

gowk, *n.* cuckoo; fool, dolt

gowling, *ppl. adj.* howling, yelling

grace-prood, *adj.* smugly conscious of divine favour, sanctimonious

gracious, *adj.* friendly, amiable

grain, see **grane**

graip, *n.* farm-yard and garden fork

graith, *n.* (1) equipment, tools, ploughing gear, goods; (2) dress, habit; **graithing,** vestments

grane, grain, *n.*, *v.* groan

Grannie, Graunie, *n.* grandmother

grape, *v.* grope, feel for, search with the hands; **grapet,** *pa. t.*

grat, see **greet**

gray-neck, *n.* a gambler, trimmer

great, *adj.* 'thick', intimate, friendly

gree, *n.* social degree, supremacy; hence **bear the gree, carry the gree,** win first place, come off best

gree, *v.* agree

greet, *v.* weep, cry; **grat,** *pa. t.*; **grutten,** *pa. pple.*; **greetie, greet-in(g),** *nn.* crying

greive, *n.* manager, farm-bailiff

grip, *v.* grasp; *n.* sharp pain; *pl.* gripes

grissle, *n.* gristle; stump of a quill pen

groanin maut, see **maut(e)**

groat, *n.* silver coin of small value, 3d. Scots; '*to get the whistle of one's groat*, to play a losing game' (B)

gr[o]usome, *adj.* horrible, 'loathsomely grim' (B)

grozet, *n.* gooseberry

grumble, *v.* begrudge; **grumbling,** *ppl. adj.* mumbling, murmuring

Grumphie, *n.* grumbler, the sow

grun', *n.* the ground, earth

grunstane, *n.* grindstone

gruntle, *n.* grunt; snout, nose

grunzie, *n.* snout

grushie, *adj.* thriving, lusty, strong

grusome, see **gr[o]usome**

grutten, see **greet**

gude, guid, *adj., adv., n., v.* good; substit. for *God*; *combs.* **gu(i)deen,** good-evening; **guid-father,** *n.* father-in-law; **gudeman, guid-man,** *n.* head of a household, master, husband; **guidwife,** *n.* mistress, wife; **gude-willy,** *adj.* generous; **gude-willie-waught,** *n.* cordial drink, 'cup of kindness' (see **waught**).

gullie, gully, *n.* large knife

gulravage, *n.* romp, uproar, horseplay

gumlie, *adj.* muddy

gumption, *n.* common sense, shrewdness

gusty, *adj.* tasty, appetizing

gutscraper, *n.* fiddler

gutty, *adj.* pot-bellied

H

ha', *n.* hall; **ha'-Bible,** 'a large family bible' (SND); **ha' folk,** *pl.* servants. See **hae**

ha'd, see **haud**

hae, ha'(e), *v.* have; *imperat.* 'here!', 'take this!'; **haen,** *pa. pple.* See **hae't**

haerse, *adj.* hoarse

hae't, haet, have it; as *neg.* or *imprec.* in *phrs.* **de(v)il h., d–mn'd h., fien(t) haet (o't),** devil a bit, devil a one, 'damn all', nothing

ha'f, see **hauf**

haff-, *adv.* half-. See **hauf**

haffet, *n.* temple; lock or hair growing on the temple

haf(f)lins(-wise), *adv.* in half measure, partly, nearly

hag(g), *n.* 'a scar or gulf in mosses and moors' (B), made by water-channels or peat-cutting

haggis, *n.* a pudding of minced liver, meal, suet, onions and spices, boiled in a sheep's stomach

hail, *n.* small shot, pellets

hail, see **hale**

hain, *v.* save, spare; *ppl. adj.* enclosed, kept for hay; **weel-hain'd,** *ppl. adj.* well-preserved, hoarded

hainch, *n.* haunch, hip

hair, *n.* whit, trifle, trace; **deil a hair, fien' a hair,** not a bit. Cf. **hae't**

hairst, *n.* harvest

hairum-scairum, *adj.* wild

haith, 'a petty oath' (B)

hal(d), *n.* hold, dwelling, refuge

hale, *n.* health

hale, hail, *adj.* healthy, sound; entire, whole

half-lang, *adj.* half-length

half-sarket, see **sark**

hallan, *n.* partition (usually of mud or clay and stones) between a cottage door and fireplace to divert the draught, or between living-room and byre

hallion, *n.* idler, rascal

Halloween, *n.* eve of All Saints' Day; **Hallow-mass,** festival of All Saints

haly, *adj.* holy

hame, *n., adv.* home; **hamely,** *adj.* familiar, plain, common, friendly; **hameward,** *adv.* homewards

hammers, *n. pl.* noisy, clumsy fellows

han(d), haun', *n.* hand, 'rare hands', artists; *phrs.* **beside our han',** 'at our own hand', by, for ourselves; **'mang hands,** at intervals; *combs.* **han'-daurk,** *n.* labour of the hands (see **daurk**); **hand-bread,** *n.* hand's breadth; **hand-wal'd,** *adj.* hand-picked, choice (see **wale**)

hang, see **hing**

Hangie, *n.* hangman; the Devil

hanker, *v.* hang about, loiter, hesitate

hansel, *n.* New Year or good-luck gift; **hansel in,** *v.* be a first gift for (the New Year)

hap, *v.* cover, shield

hap, *v.* hop; *ppl. adj.* drop in quick succession

happer, *n.* hopper (of a mill)

hap-step-an'-loup, *adv.* briskly

hardy, *adj.* bold, foolhardy

hark, *v.* listen (to); **harket,** *pa. pple.*

harn, *n.* coarse linen, sackcloth

harpy, *n.*; *attrib.* rapacious, plundering

har'sts, see **hairst**

has been, *n.* one past his best

hash, (1) *v.* hack, mangle, waste; (2) *n.* waster, impudent or dissolute fool

haslock, *n.* wool on sheep's neck

haud, ha'd, *v.* hold, keep; **haud awa,** come away (cf. **held**); **h. in,** keep in, supply with; **h. on,** persist; **h. tae,** stick to; **haud you,** stay

hauf, ha'f, *n.* half

haugh, *n.* level, fertile land by a river

haun', see **han(d)**

haurl, *v.* drag; *pres. pple.* peeling; haul off to punishment

hav[e]rel, *adj.*, *n.* simpleton, half-wit(ted)

havins, *n. pl.* behaviour; good manners, sense

hawkie, *n.* cow with white face, pet name for a cow

heal, *adj.* healthy, well; **healsome,** *adj.* wholesome

heapet, *ppl. adj.* heaped, well-filled

hech, *interj.* a sighing exclamation, 'Oh! strange!' (B)

hecht, *v.* promise, pledge, offer

heckle, *n.* flax-comb

heed, *n.* observation, care

heeze, *v.* lift, exalt, elevate

held (awa, to), *v. pa. t.* took (my) way

hem-shin'd, *ppl. adj.* with shins shaped like haims, the curved pieces of wood or metal fixed over a draught-horse's collar

herd, *n.* herd-boy

here awa, *adv.* (1) hereabouts, in this neighbourhood; (2) hither (and thither)

herry, *v.* harry, plunder; **herryment,** devastation, waste

het, *adj.* hot, burning, excited; **het and cauld,** *adv. phr.* at all times

heugh, *n.* (1) crag, steep bank; (2) ravine, pit

heuk, *n.* hook, sickle

hilch, *v.* lurch, limp

hilt and hair, (every) bit

hiltie, skiltie, *adv.* pell-mell, heedlessly

hindmost, *adj.* last, final

hiney, hinnie, hinny, *n.* honey, sweetheart, darling; *adj.* sweet

hing, *v.* hang, make (us) hang; **hang**, *pa. t.*

hirple, *v.* limp, hobble, move unevenly (as a hare)

hissel, *n.* flock of sheep on one farm or in one shepherd's care

histie, *adj.* dry, stony

hit, *v.* manage, achieve, reach (it)

hizzie, *n.* wench; silly girl; trull, whore

ho(a)st, *n., v.* cough

hoddan, *pple.* jogging along, bumping in the saddle

hoddin, *n.* coarse grey homespun cloth of mixed black and white wool

hoggie, *n.* young sheep from time of weaning till the first fleece is sheared

hog-score, *n.* distance-line in curling. See **score**

hog-shouther, *v.* push about; 'a kind of horseplay by jostling with the shoulder; to justle' (B)

Hollan(d), *n.* holland cloth, fine linen

hollow, *n.* halloo

hoodie-craw, *n.* the hooded or grey crow, black in the head, wings and tail

hoodock, *n.* the hooded crow; an avaricious person, *attrib.*

hool, *n.* membrane, pericardium

hoolie, *adv., interj.* gently, slowly, 'take leisure! stop!' (B)

hoord, *n.* hoard, drift; **hoordet**, *ppl. adj.* hoarded

horn, *n.* horn vessel, horn spoon; **Hornie**, *n.* the horned Devil

host, see **ho(a)st**

hotch, *v.* hitch, jerk about

hough, *v.* disable, by cutting the tendons of the hough

houghmagandie, *n.* fornication

houlet, *n.* owl(ct)

houpe, *n.* hope

hove, *v.* rise; *tr.* make to swell, distend

how deil, how the devil

how(c)k, *v.* dig, delve; *ppl. adj.* dug up, exhumed

howdie, *n.* midwife

howe, *n.* hollow, valley, glen; *adj.* hollow, deep; *comb.* **howe-backet,** 'sunk in the back' (B)

howk, see **how(c)k**

hoy't, *v. pa. t.* cried 'hoy!'

hoyte, *n.* 'a motion between a trot and a gallop' (B); hence *v.* move clumsily, waddle

huff, *v.* scold, berate

Hughoc, *n.* little Hugh

hum, *v.* hoax, take in, humbug

hum, *v.* mumble; **hum an' haw,** mutter inarticulately in hesitation

Humphie, *n.* nickname for a hunchback

hunder, *num. adj.* and *n.* hundred; hundredth

hung, *ppl. adj.* eloquent

hunkers, *n. pl.* hams, haunches

hurcheon, hurchin, *n.* hedgehog; mischievous child, urchin

hurdies, *n. pl.* buttocks, backside

hushian, *n.* footless stocking

hyte, *adj.* crazed, daft

I

i', *prep.* in, into

icker, see **daimen-icker**

ier-oe, *n.* great-grandchild

ilk(a), *adj.* each, every

ill-, *adj., adv.* evil; **ill-taen,** *ppl. adj.* ill-taken, resented; **Ill-thief,** *n.* the Devil; **ill-willie,** *adj.* ill-disposed, malignant, ungenerous

in for 't, liable to punishment

in to, *prep.* within, to

indentin, *pres. pple.* pledging, engaging

ingine, *n.* talent, genius, wit

ingle, *n.* fire burning on a hearth; **ingle-cheek,** *n.* chimney-corner; **ingle-low(e),** *n.* firelight; **ingle-neuk,** *n.* chimney-corner; **ingle-side,** *n.* fireside

irie, see **eerie**

I'se, I shall. See **sall**

ither, *adj.* other, another, further; *pron.* each other; **other,** *adv.* otherwise, else

J

jacket, *n.* coat of mail

jad, *n.* mare; wench, hussy

Janwar', *n.* January

jauk, *v.* 'to dally, to trifle' (B), waste time; **jaukin**, *n.* delay

jauntie, *n.* little trip, journey

jaup, *v.* 'to jerk as agitated water' (B), splash; *n. pl.*

jee, *interj., quasi-adv.* with a swing, sideways

jillet, *n.* giddy wench, jilt

jimp, *v.* jump

jimp, gimp, *adj.* slender, graceful, neat

jimps, *n. pl.* skirts

jing, by, a mild expletive

jink, *v.* dodge, dart, slip aside; move quickly, zig-zag; jerk; *n.* the act of eluding someone, the slip; **jinker**, *n.* a high-spirited beast, 'a gay, sprightly girl' (B)

jirkinet, *n.* woman's bodice

jirt, *n.* jerk

jo, see jo(e)

job, *n.* intrigue, jobbery

jocteleg, *n.* clasp-knife

jo(e), *n.* sweetheart

jog, *v.* trudge

jouk, *v.* dodge, duck

jow, *v.* toll; 'a verb, which includes both the swinging motion and pealing sound of a large bell' (B)

jowler, *n.* heavy-jawed dog, hound

jundie, *v.* elbow, jostle

K

kae, *n.* jackdaw, thief

kail, *n.* (1) borecole, green kale; (2) vegetable broth; *combs.* **kail-blade**, leaf of kale; **kail-runt**, stalk stripped of leaves; **kail-yard**, kitchen- or cottage-garden. Cf. **bow-kail, muslin-kail**

kane, *n.* payment in kind, reckoning

kebar, *n.* long pine pole; rafter

kebbuck, *n.* home-made cheese; **kebbuck-heel**, the hard end of a cheese

keckle, *v.* cackle, giggle

keek, *v.* peer, glance, peep (at); *n.* cautious glance, sly glance

kelpie, *n.* water demon in the shape of a horse

ken, *v.* (1) know, be aware of, learn; (2) be acquainted with, recognize, identify

kennin, *vbl. n.* (a) little, trifle

kep, *v.* keep, catch

ket, *n.* 'a matted, hairy fleece of wool' (B)

kettle, *n.* cauldron, pot

kiaugh, *n.* 'carking anxiety' (B)

kiln, *n.* kiln for drying grain

kilt, *v.* tuck up the skirts

kimmer, *n.* (1) gossip, woman, wife (usually familiar or contemptuous); (2) lass, wench

kin', **kind,** *adj.* kindly, agreeable, winsome; *adv.* somewhat, rather

king's-hood, *n.* second stomach in a ruminant; paunch

kintra, *adj.* country

kirk, *n.* church; **kirk-hammer,** clapper of church bell

kirn, *n.* churn

kirn, *n.* harvest-home, merrymaking at end of harvest

kirs'n, *v.* christen; dilute with water

kist, *n.* chest, coffer

kitchen, *v.* season, give relish to

kith and kin, hendiadys for *kinsfolk*

kittle, *v.* (1) tickle, excite, rouse; (2) **kittle up,** tune up, play; *adj.* (1) likely, inclined; (2) fickle, ticklish, difficult, tricky

kittlen, *n.* kitten

kiutle . . . wi', *v.* 'to cuddle, to caress, to fondle' (B)

knaggie, *adj.* knobbly, bony

knappin-hammer, *n.* hammer for breaking stones

knoit, *v.* knock

knowe, *n.* mound, hillock

knurl, **knurlin,** *n.* dim. of *knur,* dwarf

kye, *n. pl.* cows, cattle

kyles, *n. pl.* skittles

kytch, *n.* toss, jerk, upward shove

kyte, *n.* belly

kythe, *v.* make known, discover, tell

L

labo(u)r, *v.* belabour, thrash

lade, *n.* load

lag, *adj.* laggard, backward

laggen, *n.* angle between sides and bottom of a cask, dish

laid (upon), *v. pa. t.* assailed

laigh, *adv.* low

laik, *n.* lack

laimpet, *n.* limpet

laird, *n.* landed proprietor, squire

laith, *adj.* loath, unwilling, reluctant; **laithfu'**, *adj.* 'bashful, sheepish' (B)

lallan(d), *adj.* lowland; **lallans**, *n.* lowland Scots

lambie, *n.* dim. of *lamb*

Lammas, *n.* 1 August, harvest festival for the consecration of the new bread

lan', *n.* land, country; untilled soil in **lan' afore, lan' ahin**, terms for plough-horses; *pl.* estates

lane, lanely, *adj.* lonely, solitary; after *poss. prons.*, -self: **her lane**, by herself; **my lane, thy-lane**

lang, *adj.* long; *combs.* **lang-kail**, *n.* borecole, Scotch kale (see kail); **lang-kent**, *ppl. adj.* familiar; **lang-mustering**, *ppl. adj.*; **lang syne**, *attrib.* ancient (see syn(e)); **lang-tocher'd**, *ppl. adj.* well-dowered (see tocher)

lank, *adj.* thin and languid

lap, *v. pa. t.* of *loup*; leapt, leapt up

lave, *n.* rest, remainder, others

laverock, lav'rock, *n.* lark; **l.-height**, the height of the lark's flight

law, *v.* decree, determine

lawland, *n.* lowland

lay, *v.* ascribe, attribute

lay, lea, lee, *n.* untilled ground left fallow, part of the outfield, pasture; *comb.* **lea-rig**, ridge of unploughed grass between arable ridges

lea'e, *v.* leave

leal, *adj.* loyal, faithful, true

lear, *n.* learning, lore

lea-rig, see lay

learn, *v.* teach

least, *conj.* lest, for fear

leather, *n.* hide, skin; lining of the throat

lee, see **lay**

lee-lang, *adj.* live-long, whole, all day (night) through; **leesome,** *adj.* dear, tender, delightful; **leeze me on,** lief is me, I am delighted by

left-hand, *adj.* sinister

leister, *n.* pronged spear used in salmon fishing, trident

len', *v.* give, grant

let, *v.* allow; **let be,** 'to give over, to cease' (B)

leuk, *v.* look, watch; *n.* appearance, expression, glance; *pl.* looks

libbet, *ppl. adj.* castrated

licks, *n. pl.* thrashing, punishment; *v.* **lick . . . winnings,** make the best of a bad job; wallop, thrash

liein, *v. pres. pple.* telling lies

lien, *v. pa. pple.* lain

lift, *n.* sky, heavens

lift, *n.* load, large amount; **lift aboon,** boost; **gie a lift,** give a helping hand

lightly, *v.* slight, disparage

like (to), *adj.* likely to, looking as if to; *adv.* as it were, as if

limmer, *n.* rascal; jade, mistress, whore

limpan, *v. pres. pple.* limping; **limpet,** *pa. t.*

lingo, *n.* foreign or unintelligible language

link, *v.* trip, go briskly, skip

lin(n), *n.* waterfall, cataract

linnens, *n. pl.* grave cloths, winding-sheet

lint, *n.* flax plant, flax for spinning

lintwhite, *n.* linnet

lippen (to), *v.* trust, depend on

loan, loaning, *n.* strip of grass running through arable ground, serving as pasture, milking-place, and driving road

locked, *ppl. adj.* closely fastened

lo'e, *v.* love; **loosome,** *adj.* sweet, charming

logger, *adj.* thick, stupid

loof, *n.* palm; hand given in pledge; paw. Cf. **aff-loof**

loon, loun, *n.* (1) rascal, rogue; (2) fellow

loosome, see **lo'e**

loot, *v. pa. t.* of *lat,* let, allowed; let out, uttered; **loot on,** showed, disclosed

loove, *n.* love; **looves,** see **loof**

lough, *n.* loch, lake

loun, see **loon**

loup, lowp, *v.* leap, jump

lour, *v.* look threateningly

louse, lowse, *v.* loose

lowe, *n.* flame; *v.* blaze, rage. See **ingle**

lowp, see **loup**

lowse, see **louse**

lucky, *n.* familiar term of address to an old woman; ale-wife

lug, *n.* ear; **chimla lug,** side wall of chimney recess, chimney-corner; *ppl. adj.* **lugget (caup),** (shallow wooden dish) with handles (see **caup); luggie,** *n.* wooden dish with staves projecting to form handles

lum, *n.* chimney

lum, see **warklum**

Lunardi, *n.* a kind of bonnet named after the Italian balloonist

lunch, *n.* large slice, thick piece

lunt, *v.* smoke (a pipe); *n.* puff of smoke; *n.* steam

lyart, *adj.* streaked with white, grizzled; grey; streaked, red and white

M

mae, *adj., quasi-n.* more

Mahoun, *n.* the Devil

mailen, mailin, *n.* piece of arable land held on lease, small-holding

maingie, *adj.* having the mange, scabby

mair, *adj., adv.* greater, more; **mair for token,** especially, in particular

maist, *adv.* almost

maist(ly), *adv.* mostly

mak, *v.* make, do; **mak to through,** see through, make good

mamie, *n.* mother

'mang, *prep.* among; **'mang hands,** see **han(d)**

manteele, *n.* mantle, cape

mantling, *ppl. adj.* foaming, creaming

mark, *n.* coin worth 13s. 4d. Scots

mashlum, *n.* maslin, mixed meal

mason, *n.* mason, freemason; *attrib.* masonic

maukin, *n*. the hare

maun, *auxil. v*. must; **maun(n)a**, must not

maut(e), *n*. malt, barley prepared for brewing, ale; **groanin maut**, ale provided for visitors at a lying-in

maw, *v*. mow, reap

meere, *n*. mare

meikle, mickle, mu(c)kle, *adj*. great, plentiful, much; *adv*. much, greatly; **meikle corn**, oats; **mickle a do**, much to do

melder, *n*. quantity of meal ground for a customer at one time; the occasion of grinding a customer's corn at the mill

mell, *v*. consort, have friendly dealings; meddle, tamper

melvie, *v*. 'to soil with meal' (B)

men', mend, *v. tr*. cure, heal; *intr*. mend one's ways, repent

mense, *n*. decorum, sense, moderation, tact; **menseless**, *adj*. ill-bred, boorish

Merran, *n*. Marion

Mess John, Mass John [Maister of Arts], the priest, minister

messan, *n*. lap-dog; cur

mickle, see **meikle**

midden-creel, *n*. manure-basket

midden-hole, *n*. 'a gutter at the bottom of the dung-hill' (B)

mim, *adj., adv*. demure(ly); **mim-mou'd**, 'affectedly prim or demure' (SND)

min, min', *n*. mind, recollection

mind, *v*. remind, remember; watch, take care of, see to; **mind't**, *ppl. adj*. disposed, inclined

minnie, minny, *n*. familiar word for mother

mirk, *n*. darkness; *adj*. dark

misca', miska', *v*. abuse, malign

mis(c)hanter, *n*. misadventure, mishap

misguidin, *vbl. n*. mismanagement, squandering

miska', see **misca'**

mislear'd, *ppl. adj*. unmannerly, mischievous

miss, *n*. mistress, whore

mist, *v. pa. t*. missed

mistak', *v*. mistake

mite-horn, *n*. horn on the harvest-bug

mither, *n*. mother

mix(t)ie-max(t)ie, *adj.* jumbled, confused, incongruous

mizl'd, *ppl. adj.* confused, mystified, misinformed

mock, *n.* derision, abuse

modewurk, *n.* mouldwarp, mole

monie, mony, *adj., n.* many

mool, *n.* earth, clod; grave-clods, grave

moop, *v.* 'to nibble as a sheep' (B)

moss, *n.* swamp, peat-bog

mottle, *adj.* full of specks, spotty, dusty

mou', *n.* mouth

much about it, about the same

mu(c)kle, see meikle

muir, *n.* moor; muirfowl, *n.* red grouse

muscle, *n.* mollusc, mussel

musie, *n.* dim. of *muse*

muslin-kail, *n.* thin broth, of water, shelled barley and greens only

mutchkin, *n.* quarter-pint (Scots), *c.* three-quarters of the imperial pint

muve, *v.* move; *ppl. adj.* affecting

mysel, *pron.* myself

N

na', nae, *adv., conj.* not, by no means. See deil na, whatn(a)

na(e), *adj.* no; naebody, *n.* no one; naething, *n.* nothing

naig, *n.* small horse, pony

nail('t), *v.* clinch, prove (it)

nane, *pron., adj., adv.* none

nappy, *n.* ale

near(-)hand, *adv.* almost

neebo(u)r, nibor, *n.* neighbour

negleckit, negleket, *pa. pple.* neglected

neist, see niest

neuk, newk, *n.* corner, recess

new-ca'd, *ppl. adj.* newly calved

nibor, see neebo(u)r

nice, *adj.* fine, delightful; dainty, refined, fastidious, precise

nick, *n.* cut; *v.* cut through, slit; *pres. pple.* cutting down, reaping; *pa. pple.* seized, nabbed

Nick, Auld Nick, Nickie-ben, familiar names for the Devil

niest, neist, *adj., adv.* next

nieve, *n.* fist, clenched hand; **nievefu',** *n.* handful

niffer, *n.* 'an exchange; to exchange, to barter' (B); comparison

nightly, *adj.* appearing at night, travelling at night; *adv.* at night(s)

nine(s), to the, to the highest degree, to perfection

nit, *n.* nut; standard boss

no, *adv.* not

nocht, *n.* nothing; *adv.* not

noddle, *n.* head, brain, pate

nor, *conj.* than. See **deil nor**

norland, *adj.* northern, from the north

nor-west, *n.* north-west wind

notion, *n.* understanding, fancy, desire

nowt(e), *n.* cattle, oxen

O

och, *interj.* expressing surprise, sorrow, regret

ochon, oh-hon, *interj.* alas

o'er, see **owre**

o'erword, *n.* burden, refrain

offer, *v.* promise, seem likely to turn out

oh-hon, see **ochon**

onie, ony, *adj., pron.* any

or, *prep.* ere, before

orra, *adj.* odd, spare, extra

o't, of it

other, see **ither**

ought, *n.* anything (*var.* **aught**); **oughtlins,** *adv.* anything in the least, at all

ourie, *adj.* poor, dreary, wretched

oursel(ls), *pron. pl.* ourselves

outcast, *n.* quarrel

outler quey, *n.* young cow lying out at night

out(-)owre, *prep.* over across, above, beyond; *adv.* over; **out thro',** *adv.* right through

outspak, *v. pa. t.* spoke out, up

owre, ower, *adv., prep*. over; *adj., adv*. too; **o'er far,** too surely
owrehip, *adv*. over the hip
owsen, *n. pl*. oxen, cattle
owther, *n*. author

P

pack, *adj*. 'intimate, familiar' (B)
pack (aff), *v*. go packing, depart
paidle, *v*. paddle, wade; dabble
pai(r)trick, paetrick, *n*. partridge; *fig*. girl
palaver, *n*. idle chatter, nonsense
pang, *v*. cram, stuff
parishon, *n*. parish
(a) **parliamentin,** *ppl*. attending, serving in parliament
parritch, pirratch, *n*. porridge; **p.-pat,** *n*. porridge-pot
part's be, part, share shall be
party-match, *n*. card contest
pat, *n*. pot. See **pit**
pattle, pettle, *n*. small long-handled spade used to clean the plough
paughty, *adj*. proud, insolent
pawkie, *adj*. cunning, crafty, sly
pay, *v*. give deserts, flog; **pay't hollow,** beat thoroughly
pech, pegh, *v*. 'to fetch the breath short *as in an asthma*' (B)
peer, *v*. equal, rank with
peghan, *n*. stomach
pell [*and*] mell, *adv*. in violent disorder
pendle, *n*. pendule, pendant
penny-fee, *n*. wages paid in money
penny-wheep, *n*. small beer
pennyworths, *n. pl*. good bargain
perish, *v*. make to perish, destroy
pet, *v*. take the pet, sulk
pettle, see pattle
philibeg, *n*. kilt
phiz, *n*. countenance, expression of face
phrase, *v*. flatter (make a phrase about); **phraisin,** *adj*. exaggerating,
    extravagant

pibroch, *n.* classical bagpipe music

pickle, *n.* small quantity of

pictur'd beuk, *n.* playing card

pike, pyke, *v.* pick (at); pluck

pin, *n.* skewer; gallows-peg; latch pin

pine, *n.* pain, sorrow

pint-stowp, see **stoup**

pirratch, see **parritch**

piss, pish, *v.* urinate; *ppl. adj.* soaked with urine

pit, *v.* put, make; **pat,** *pa. t.*; **pat to,** put to it, drove

plack, *n.* small coin (4 pennies Scots), copper, farthing, nothing worth; **plackless,** *adj.* penniless

plaid(ie), *n.* long piece of woollen cloth, chequered or tartan, used as a cloak; **plaiden,** *adj.* with check or tartan pattern; *n.* cloth of this kind

plaister, *n.,* *v.* plaster

planted, *pa. pple.* settled in

play, *n.* joy, pleasure, source of delight

plea, *n.* action at law

pleugh, plew, *n.* plough; ploughing-team; **p.-pettle,** see **pattle**

pliskie, *n.* trick

pliver, *n.* green plover; lapwing, peewit

plumpet, *v. pa. t.* plunged, sank

plush, *adj.* long-knapped velvet

poacher-court, *n.* kirk session

pock, *n.* poke, bag

poind, *v.* distrain, seize goods and sell them under warrant

poortith, *n.* poverty

Poosie, *adj.* pejorative term for a woman; **Poossie, puss(ie),** *n.* Puss, the hare

pot, *n.* pot-still, to which heat is applied directly and not by a steam-jacket

potato-bing, *n.* heap of potatoes for winter storage

pou, pow, pu', *v.* pull

pouchie, *n.* dim. of *pouch*

pouk, *v.* poke, prod

pouther, powther, *n.* powder; **pouthered,** *ppl. adj.*; **pouthery,** *adj.*

pow, *n.* head. See **pou**

pownie, *n.* pony, 'specifically a riding horse' (SND)

powt, *n.* poult, chicken

powther, see **pouther**

pree, see **prie**

preen, *n.* pin; something of little value

Premier, *n.* prime minister; *v.* play the prime minister (nonce-word)

prent, *n., v.* print

pride, *v.* make proud; **pridefu',** *adj.* proud

prie, pree, *v.* try, taste; p. (her) mou', kiss (her)

prief, *n., adj.* proof

priestie, *n.* priest (dim. used contemptuously)

priggin, *pres. pple.* chaffering, haggling

primsie, *adj.* 'demure, precise' (B), affected

proper, *adj.* handsome, elegant, fine

proves, *n.* provost, chief magistrate

pu', see **pou**

puddock-stool, *n.* toadstool

puir, *adj.* poor

pun(d), *n. pl.* pounds

pursie, *n.* little purse

puss(ie), see **Poosie**

pyet, *n.* magpie

pyke, see **pike**

pyle, *n.* spike, blade; grain, glume or pale of chaff

Q

quarrel, *v.* dispute, challenge

quat, *v.* (Engl. *quit*) leave, put by; *pa. t.* left, abandoned

quaukin, *pres. pple.* quaking

quean, quine, *n.* (1, Sc. sense) young girl, sturdy lass; (2, Engl. sense) jade, hussy

queer, *adj.* (1) odd in appearance; (2) roguish

queir, *n.* choir

questions, *n. pl.* the catechism

quey, *n.* 'a cow from one year to two years old' (B), heifer

quietlenswise, *adv.* quietly

quine, see **quean**

quo, *pa. t.* of *quethe*, said

R

racked, *ppl. adj.* excessive, extortionate

raep, rape, *n.* rope

ragged, *adj.* unkempt, shaggy

ragouts, *n. pl.* highly seasoned dishes of stewed meat and vegetables

ragweed, *n.* ragwort

raible, *v.* gabble

rair, *v.* roar, complain; **rair't,** *pa. pple.*

ra(i)se, *v. pa. t.* rose; **rais'd,** made . . . get up

raize, *v.* provoke, rouse

ramblan, *ppl. adj.* roving

ramfeezl'd, *ppl. adj.* exhausted

ram-stam, *adj.* headstrong, reckless

random-splore, *n.* careless frolic, carousal. See **splore**

randy, *n.* rough, rude fellow; **randie,** *adj.* rude, coarse-tongued, riotous

rant, *v.* make merry; **ranter,** *n.* riotous fellow, merry singer

rap, *n.* knock

rape, see **raep**

raploch, *adj.* coarse, homely

rase, see **ra(i)se**

rash, *n.* rush; **rash-buss,** clump of rushes

rattan, ratton, rottan, *n.* rat

rattlin(g), *adj.* loquacious, lively in speech or manner

raucle, *adj.* rough, coarse, rudely strong

raught, see **ryke**

raw, *n.* row, file

rax, *v.* stretch; *ppl. adj.* elastic

ream, *n.* cream, froth; *v.* foam

reave, see **rief**

reck, *v.* regard, care for, heed

red(e), *v.* advise, counsel, warn

red-wat-shod, *adj.* shod with wet blood. See **wat**

red-wud, *adj.* violently distracted, stark mad. See **wud**

reek, *n.* smoke; *ppl. adj.* **reekan,** dripping, bloody; *ppl. adj.* **reeket, reekit,** smoked, smoky; **reekin-red,** *adj.* steaming with warm blood; **warm-reekin,** *adj.*

reest, *v.* 'to stand restive' (B)

reestet, *ppl. adj.* smoke-dried, 'cured'

reif, see **rief**

remarkin, *vbl. n.* observation, entertainment

remead, remeid, *n.* remedy, redress

respeckit, *ppl. adj.* considered worthy

ribban, *n.* riband, ribbon

rickle, *n.* pile of sheaves, stack

rief, *n.* plunder; **reif**, *adj.* thieving, despoiling; **reave**, *v.*

rig, *n.* arable ridge; **riggin**, *n.* ridge, roof

rig-woodie, *n.* ridge- or back-band for a cart-horse, made of twisted withes; *attrib.* abusive epithet, prob. withered, coarse, yellow

rin, *v.* run

ripp, *n.* 'a handful of unthreshed corn, etc.' (B)

ripple, *v.* draw flax through a comb to remove seed

risk, *v.* 'to make a noise like the breaking of small roots with the plough' (B)

rive, *v.* break up; reave, take by force; burst, part asunder

roaring, *adj.* brisk, vigorous, riotous

rock, *n.* distaff; **rockin**, spinning party

rood, *n.* quarter-acre

rook, *n. fig.* impudent cheat

roon, *n.* round, circuit

roose, *v.* praise

roose, rouse, *v.* stir up, agitate

roosty, *adj.* rusty

rottan, see **rattan**

round, *adv.* confidently, roundly

roupet, rupit, *ppl. adj.* husky, hoarse

rouse, see **roose**

rousing, *adj.* outrageous

rout, *n.* road, course, way

routh(ie), see **rowth**

row(e), *v.* roll, wrap

rowte, *v.* bellow, roar, low

rowth, routh, *n.* abundance, plenty; **routhie**, *adj.* plentiful

rozet, *n.* resin

run(-)deil, *n.* complete, thoroughgoing devil

rung, *n.* cudgel

runkl'd, *ppl. adj.* wrinkled

runt, *n.* cabbage stalk; *ppl. adj.* stunted

rupit, see **roupet**

ruth, *n.* pity

ryke, *v.* reach; **raught,** *pa. t.*

S

's, shortened form of (1) *is,* is, are; (2) *as;* (3) *us*

sab, *v.* sob

sae, *adv., conj.* so

saft, *adj.* soft; silly, lax; soft to the touch

sair, *v.* serve, suffice; **sairs,** *pres. pl.* avail; **sair't,** *pa. pple.*

sair, *adj., adv.* sore(ly); *adj.* sorry; sad, aching; hard, harsh, heavy;
    adv. severely, quite, desperately, violently; *combs.* **sairwark,** *n.*
    hardship, labour; **sair-won,** *adj.* hard-won

sairie, *adj.* dismal

sal-alkali, *n.* soda-ash; **sal-marinum,** *n.* common salt

sad, *v. pt. t.* sold; **sell't awa,** *pa. pple.* disposed of by sale

sall, *v.* shall; reduced enclitic forms **-s(e), -s',** mis-written **-'s(e), I'se,
    we'se, ye'se, it's**

sample, *n.* example

sang, *n.* song

Sannock, Sawnie, *n.* abbreviations of *Alexander*

sappy, *adj.* plump, succulent

sark, *n.* shirt; chemise, shift; **half-sarket,** *ppl. adj.* half-clothed;
    sark-necks, *n. pl.* collars

saugh, *n.* sallow, willow; **saugh-woodies,** *n. pl.* ropes of twisted
    sallow-withes

saul, *n.* soul

saumont, sawmont, *n.* salmon; **s.-coble,** *n.* flat-bottomed rowing-
    boat used in spearing salmon on the river, or in net-fishing by the
    coast

saunt, *n.* saint; puritan, *pl.* the elect

saut, *n., adj.* salt; **sautet,** *ppl. adj.;* *comb.* **saut-backet,** *n.* small
    wooden box for holding salt water, kept near the kitchen fireplace

saw, *v.* sow

sawmont, see **saumont**

Sawnie, see **Sannock**

sax, *adj.*, *n.* six; **saxpence**, *n.*

scaith, see skaith

scandal-potion, *n.* tea

scant, *adj.* stinted, deficient, poor, scarce; *n.* dearth, poverty

scar, *n.* cliff, bank, rock

scar, *v.* scare, frighten off; **scaur**, *adj.* afraid

scaud, *v.* scald

scawl, *n.* scolding, abusive woman

scho, *pron.* she

schulin', *n.* schooling

sconner, *v.* feel sick, feel disgust; *n.* disgust, revulsion

score, *n.* indentation

scow'r, *v.* roister; **scour'd**, *pa. t.* ran, ranged

scraichan, *ppl. adj.* screaming

screed, *n.* tear; *v.* repeat readily, rattle (off)

scriegh, *v.* 'to cry shrilly' (B), neigh; **scriechan**, *pres. pple.* screeching

scri(e)ve, *v.* 'to glide swiftly along' (B)

scrimp, *v.* be sparing of, cut down on; **scrimpet**, *ppl. adj.* stunted; **scrimply**, *adv.* scarcely, barely

scroggie, scroggy, *adj.* covered with stunted bushes

sea-way, *n.* the progress of a ship through the waves

see'd, *v. pa. t.* saw; **far seen**, *ppl. adj.* well versed

seisin, *n.* sasine, in Sc. law 'the act or procedure of giving possession of feudal property' (SND)

sell't, see **sald**

sen, see sin

sen', *v.* send; **sen't**, send it

sense, in a, in any respect

servan', *adj.* servant, menial

service, *n.* toast in homage

set, *v.* set out, start off; suit, become; **sets . . . ill**, ill becomes; **set up a face**, put on a favourable appearance, make a pretence; **settlin'**, *vbl. n.* quieting, fixing

shachl't, *ppl. adj.* shapeless, twisted by shuffling

shaird, *n.* shard; fragment, remnant

shank (it), *v.* walk

shanna, sha'na, *v.* shan't

shaul, *adj.* shallow

shaver, *n.* young wag, roisterer, joker; **shavie**, *n.* trick

shaw, *n.* 'a small wood in a hollow place' (B)

shaw, *v.* show, reveal

shear, *v.* reap with a sickle; **shure**, *pa. t.*

sheep-shank (bane), nae, *n.* person of no little importance

sheerly, *adv.* wholly, entirely

sheuch, sheugh, *n.* trench, ditch

sheuk, *v. pa. t.* shook

shiel, *n.* hut, shanty

shift, *v.* change places

shill, *adj.* resonant, shrill

shog, *n.* jog, shock

shool, *n.* shovel; **fire-shool**, *n.*

shoon, *n. pl.* shoes

shore, *v.* (1) threaten; (2) offer

shouther, *n.* shoulder

shure, see **shear**

sic, *adj.* such; **siccan**, *adj.* such-like

sicker, *adj.* secure, safe, steady; *adv.* effectively, severely

sidelins, *adv.* sideways, obliquely

sie, *v.* see

siller, *n.* silver, wealth

silly, *adj.* poor, hapless, pitiful; frail, sorry, helpless, harmless; foolish;
   weak, feeble

simmer, *n.* summer

sin, *n.* son

sin, sin', sen, *adv., prep., conj.* since, from the time that; **sinsyne**,
   adv. since then. See **syn(e)**

sinn, *n.* sun

sinsyne, see **sin**

sirnam'd, *pa. pple.* surnamed

skaith, scaith, *n.* hurt, damage; *v.* harm

skeigh, skiegh, *adj.* 'mettlesome, fiery, proud' (B), disdainful

skellum, *n.* rascal, scoundrel

skelp, (1) *v.* strike, beat, thrash; *ppl. adj.* smacking (kiss); *n.* slap;
   smack! bang!; (2) *v.* hurry, rush; **skelpie-limmer**, *n.* hussy, 'a
   technical term in female scolding' (B). See **limmer**

skiegh, see **skeigh**

skinking, *adj.* watery

skinklin, *ppl. adj.* glittering, showy

skirl, *v.* shriek, yell

sklent, *v.* squint greedily, direct aslant with malice; *ppl. adj.* falling obliquely, slanting; *n.* side-look

skouth, *n.* scope, liberty

skyre, *v.* to shine; **skyrin,** *ppl. adj.* flaunting, bright-coloured

skyte, *n.* skite, 'rebound, ricochet' (SND)

slade, *pa. t.* of *slide,* slip, steal away

slae, *n.* the blackthorn, its fruit

slap, *v.* drive, strike; *adv.* directly, suddenly

slap, *n.* gap in a dyke or fence

slaw, *adj., adv.* slow

slee, *adj.* clever, wise, witty, sly; **sleest,** *superl.*

sleeket, sleekit, *ppl. adj.* smooth, glossy; sly

slight, *n.* skill, dexterity; artifice

slip, *n.* quick-release leash

slype, *v.* 'to fall over *as a wet furrow from the plough*' (B)

sma', *adj.* little, slight; slender, narrow

smeddum, *n.* fine powder used as medicine or insecticide

smeek, *n.* smoke

smiddie, *n.* smithy

smirking, *ppl. adj.* smiling

smoor, *v.* smother; *pa. t.* was smothered

smoutie, *adj.* 'smutty, obscene; ugly' (B)

smytrie, *n.* numerous collection

snap, *adj.* quick, smart

snapper, *v.* stumble

snash, *n.* abuse, insolence

snaw, *n.* snow; **snawy,** *adj.*; *comb.* **snaw-broo,** see **broo**

sned, *v.* cut off, lop, prune

sneeshin (mill), *n.* snuff (box)

snell, *adj.* keen, bitter

snick, *n.* latch, bar; **snick-drawing,** *adj.* crafty

snirtle, *v.* laugh quietly, snigger

snool, *v.* 'subdue, keep in subjection' (SND)

snoove, *v.* go steadily on

snore, *v.* snort

snowck, *v.* snuff, poke about with the nose

snuff, *v.* sniff

sobbin, see **sab**

so(d)ger, *n.* soldier

some(thing), *adv.* somewhat, a bit

sonnet, *n.* song

sonsie, sonsy, *adj.* good-natured, tractable; buxom, comely

s(o)ugh, *n.* rushing sound of wind; deep breath

souk, *n.* suck, swig

soup(e), sowp, *n.* sup, drink, mouthful

souple, *adj.* soft, pliant, supple

sour-mou'd, *ppl. adj.* peevish, bitter-tongued

s(o)uter, sowter, *n.* shoemaker, cobbler

so(we)ns, *n.* sour pudding of oats and water

sowp, see **soup(e)**

sowter, see **s(o)uter**

sowth, *v.* 'to try over a tune with a low whistle' (B)

sowther, *v.* solder, patch up

spae, *v.* divine, foretell

spail, *n.* spale, splinter

spair, *v.* spare; *ppl. adj.* restrained, reticent

spairge, *v.* plaster, sprinkle; bespatter

spak, *v. pa. t.* spoke

span-lang, *adj.* small (lit. the measure of the extended hand, 9 inches)

spavie, *n.* spavin, tumour caused by inflammation of a horse's shank cartilage, or of the hock-bone; **spavet,** *ppl. adj.* spavined

spean, *v.* wean

speat, *n.* spate, flood

speed, come speed, prosper, attain a desire; **speedy,** *adj.* quick, brief

speel, *v.* climb

speet, *v.* spit, transfix

spell, *v.* study, contemplate

spell, tak a, take turns at the work, work continuously

spence, *n.* parlour, inner room

spier, speir, *v.* ask, inquire; **s. at,** ask of

spin'le, *n.* spindle, axle

splatter, *v.* sputter, bespatter; *n.* splash, noisy splutter

spleuchan, *n.* tobacco-pouch, purse

splore, *n.* frolic, uproar, carousal. See **random-splore**

sport, *v.* spend in pleasure; **sportin,** *vbl. n.* sexual fun, games, jesting; **sportin' lady,** *n.* whore

spotting, *ppl. adj.* staining

sprattle, *v.* struggle, scramble

sprawl, *v.* struggle, crawl

spring, *n.* dance, lively tune

sprittie, *adj.* 'rushy' (B)

spunk, *n.* spark, match; **spunkie,** *adj.* spirited, mettlesome; *n.* will o' the wisp

spurtle, *n.* wooden instrument for turning oat-cakes, porridge-stick; **spurtle-blade,** *n.* sword

squad, *n.* company, party; set

squatter, *v.* 'flutter in water' (B)

squattle, *v.* squat, nestle down

stacher, *v.* toddle, totter, stagger

stack, *pa. t.* of *stick*

sta(i)g, *n.* young horse; **staggie,** *dim.*

stammer, *v.* stumble (of a horse)

stan', *v.* stand, stop, stick; **he wad stan't,** he would have stood; **stan',** *n.* pause, halt

stane, *n.* stone; measure of weight

stang, *n., v.* goad, sting

stank, *n.* pond, 'a pool of standing water' (B)

stap, *v.* stop; **stapple,** *n.* stopper, bung

stare, *v.* express clearly; **stare in the face,** confront

stark, *adj.* strong, hardy

starn, *n.* star; **starnies,** *n. pl.* little stars

startle, *v.* take fright; 'to run *as cattle stung by the gadfly*' (B), caper

statuary, *n.* sculptor

staukin, *pres. pple.* stalking, walking stealthily

staumrel, *adj.* stammering, half-witted, silly

staw, *v. pa. t.* stole; crept, slipped away; **stown,** *pa. pple.*; **stownlins,** *adv.* by stealth, secretly

steek, *n.* stitch

steek, *v.* shut

steer, *v.* stir, agitate, rouse; affect, afflict; **a steerin,** in motion

steer, *v.* take one's way

steeve, *adj.* firm, strong

stegh, *v.* cram the stomach with food

stell, *n.* still, apparatus for distillation; stills, *pl.*

sten', *n.* leap, bound; sten't, *v. pa. t.* reared, turned

stent, *n.* impost, duty

stey, *adj.* steep, difficult

stibble, *n.* stubble; stibble-field, stibble-rig, stubble field, 'the reaper who takes the lead' (B)

stick, *n.* cudgel, splinter, fragment; a' to sticks, stick an' stow, *adv. phr.* utterly

stills, see stell

stilt, *v.* lift the legs high, prance

stimpart, *n.* measure of grain, quarter-peck, 'heapet' or 'straiked'

stir, *n.*; corruption of *sir*

stirk, *n.* young bullock

stock, *n.* plant, stem

stoited, stoiter'd, see stoyte

stomach, *n.* spirit, temper

stook, *n.* set of corn sheaves placed on end in two rows, against each other, in the field

stoor, *adj.* harsh, 'sounding hollow, strong and hoarse' (B). See stoure

stops . . . o', *v.* keeps from, deprives of

store, in, in plenty

stoup, stowp(e), *n.* tankard, measure; *comb.* pint-s.

stoure, stoor, *n.* battle, tumult, storm; adversity; dust; like s., *adv. phr.* swiftly; stourie, *adj.* dusty

stow'd, *pa. pple.* (have) filled, crammed

stown(lins), see staw

stowp(e), see stoup

stoyte, stoit(er), *v.* lurch, stagger

strae, *n.* straw; strae-death, *n.* natural death in bed

straik, *v.* stroke

strak, *v. pa. t.* struck

strang, *adj.* strong; violent

strappan, *ppl. adj.* strapping, sturdy

straught, *adv.* straight

streek, *v.* stretch

striddle, *v.* straddle, stride

string, *n.* string used as a measure

stroan't, *v. pa. pple.* pissed

strunt, *n.* liquor

strunt, *v.* move with assurance

studdie, *n.* stithy, anvil

stuff, *n.* provision, store of corn

stump, *v.* walk clumsily; **stumpie (pen),** worn quill pen

sturt, *v.* fret, trouble; *ppl. adj.* troubled, afraid; *n.* contention, quarrelling, violence, esp. in traditional allit. phr. **sturt and strife**

styme, see a, see at all

sucker, *n.* sugar

sud, *v.* should (have)

sugh, see s(o)ugh

summon, *n.*; *obs. sing.* of *summons*

sune, *adv.* soon

suter, see s(o)uter

Suthron, *adj., n. pl.* southerners, Englishmen

swaird, *n.* sward

swank, *adj.* limber, agile; **swankie,** *n.* strapping lad

swap, *v.* strike, strike a bargain; exchange

swarf, *v.* swoon

swat, *v. pa. t.* sweated

swatch, *n.* sample

swats, *n. pl.* new small beer

swinge, *v.* flog

swirl, *n.* 'a curve, an eddying blast or pool, a knot in wood' (B); **swirlie,** *adj.* 'knaggy, full of knots' (B)

swith, *adv., interj.* quickly!, away!

swither, *n.* state of agitation, flurry

swoor, *v. pa. t.* swore

syke, *n.* small stream, ditch

syn(e), *adv., conj.* then, since; **lang syn(e),** long since, long ago

T

tack, *n.* leasehold, tenure

tacket, *n.* hob-nail for boots

tae, *n.* toe; **three-tae'd,** *ppl. adj.*

tae, *prep., conj.* to

ta'en, see tak(e)

taet, *n.* tuft, small handful

tail, *n.* female genitals

ta(i)rge, *v.* discipline, constrain

tak(e), *v.* take, seize; take one's way; **tak aff**, drink off, up; carry away; **tak the gate**, take to the road, get home; **ta'en**, *pa. pple.* (have) taken

tald, see tell

tane . . . tither, *pron., adj.* one . . . other

tangle, *n.* sea-weed

tangs, *n.* tongs

tap, *n.* (1) top, head; (2) portion of lint put on the distaff; **tapma(i)st, tapmost**, *adj.* topmost; **tap-pickle**, *n.* the grain (*pickle*) at the end of a stalk of wheat, barley, oats

taper, *adj.* tapering, slender

tapetless, *adj.* 'heedless, foolish' (B)

tappit-hen, *n.* hen with a top-knot; drinking-vessel with a knobbed lid

tapsalteerie, *adv. comb.* topsy-turvy, upside down, in disorder

targe, *n.* light shield

tarrow, *v.* hesitate, show reluctance; **tarrow't**, *pa. pple.* 'murmured' (B)

tarry-breeks, *n.* nickname for a sailor

tassie, *n.* dim. of *tass*, silver goblet

tauld, see tell

tauted, tawtied, *ppl. adj.* matted, shaggy

tawie, *adj.* (of a horse) 'that handles quietly' (B)

tawpie, *n.* senseless girl

tawtied, see tauted

teethin, *pres. pple.* putting fresh teeth into

tell, *v.* relate, enumerate; count the price out (and drink off); **ta(u)ld**, *pa. t.* and *pa. pple.*

temper-pin, *n.* turning screw

ten-hours bite, *comb.* 'a slight feed to the horses while in the yoke in the forenoon' (B); **tenpund**, *adj.* of the annual value of ten pounds

tent, *n.* 'a field pulpit' (B)

tent, *v.* heed, care, tend; watch, take heed; *n.* caution, care; **tentie**, *adj.* watchful, careful

tester, *n.* sixpence

tether, *n.* rope, noose

teugh, *adj.* tough, hardy, violent

thack, *n.* thatching

thae, *dem. pron., adj.* those

thairm, *n.* intestine; *pl.* fiddle strings; **thairm-inspiring,** *adj.* gifted on the fiddle

thanket, thankit, *pa. pple.* thanked

theek, *v.* collateral form of *thatch*; **theekit,** *pa. pple.* and *ppl. adj.*

thegither, *adv.* together; at a time, continuously

thick, *adj.* (1) familiar, intimate; (2) going in quick succession, rapid

thieveless, *adj.* cold, without warmth

thig, *v.* take, accept; beg

thir, *dem. adj.* these

thirl, *v.* pierce, penetrate

thole, *v.* endure, suffer

thou's(e), *v.* thou art, thou hast, thou shalt. Cf. **I'se, ye'se.** See **sall**

thowe, *n.* thaw

thowless, *adj.* spiritless

thrang, *n.* crowd, press of people; *adj.* crowding, in a crowd, busy; **thick an' thrang,** close engaged together; *v.* crowd in, jostle; *adv.* busily, earnestly

thrapple, *n.* throat

thrave, *n.* two stooks of corn, hence a measure of straw, etc.

thraw, *v.* turn, twist; worst, frustrate; *n.* twist, turn; **for thrawin,** to prevent warping

threap, *v.* argue obstinately, 'maintain by dint of assertion' (B)

three-tae'd, see **tae**

thresh, *v.* beat, belabour

thretteen, *adj.* thirteen

thretty, *adj.* thirty

thrissle, thristle, *n.* thistle

thrist, *v.* thirst

through, mak to, see **mak**

(a') throw'ther, a' throu'ther, *adv. phr.* 'through each other', in confusion, disorder

thrum, *v.* sound monotonously, hum

thump, *v.* strike; *pa. t.* fired

thysel, *pron.* yourself

tickle, *v.* rouse; please, amuse

tight, *adj.* (1) neat, shapely; (2) tidy, cosy, snug; (3) capable, able, ready; *adv.* closely, strictly

till, *prep.* to; **till 't,** to it

timmer, *n.* timber; trees; material; wooden edge

tine, tyne, *v.* lose, get lost; **tint,** *pa. t., pa. pple.*

tinkler, *n.* itinerant mender of pots and pans, usually a gypsy; low rascal; *combs.* **tinkler-gipsey, tinkler-hizzie** (see **hizzie**)

tint, see **tine**

tip, see **toop**

tippence, *n.* twopence; **tippeny,** *n.* ale originally sold at 2d a Scots pint (3 imperial pints)

tirl, *v.* strip, uncover, unthatch

tirl, *v.* rattle at a door, by turning or lifting the latch

tither (the), *pron., adj.* the other (of two), the other (day)

tittie, titty, *n.* (*colloq.*) sister

tittlan, *ppl. adj.* tattling, whispering

tocher, *n.* dowry; *v.* furnish with a dowry

tod, *n.* fox

toddlan, todlin, *pres. pple.* toddling; walking unsteadily; *ppl. adj.* hurrying, pattering

toddy, *n.* whisky, hot water and sugar

toolzie, see **tulzie**

toom, *adj., v.* empty

toop, tip, tup, *n.* ram

touch, a wee, a very little

toun, town, *n.* village, farm, town; **towns-bodies,** town dwellers (SND)

tout, *n.* blast (of a trumpet)

touzle, *v.* ruffle, handle roughly; **towsing,** *vbl. n.* rumpling, handling indelicately; **towzie,** *adj.* unkempt, shaggy

tow, *n.* bell-rope; rope; gallows-rope

tow, *n.* fibre of flax prepared for spinning

towmond, towmont, *n.* twelvemonth, year

towns-bodies, see **toun**

towsing, towzie, see **touzle**

toy, *n.* close-fitting cap, 'a very old fashion of female head dress' (B)

toyte, *v.* 'walk like old age' (B), totter

tozie, *adj.* warm, cosy, tipsy

trac'd, *pa. pple.* harnessed

tram, *n.* cart or barrow shaft

transmugrify'd, *ppl. adj.* transformed, metamorphosed

trashtrie, *n.* trashery, rubbish

tread, *v. pa. t.* trod

trepan, *v.* inveigle, beguile

trews, *n.* close-fitting trousers, worn with stockings

trick, *n.* habit, turn; **trickie,** *adj.* crafty, deceitful

trig, *adj.* trim, smart

trin'le, *n.* wheel of a barrow

trot, *v.* run, bustle (of a stream)

trow, *v.* trust; believe; **trow't,** believe it; **in trouth, trowth,** *adv.*, *interj.* truly, indeed

trustee, *n.* administrator

tryst(e), *n.* meeting, assembly; cattle-fair, market; **trysted,** *ppl. adj.* appointed; **trystin(g),** *ppl. adj.*

tug, *n.* 'raw hide, *of which, in olden times, plough-traces were frequently made*' (B)

tulzie, toolzie, *n.* quarrel, contest, brawl

tup, see **toop**

twa, see **twa(y)**

'twad, see **wad**

twal, *num. adj.*, *n.* twelve, midnight; **twal hundred,** woven in a reel of 1,200 divisions; **twalpennie,** *attrib.* shilling('s); **twal-pint,** *adj.* giving 12 pints at a milking; **twalt,** *adj.* twelfth

twa(y), *num. adj.*, *n.* two; **twafauld,** *adv.* bent double; **twa-three,** *adj.* two or three, a few

twin, *v.* separate (from), deprive (of)

twissle, *n.* wrench, twist

tyke, *n.* dog, cur, mongrel

tyne, see **tine**

tyta, *n.* pet name for 'father'

U

ulzie, *n.* oil

unco, *adj.* odd, strange; *adv.* very; **uncos,** *n. pl.* strange tales, news

under hidin, in hiding

unkenn'd, unkend-of, *ppl. adj.* unknown, unnoticed. See **ken**

unsicker, *adj.* unsure, fickle. See **sicker**

unskaith'd, *ppl. adj.* unscathed. See **skaith**

up wi', here's to; **up wi't a',** here's to (you)

upo', *prep.* upon

urinus-spiritus, *n.* spirit of urine

use't, *pa. pple.* used, treated; **us'd,** *ppl. adj.* experienced

usquabae, usquebae, *n.* whisky

V

vapour, *n.* fancy, whimsy; **vap'rin,** *ppl. adj.* blustering, fuming

vauntie, *adj.* vain, proud

vend, *v.* sell; advance, utter

vera, *adj.* very, actual; true, real

viewin, *vbl. n.* view, sight

virl, *n.* band of metal or ivory

vittel, vittle, *n.* grain, fodder

vogie, *adj.* vain

vow, see **wow**

W

wa', waw, *n.* wall

wab, *n.* web, woven fabric

wabster, *n.* weaver

wad, *v.* covenant; wager, stake; wed, marry.

wad, *v.* would (have); (who) would; **wadna,** would not; **'twad,** it would (have)

wae, woe, (1) *interj., adv.* **waes, woe is** (me), alas; **wae sucks** (sakes), alas; **wae gae by, w. on, w. worth,** may evil befall, cursed be; (2) *n.* misery, misfortune; **wae(fu'),** *adj.* bringing misery

waft, *v.* carry by water; *n.* sea-trip

waft, *n.* weft in a web, *fig.*

wag, *v.* nod, shake; **wag-wits,** *n. pl.* scandal-mongers, jokers

wail, *v. tr.* bewail

wair, ware, *v.* spend, lay out, bestow

wale, *n.* choice, choicest one (kind); *v.* choose, pick out

walie, wa(w)ly, waulie, *adj.* handsome, fine, ample

wallop, *v.* kick the heels, thrash about, be hanged; *n.* leap, beat

waly, see **walie**

wame, *n.* belly, stomach; **wamefou**, *n.* belly-full, meal

wan, *v. pa. t.* won

wanchancie, *adj.* dangerous, unlucky

wanrestfu', *adj.* restless

wapon-shaw, *n.* muster, review of men under arms

war, see **wa(u)r**

ware, see **wair**

wark, *n.* work, labour; business in hand

warklum, *n.* instrument, tool for work; *fig.* penis

warl(d), *n.* world; **warly**, *adj.* worldly

warlock, *n.* witch, wizard; **warlock-breef**, *n.* charter conveying magical powers, charm

warly, see **warl(d)**

warp, *v.* weave; **warpin**, *vbl. n.*

warran, *v.* warrant, guarantee

warsle, *v.* wrestle, struggle, contend (with)

warst, see **wa(u)rst**

was, *v. pa. t.* were

wastrie, *n.* wastefulness, extravagance

wat, *adj., pa. pple.* wet

wat, *v.* know, be aware of, be sure; **watna**, don't know

water, *n.* urine; **water-brose**, made with water; **water-fit**, mouth of a river; **water-kelpie**, see **kelpie**

watna, see **wat**

wattle, *n.* wand, stick

wauble, *v.* 'to swing' (B), move unsteadily from side to side

waught, *n.* draught, heavy drink

wauk, **wauken**, *v. intr.* be or stay awake, wake up; *tr.* wake, arouse; *pres. pple.* staying awake to keep watch (on); *ppl. adj.* **waukin**, awake, sleepless; **waukrife**, *adj.* wakeful, vigilant

wauket, *ppl. adj.* made callous, horny

waulie, see **walie**

wa(u)r, *adj., adv.* worse; *v.* worst, excel, surpass

wa(u)rst, *adj., adv.* worst

wavering, *pres. pple.* wandering, fluttering

waw, see **wa'**

wawly, see **walie**

wean, *n.* child; **weanies,** *dim. pl.* infants

wearing, *pres. pple.* passing (of time)

weary, *v.* grow weary, bored; *adj.* tiring, toilsome; *adv.* utterly, miserably; *phr.* **weary fa',** a curse on

weason, *n.* gullet

wecht, *n.* sieve

wee, *n., adj.* little bit, while; **wee-bit,** *quasi-adj.* little bit of a; **(a) wee thing,** *adv. phr.* a little; **wee-thing,** *n.* child, infant

weel, *adv., adj.* well, fine, satisfied; *n.* well-being, welfare, prosperity; **as weel 's,** as well as; **weel-gaun,** *ppl. adj.* good-going, active (see **gae**); **weel-hain'd,** see **hain**; **weel-hoordet,** *ppl. adj.* closely hoarded; **weel-swall'd,** *ppl. adj.* fully stretched; **weel-tocher'd,** *ppl. adj.* well-dowered (see **tocher**)

weepers, *n. pl.* cuffs

weet, *v., adj.* wet; *n.* dew, rain

we'se, *v.* we'll. See **sall**

westlin, *adj.* west(ern), westerly; west country; westward

wether, *n.* castrated ram; **wether-haggis,** *n.* haggis made in a wether's stomach

wha, whae(v)er, *pron.* who; **wham,** whom; **whase,** *pron.* whose; **whase,** who is

whaizle, *v.* 'to wheez' (B)

whalp, *v.* whelp

wham, see **wha**

whan, *adv.* when

whang, *n.* thick slice of cheese; *v.* to beat (as with a thong), flog

whare, wha(u)r, *adv., conj.* where

whase, see **wha**

whatfore no, *why not?*

whatn(a), (on, by) what (a)

whatt, *v. pa. t.* whetted, put an edge on

whaup, *n.* curlew

whaur, see **whare**

whid, *n.* word (thieves' cant); a lie

whid, *v.* move nimbly and noiselessly (of a hare); *n.* 'the motion of a hare running but not frightened' (B)

whig, *n.* Puritan, hypocrite; **whiggish,** *adj.* rigid, precise

whigmeleerie, *n.* whimsical ornament

whiles, see **whyle**

whin, *n.* gorse, furze-bush

whinge, *v.* whine; *ppl. adj.* canting, complaining

whin-rock, whunstane, *n.* whinstone, hard dark rock (e.g. greenstone, basalt)

whipper-in, *n.* huntsman responsible for keeping the hounds in pack

whirl, *n.* rush, rapid trip

whirlygigums, *n. pl.* fantastic ornaments

whirry, *v.* hurry, drive

whissle, gat the, see **groat**

whist, held my, kept silent

whitter, *n.* draught of liquor

whittle, *n.* knife used as a weapon; clasp-knife; surgical knife

whunstane, see **whin-rock**

whyle, whiles (*n., adv. gen.*), *adv.* at times, sometimes; **wh. ... wh.,** now ... then, at times ... at times

wi', *prep.* with; **wi'm, wi's, wi't,** with him, his, it

wick (a bore), *v.* 'to strike a stone in an oblique direction, *a term in curling*' (B)

wicker, *n.* branch

widdefu', see **woodie**

widdle, *n.* strife, trouble

wiel, *n.* eddy

wierd, *n.* fate, fortune

wifie, *n.* dim. of *wife* (affectionate term)

wight, *n.* creature, fellow

wight, *adj.* strong, stout

wil-cat, *n.* wild-cat

willyart, *adj.* shy, awkward

wi'm, see **wi'**

wimble, wumble, *n.* gimlet; *fig.* phallus

wimple, *v.* meander; *ppl. adj.* twisting, turning

win, *v.* reach, gain, get; **win,** *pa. pple.* earn

win', *v.* wind; **win't,** *pa. t.* wound

win', *n.* wind, breath

winkers, *n. pl.* eye-lashes, eyes

winn, *v.* winnow

winna, *v.* will not, won't

winnock, *n.* window; **winnock-bunker**, window-seat

win't, see **win'**

winter-hap, *n.* covering for the winter. See **hap**

wintle, *v.* swing from side to side, roll; *n.* 'a wavering, swinging motion' (B)

winze, *n.* curse

wi's, see **wi'**

wiss, *v.* wish

wit, *v.* know

wi't, see **wi'**

witchin(g), *ppl. adj.* bewitching, fascinating

withoutten, *prep.* without

witty, *adj.* jocular, merry

woe, see **wae**

won, *v.* dwell

wonner, *n.* wonder, marvel, fine specimen (contemptuous)

wonted, *pa. pple.* habituated, accustomed

woo', **woo**, *n.* wool

woodie, **woody**, *n.* withy, rope, halter for hanging; **widdefu'**, *adj.* deserving hanging, rascally

wooer-bab, *n.* garter at the knee tied with two loops and worn by a suitor

woor, *pa. t.* wore out

wordie, *n.* little word

wordie, **wordy**, *adj.* worthy

worms, *n. pl.* long spiral tubes at the head of a whisky still, in which the vapour is condensed

worset, *adj.* worsted, woollen fabric, *attrib.*

wow, **vow**, *interj.* (emphatic)

wrack, *n.* wreckage, waste washed on a flood; *v.* wreck, destroy

wrang, *n., v., adj.* wrong; *pa. pple.* (have) wronged

wreeth, *n.* snow-drift

write, *n.* writing; **writer(-chiel)**, *n.* lawyer; **wrote**, *pa. pple.* written

wud, *adj.* enraged, angry. Cf. **red-wud**

wumble, see **wimble**

wyle, *v.* lure

wylecoat, *n.* 'a flannel vest' (B)

wyte, *v.* blame, reproach (with, for)

yard, *n.* garden; **yerd,** *n.* churchyard; **kail-yard,** see kail
yealing, *n.* contemporary in age
year, *n. pl.* years
yearn, *n.* eagle
yell, *adj.* barren; milkless, dry
yerd, see yard
yerk, *v.* lash, stir up
ye'se, *v.* you shall. See **sall**
yestreen, *adv.* yesterday even(ing)
yet(t), *n.* gate
yeuk, *v.* itch; **yeuks,** *n. pl.* itch
yill, *n.* ale; *comb.* **yill-caup,** see **caup**
yird, yirth, *n.* earth
yirr, *n.* a bark
yokin, *vbl. n.* contest, turn
'yont, *prep.* beyond, on the far side of
youngkers, *n. pl.* young folk
yoursel, *pron.* yourself, yourselves
yowe, *n.* ewe; **yowie,** *dim.* ewe-lamb
Yule, *n.* Christmas

BIBLIOGRAPHY

The foundations of Burns scholarship are supplied by:

J. De Lancey Ferguson and G. Ross Roy, eds., *The Letters of Robert Burns*, 2 vols., Oxford, 1985.

James Kinsley, ed., *The Poems and Songs of Robert Burns*, 3 vols., Oxford, 1968.

Donald A. Low, ed., *Robert Burns: The Critical Heritage*, London and Boston, 1974.

Donald A. Low, ed., *The Kilmarnock Poems*, London, 1985.

The letters are available more cheaply, and arranged differently, in:

James A. Mackay, ed., *The Complete Letters of Robert Burns*, Ayr, 1987.

The bases of contemporary critical understanding are found in:

Thomas Crawford, *Burns: A Study of the Poems and Songs*, Edinburgh, 1960, reprinted 1978.

David Daiches, *Robert Burns*, London, 1952, revised 1966, reprinted 1981.

Useful recent studies are:

Raymond Bentman, *Robert Burns*, Boston, 1987.

Mary Ellen Brown, *Burns and Tradition*, London, 1984.

R. D. S. Jack and Andrew Noble, eds., *The Art of Robert Burns*, London and Totowa, NJ, 1982.

Maurice Lindsay, *The Burns Encyclopaedia*, London, 1980.

Donald A. Low, *Burns*, Edinburgh, 1986.

Donald A. Low, ed., *Critical Essays on Robert Burns*, London and Boston, 1974.

Carol McGuirk, *Robert Burns and the Sentimental Era*, Athens, Ga., 1985.

Burns's songs may be better understood through:

Thomas Crawford, ed., *Love, Labour and Liberty: The Eighteenth-Century Scottish Song Lyric*, Cheadle (Cheshire), 1976.

Thomas Crawford, *Society and the Lyric: A Study of the Song Culture of Eighteenth-Century Scotland*, Edinburgh, 1979.

James C. Dick, ed., *The Songs of Robert Burns*, Harboro, Pa., 1962.

William Donaldson, *The Jacobite Song: Political Myth and National Identity*, Aberdeen, 1988.

Jean Redpath's singing of Burns is recorded in two series:

Burns Songs from the 'Scots Musical Museum', Scottish Records, Brig o' Turk, Perthshire.

The Songs of Robert Burns (researched and arranged by Serge Hovey), Greentrax Records, Edinburgh, and Philo/Rounder Records, USA.

The standard biography is still:

Franklin B. Snyder, *The Life of Robert Burns*, New York, 1932, reprinted Hamden, Conn., 1968.

For the cultural and historical background see:

William Ferguson, *Scotland 1689 to the Present*, revised edn, Edinburgh, 1978.

1800, Aberdeen, 1987.

Bruce Lenman, *Integration, Enlightenment and Industrialisation: Scotland 1746–1832*, London, 1981.

T. C. Smout, *A History of the Scottish People 1560–1830*, London, 1969.

Roderick Watson, *The Literature of Scotland*, London, 1984.

INDEX OF TITLES

INDEX OF FIRST LINES